INTERNATIONAL BUOYAGE SYSTEM

BUOY PLACEMENT	USER'S GUIDE	ILLUSTRATION OF USE	LEGEND
Used to mark the port (left) side of a channel when proceeding in the upstream[2] direction	Keep this buoy on your port (left) hand side when proceeding in the upstream[2] direction		The following are the meanings of the light character abbreviations **Fl** **Flashing** A light in which a flash is regularly repeated at a rate of 15 flashes per minute (a flash every 4 seconds)
Used to mark the starboard (right) side of a channel when proceeding in the upstream[2] direction	Keep this buoy on your starboard (right) side when proceeding in the upstream[2] direction	UPSTREAM	**Q** **Quick Flashing** A light in which a flash is regularly repeated at a rate of 60 flashes per minute (a flash every second) **VQ** **Very Quick Flashing** A light in which a flash is regularly repeated at a rate of 120 flashes per minute (a flash every $1/2$ second)
Used to indicate that there is safe water all around the buoy (e.g. landfalls, mid channels)	You may pass this buoy on either side but when it is marking the middle of a channel it should be kept on your port (left) side when proceeding in either direction	LANDFALL MID CHANNEL	**Mo(A)** **Morse "A"** A light in which a short flash is followed by a long flash to form the letter "A" in the Morse Code 10 times per minute (every 6 seconds)
Used, at a point where a channel divides, when proceeding in the upstream[2] direction, to indicate that the preferred channel is to starboard (i.e. to the right)	You may pass this buoy on either side when proceeding in the upstream[2] direction but the main or preferred channel will be entered by keeping this buoy on your port (left) side. Consult your chart for details of the danger being marked	SECONDARY CHANNEL UPSTREAM MAIN CHANNEL	**LFl** **Long Flash** A light in which a flash of 2 seconds duration is repeated at a rate of 6 flashes per minute (a flash every 10 seconds) **Fl (2+1) 5S** **Composite Group Flashing** A light in which a group of 2 flashes is followed by a single flash, the whole sequence being regularly repeated 12 times per minute (every 5 seconds)
Used, at a point where a channel divides, when proceeding in the upstream[2] direction, to indicate that the preferred channel is to port (i.e. to the left)	You may pass this buoy on either side when proceeding in the upstream[2] direction but the main or preferred channel will be entered by keeping this buoy on your starboard (right) side. Consult your chart for details of the danger being marked.	MAIN CHANNEL SHOAL UPSTREAM SECONDARY CHANNEL	**Fl (2+1) 10S** **Composite Group Flashing** A light in which a group of 2 flashes is followed by a single flash; the whole sequence being regularly repeated 6 times per minute (every 10 seconds)
Cardinal Buoys are Used: (a) To indicate that the deepest water in that area is on the named side of the mark (e.g. to the north of a north cardinal) (b) To indicate the safe side on which to pass a danger (c) To draw attention to a feature in a channel such as a bend, a junction or the end of a shoal	Keep to the named side of all cardinal buoys (i.e. keep to the north of north cardinal buoys, keep to the east of east cardinal buoys, etc.) and the buoy will be between you and the danger. Consult your chart for details of the danger. *Memory aids* (a) The points of the topmark cones point toward the black parts of the buoy (b) The cones on the north cardinal point north and those on the south cardinal point south. (c) The number of short light flashes in each group on the east, south and west cardinals is the same as the hour at the corresponding point on a clock face (e.g. the 3 flashes for the east cardinal corresponds to 3 o'clock) *Clock Face* EAST SOUTH WEST	 N NW NE Danger SW SE	**Q(3) 10S** **Group Quick Flashing** A quick flashing light in which a group of 3 flashes is regularly repeated 6 times per minute (every 10 seconds) **VQ(3) 5S** **Group Very Quick Flashing** A very quick flashing light in which a group of 3 flashes is regularly repeated 12 times per minute (every 5 seconds) **Q(6) + LFl 15S** **Group Quick Flashing plus Long Flash** A light in which a group of 6 quick flashes is followed by a single long flash; the whole sequence being regularly repeated 4 times per minute (every 15 seconds) **VQ(6) + LFl 10S** **Group Very Quick Flashing plus Long Flash** A light in which a group of 6 very quick flashes is followed by a single long flash; the whole sequence being regularly repeated 6 times per minute (every 10 seconds) **Q(9) 15S** **Group Quick Flashing** A quick flashing light in which a group of 9 flashes is regularly repeated 4 times per minute (every 15 seconds) **VQ(9) 10S** **Group Very Quick Flashing** A very quick flashing light in which a group of 9 flashes is regularly repeated 6 times per minute (every 10 seconds)

Small Craft
Piloting &
Coastal
Navigation

*"If a man does not know his part,
no wind will be favourable."*

PRINCE HENRY THE NAVIGATOR

Small Craft Piloting & Coastal Navigation

A.E. SAUNDERS

Illustrated by JOHN SARAFIAN

VAN NOSTRAND REINHOLD
TORONTO NEW YORK

Copyright © 1982 A.E. Saunders

Illustrations by John Sarafian

Published by
Van Nostrand Reinhold Publishers
A Division of International Thomson Limited
1410 Birchmount Road
Scarborough, Ontario, Canada M1P 2E7
ISBN 0-7706-0003-4
Published in the United States of America by
Van Nostrand Reinhold Company Inc.,
New York.
ISBN 0-442-29699-1

Library of Congress Number 81-71657

Canadian Cataloguing in Publication Data

Saunders, Al, 1927–
   Small craft piloting and coastal navigation

ISBN 0-7706-0003-4

1. Navigation   2. Boats and boating.   I. Title.

VK559.S38   623.89   C82-094170-0

Printed and bound in the United States of
America.

82 83 84 85 86 87   7 6 5 4 3 2 1

Contents

Preface

"But for friends, we would be limited to doing that which we are capable of doing." BOYD'S BASICS

Although I have been "messing about in boats" for the past thirty-five years and have had some experience in canoes, sailing dinghies, runabouts and cruisers both sail and power, it was 1969 before I realized the extent of my ignorance of boating safety, seamanship and navigation. It was then that I enlisted in the Canadian Power Squadron Piloting Course. This opened for me a whole new horizon of boating safety, interest and enjoyment. While continuing studies with the Power Squadron in the field of small craft piloting and coastal navigation, I became involved with Frenchman's Bay Squadron as a lecturer in piloting and coastal navigation.

It was during this period of teaching that I came to the conclusion that, although there are many good books on the market in this field, most of them either delve into the topic to satisfy the master mariner or else they tend to be very shallow in their coverage and do not tell the reader how and why. This book is an attempt to bridge that gap.

In the interest of continuity and maintaining the objective of not encumbering the reader unnecessarily with either trivia, unduly complex definitions or data which may be of importance to a serious student of advanced celestial navigation, I have taken a certain amount of "poetic licence." For example, my definition of a nautical mile is not absolutely accurate, because the earth is an oblate spheroid rather than a sphere. For the purposes of small craft piloting and navigation, however, such inaccuracies are inconsequential.

The two principal sections take the reader from an introduction to regulations and rules of the road, through elementary or basic piloting involving the compass, charts and positioning, up to more advanced piloting techniques generally used in coastal navigation. A final cruise allows the reader to reinforce the knowledge gained through the study of this book. At the conclusion the reader should have a sound knowledge of all aspects of small craft navigation except for celestial and advanced electronic methods.

This book would not have been possible without the encouragement, support and assistance of a great many persons too numerous to acknowledge here. However, I must pay special tribute to some persons and organizations whose outstanding contributions must be recognized: to Agincourt Power Squadron Commander Retired R. R. Short, who opened my eyes to my ignorance of the subject of navigation and taught me "deviation per ship's heading;" to Frenchman's Bay Power Squadron Commander Retired F. Crowe, who, together with the press gang of the squadron, shanghaied me into the training department of that squadron; to many members and the executive, past and present, of Frenchman's Bay Squadron; to the Canadian Hydrographic Service, and in particular Boyd Thorson, Chief, Chart Production and G. Ross Douglas, Regional Hydrographer; to the Canadian Coast Guard, and in particular Alfie Yip, Regional Superintendent, Navigational Aids; to my wife for her patience during the time that I spent in learning something, in attempting to teach others and in writing this book; to fellow sailor Sheila Rowe for "getting this vessel away from the dock"; and Jim Wills for his editorial advice.

In particular I wish to acknowledge the help and advice of Roy Cunningham, Charlie Ellins and Donna Read, who so ably reviewed the manuscript and were more than helpful with their many suggestions and technical assistance.

I would especially thank my sister, Madelon Muir, whose untiring efforts in the preparation and typing of the manuscript is beyond my ability to express thanks. Any errors or omissions are solely the responsibility of the writer.

A. E. Saunders
Agincourt, Ontario
February 1982

1. Basic Regulations and Rules of the Road

"There's a difference between right and wrong, but sometimes it's difficult to tell which is which."   SAUNDERS' LAW OF NAVIGATION *#1*

BASIC REGULATIONS

Due to the continuous updating of rules and regulations relating to such things as the licensing of vessels and/or operators, requirements of safety equipment, etc., it is not possible here to be specific and detailed on this subject. Rather, you should be aware of the general scope of regulations and where to obtain them.

The Canadian Coast Guard annually publish a booklet entitled *Canadian Coast Guard Boating Handbook* which, at the current time, is available free of charge. This handbook is a summary of the legislation pertaining to boating safety and has been produced specifically for pleasure vessels. It is well illustrated and extremely easy to understand.

Included in this handbook are such things as:

- Vessel and registration requirements, capacity plates.
- Minimum required safety equipment for various sizes of boats.
- Rules of the road.
- Requirements with respect to charts and other publications which must be aboard each vessel.
- Lighting requirements.
- The Canadian system of buoyage.

This booklet is generally available on request at such locations as marinas, boat dealers and brokers, marine supply stores, chart dealers, yacht clubs, boat shows, Canadian Coast Guard or Federal Ministry of Transport offices and at many lockmaster's offices of the various canal systems in Canada. The handbook is also included as a part of the kit of material supplied for the Canadian Power Squadron "Basic Boating Course."

In addition to the rules and regulations included in the *Boating Handbook*, boaters must comply with the regulations or by-laws applicable in some specific locations. For example, a number of major ports, such as Toronto, Hamilton and some East and West Coast areas, come under additional local regulations. In the case of Toronto Harbour, there is a requirement that the vessel operator be licensed by the Toronto Harbour Commission. Such additional regulatory requirements are generally listed in the local "Sailing Directions" or on the harbour chart applicable. Visitors to such areas are generally exempt from licensing during short, infrequent visits.

The United States Coast Guard issues a publication similar to the *Canadian Coast Guard Boating Handbook* which covers the principal regulations and safety tips applicable to recreational boating in the United States.

In general, Canadian vessels are considered to be in compliance with the safety equipment regulations of other countries while visiting, provided that they are in compliance with Canadian regulations. Similarly, vessels visiting Canadian waters are considered to meet Canadian regulations if they meet those in their home country. One exception is that all vessels in Canadian waters must be in compliance with Canadian regulations concerning the discharge of sewage.

RULES OF THE ROAD

The rules of right of way on the water are much more important than the rules of the road on the highway when you consider that there are no prescribed lanes and roadways for pleasure vessels. Operating a boat is somewhat akin to continuously driving your automobile in the largest and busiest parking lot you can visualize. Vessels without licensed operators (as a rule) are being propelled in all directions at varying rates of speed with various levels of competency and without brakes.

The rules of the road on the waterway are generally taken from the *Collision Regulations for the Prevention of Loss of Life at Sea*. They are very similar to the rules of the road for highways as found in various highway traffic acts.

The rules can be simply stated in four phrases or ten words:

- Keep Right
- Give Right
- Big Is Right
- Nobody Is Right

Keep Right When approaching a vessel "head on," or nearly so, each vessel must alter course to starboard (right) and keep to the right hand (starboard) side of the channel or area of operations. The vessels

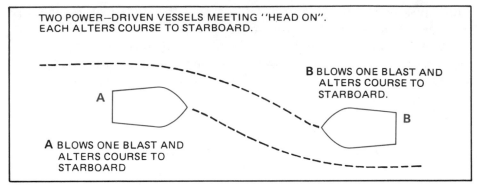

TWO POWER—DRIVEN VESSELS MEETING ''HEAD ON''.
EACH ALTERS COURSE TO STARBOARD.

B BLOWS ONE BLAST AND
ALTERS COURSE TO
STARBOARD.

A

B

A BLOWS ONE BLAST AND
ALTERS COURSE TO
STARBOARD

FIG. 1

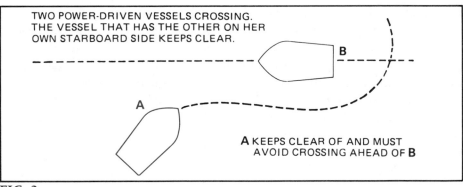

ANY VESSEL OVERTAKING ANOTHER
MUST KEEP CLEAR

A

B

FIG. 2

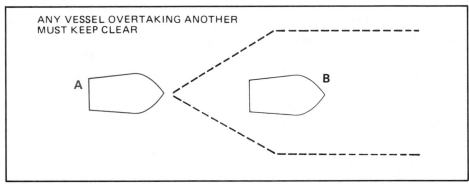

TWO POWER-DRIVEN VESSELS CROSSING.
THE VESSEL THAT HAS THE OTHER ON HER
OWN STARBOARD SIDE KEEPS CLEAR.

B

A

A KEEPS CLEAR OF AND MUST
AVOID CROSSING AHEAD OF **B**

FIG. 3

will pass "port to port." This is the same as the general rule involving automobiles in North America: keep to the right. (See Fig. 1.)

When overtaking another vessel, you must yield the right of way to the overtaken vessel. (See Fig. 2.)

Give Right When two vessels are each on a course such that their courses (paths) will cross, the vessel that has the other vessel on her starboard (right) side must give the right of way to the vessel on the right. (See Fig. 3.) This is similar to two vehicles approaching an unmarked or "courtesy" stop intersection. The vehicle on the right has the right of way.

Big Is Right There are times that a large vessel, merely because of its size, has the right of way. For example, a large freighter or ferry boat may be sailing through a channel where its movements may be restricted. Regardless of the rules, the larger vessels will have the right of way. This is one instance where a power vessel has the right of way over sailing vessels. According to *The Canadian Boating Handbook*, "In a narrow channel, a power-driven vessel less than 20m long or a sailing vessel must not hamper the safe passage of a vessel which can navigate only inside such a channel."

Nobody Is Right It is the responsibility of the skipper of any vessel to take whatever action that may be expected of a prudent seaman to prevent a collision at sea. Even though you may clearly have the right of way in a particular situation according to the regulations, you may be judged to have some legal responsibility (and you will most certainly have a moral responsibility) if you fail to take all reasonable action to prevent a collision. Also, in fog no one has the right of way until each can actually see each other (not by radar). In fog, the rate of speed should be slow enough so that the vessel can be stopped within one-half the distance of visibility.

Additional Considerations

- A vessel having the right of way must maintain her course and speed until the danger of collision no longer exists.
- Generally speaking, a power vessel must yield the right of way to a sailing vessel.
- A vessel headed downstream in a river with a significant current or headed in the same direction as the tidal current will have the right of way over a vessel headed upstream or against the tidal current.
- A sailing vessel on a starboard tack (having the wind coming from the right hand side of the vessel) will have the right of way over a sailing vessel on a port tack. (See Figs. 4b and 4c.)
- A sailing vessel beating into the wind will have the right of way over a sailing vessel running free with the wind. (See Fig. 4a.)
- When two sailing vessels are running free, or when on the same tack, the one furthest upwind must yield the right of way to the other.

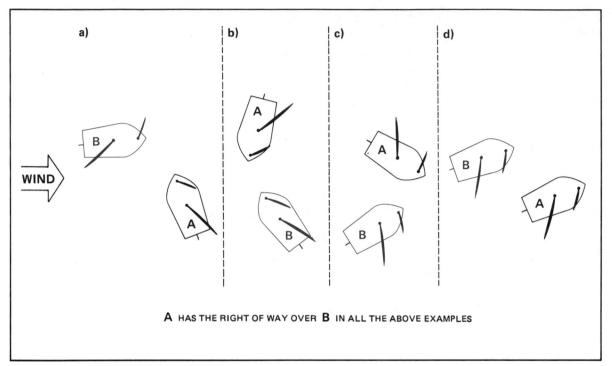

FIG. 4

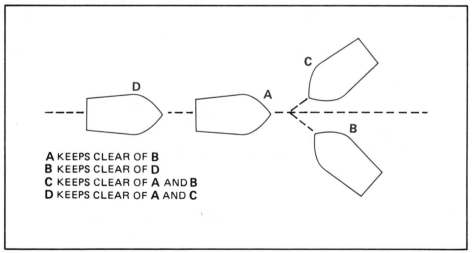

FIG. 5

- Sailing vessel regulations quoted here are generally the "International Rules of the Road." (See Fig. 4.) Special rules prevail for sail craft engaged in a race.

SUMMARY
Regulations are constantly under revision.
Some areas are subject to local regulations in addition to national regulations.
Regulations differ, country to country.
Obtain the latest regulations annually. In Canada, obtain the Canadian Coast Guard *Boating Handbook* free of charge from your local marina or chart dealer. In the U.S., obtain the equivalent publication of the United States Coast Guard.
Ask your chart dealer about other applicable local regulations.
Obtain regulations of foreign countries to be visited from your chart supplier.

In general:

- Keep to the right-hand side of channels or waterways.
- Vessels approaching from your right-hand side have the right of way.
- Yield the right of way to large vessels (over 65 feet).
- You have the final responsibility to avoid a collision.

Obtain and study an up-dated copy of *Collision Regulations for the Prevention of Loss of Life at Sea*.

2. Buoyage Systems

"Rocks have an affinity for propellers."

SAUNDERS' LAW OF NAVIGATION *#2*

LATERAL SYSTEM — NORTH AMERICAN

The system of buoyage used in Canadian waters is referred to as the "Lateral System of Buoyage." This term comes from the Latin origin of the word lateral — "side."

There are two principal colours of buoys, and we leave one colour on one side as we pass it, and the other colour on the other side.

Channel Buoys First, let us consider the two principal colours and shapes of buoys and their light colours and characteristics if lighted. There are red buoys which, when possible, are conical in shape or have pointed top spars (poles). If lighted, they will carry a red light. If a red buoy is numbered, it will bear an even number either with or without a prefix or suffix letter. If unlighted, such a buoy may be painted with a fluorescent band of orange near the top.

There are black buoys which, when possible, are can- or barrel-shaped or have flat top spars. If lighted, they will carry a green light. If a black buoy is numbered, it will bear an odd number either with or without a prefix or suffix letter. If unlighted, a black buoy may be painted with a fluorescent band of green near the top.

The general rule applicable to these red and black buoys *in U.S. and Canadian waters* is to leave the red buoys on your starboard side as you proceed:

- Upstream
- Into port
- Against an ebb tide
- Proceeding Southerly on the East Coast
- Proceeding Northerly on the West Coast

An easy way to remember this is: Red Right Returning
Consider returning (to port) as being:

- Proceeding upstream
- Entering a harbour

- Heading toward the mainland, and therefore against an ebb tide, or with a flood tide
- Travelling clockwise around the North American coast.

A few examples may help to clarify this rule. As you enter Toronto Harbour through the Western Gap, you will note that the red buoys and red lights are on your starboard side and the green lights and black buoys are on your port side. (See Fig. 6.) As you proceed upstream through the St. Lawrence Seaway along the Detroit River from Lake Erie to Lake St. Clair, you will again be in the proper channel if you pass all red lights and red buoys leaving them on your starboard and pass all green lights and black buoys leaving them on your port side. As you proceed through Captains' Passage on the West Coast (Chart 3450T) against the current from the ebb tide, you will follow the preferred channel if you leave the green light (black buoy) on your port side as you pass it. As you proceed North from Hangdog Bank to Byng Inlet on the East side of Georgian Bay, following the "Small Craft Route," you will see from the charts that the only safe passage is by leaving the red buoys on your starboard side. Remember the East side of Georgian Bay is considered a West coast because the bay is West of the Ontario mainland.

There exist, however, many exceptions to this rule, and caution should be exercised. You cannot assume that going between any two buoys, whether of the same colour or not, will result in a safe passage. Nor can you assume that leaving a buoy between you and shore will be correct. The *only* way to be certain is to obtain an updated chart and determine where the hazards are shown relative to the various aids to navigation (buoys and lights).

Day Beacons There are many locations where it is convenient and less costly to mount a day beacon on an island, wharf, or shore in lieu of mooring a buoy or building a lighthouse. Starboard-hand beacons (leave to starboard heading upstream or inbound) are triangular in shape with a red/orange border and are mounted pointed side up. The Port-hand beacons are square with a black/green border and are mounted with a flat side up.

Junction Buoys There are many other locations where the skipper may have the option of alternate channels. One, perhaps, may proceed into a major shipping terminal location, while an alternate channel may lead to a small craft mooring area, marina or yacht club. A junction buoy will be located at the point where the main channel divides into

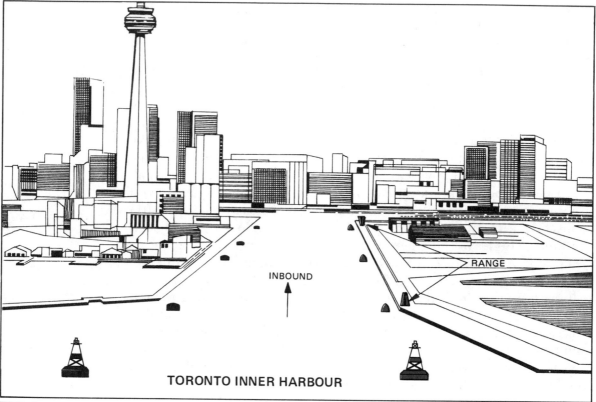

INBOUND

RANGE

TORONTO INNER HARBOUR

FIG. 6

these two options as you enter the harbour, and it will be painted with horizontal, alternating red and black stripes.

There are two possible colour combinations for junction buoys:

- Top stripe red, conical or pointed top. If lighted, a red light. If numbered, an even number. The major or main channel will be followed if you leave this buoy on your starboard side as you proceed into the harbour.
- Top stripe black, flat top or can-shaped. If lighted, a green light. If numbered, an odd number. By leaving this buoy on your port side you will follow the main channel when proceeding upstream.

Fairway Buoy   A fairway buoy is used to identify an area of deep water; generally it marks the centre of a main channel. It is frequently seen just outside a main harbour entrance.

For a detailed description of the "Lateral System of Buoyage," you should obtain a copy of the booklet, *The Canadian Aids to Navigation*

System, published by the Department of Transport and available from your chart dealer at no charge. Also, you should purchase from your dealer the booklet entitled, "Chart #1, Symbols and Abbreviations" to assist in locating and identifying these aids.

An excerpt from *The Canadian Aids to Navigation System* is illustrated as an example of the lateral systems in Canada and the U.S.A. (Fig. 7).

OTHER SYSTEMS OF BUOYAGE

There are several other systems of buoyage throughout the world:

- Intercoastal waterways (U.S.A.) — complex lateral system.
- State waters (U.S.A.) — combined cardinal and lateral system.
- Western rivers (U.S.A.) — essentially a lateral system, the same as the North American System.
- Cardinal system (European) — recommended reading for further details: *The American Practical Navigator*, Vol. 1, Bowditch.
- Uniform cardinal system (European and others).

Further information on U.S.A. systems and the symbols and abbreviations used on U.S. charts are available in "Chart No. 1 United States of America Nautical Chart Symbols and Abbreviations." This publication should be obtainable from most marine supply stores and chart dealers. Additional information on the "Cardinal System of Buoyage" can be found in the *American Practical Navigator*, Publication H.O.9, commonly referred to as "Bowditch," or in *Reed's Nautical Almanac*, published in various editions covering many countries and areas world wide.

COLOURS OF BUOY LIGHTS

Three main colours of lights are used on navigation buoys: red, green and white.

Red Light   Red lights are used on lighted red buoys and on lighted red and black horizontally banded buoys indicating that the safe or preferred channel will be followed by keeping the buoy on the vessel's starboard (right) hand when proceeding upstream.

Green Light   Green lights are used on lighted black buoys and on lighted red and black horizontally banded buoys indicating that the safe or preferred channel will be followed by keeping the buoy on the vessel's port (left) hand when proceeding upstream.

White Light   White lights are used on black and white vertically striped buoys, solid white buoys and on other special purpose buoys.

The Canadian Aids to Navigation System

Aids to navigation must be used in conjunction with charts, light lists and sailing directions to understand and interpret their function properly.

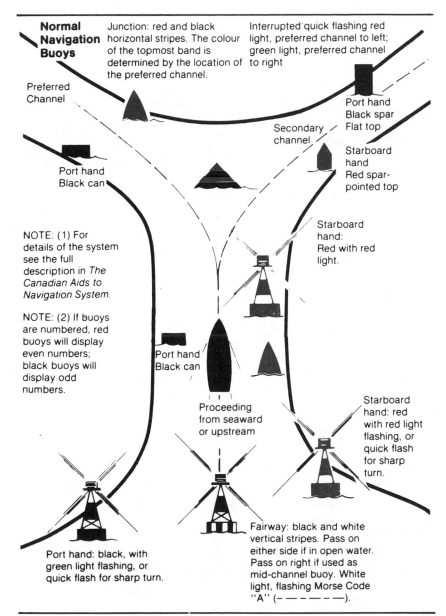

Normal Navigation Buoys

Junction: red and black horizontal stripes. The colour of the topmost band is determined by the location of the preferred channel.

Interrupted quick flashing red light, preferred channel to left; green light, preferred channel to right

Preferred Channel

Port hand Black spar Flat top

Secondary channel

Starboard hand Red spar- pointed top

Port hand Black can

Starboard hand: Red with red light.

NOTE: (1) For details of the system see the full description in *The Canadian Aids to Navigation System*.

NOTE: (2) If buoys are numbered, red buoys will display even numbers; black buoys will display odd numbers.

Port hand Black can

Proceeding from seaward or upstream

Starboard hand: red with red light flashing, or quick flash for sharp turn.

Port hand: black, with green light flashing, or quick flash for sharp turn.

Fairway: black and white vertical stripes. Pass on either side if in open water. Pass on right if used as mid-channel buoy. White light, flashing Morse Code "A" (– — – — – —).

FIG. 7

LIGHT PHASE CHARACTERISTICS

Fixed Light A fixed light, marked as (F) on charts, has the characteristic of being constantly lit and is a white light unless otherwise specified by the use of a letter symbol denoting some other colour. It is used generally as a part of the overall pattern of lights to direct the vessel to the proper side of a hazard, or as a part of a general traffic scheme.

Flashing Light A flashing (Fl) light is used on port, starboard-hand and anchorage buoys. It flashes 15 times per minute.

Quick Flashing Light A quick flashing (QkFl) light is used on port and starboard-hand buoys where a distinct cautionary emphasis is desired, such as, a sharp turn in a channel, a wreck or other obstruction. It is also used on a number of special purpose buoys. It flashes 60 times per minute.

Interrupted Quick Flashing Light An interrupted quick flashing (IntQkFl) sequence is used on junction or middle-ground buoys marking locations, such as wrecks or other obstructions, that can be passed on either side. It consists of a series of 8 quick flashes followed by a dark period. This pattern is repeated every 12 seconds.

Morse Code Letter "A" The Morse Code letter A (MO(A)) is used on fairway buoys. It is identifiable by a short flash followed by a long flash every 6 seconds.

These light characteristics, excerpted from *Canadian Aids to Navigation*, are generalizations. The appropriate chart and "Symbols and Abbreviations" should always be consulted to ensure a safe passage.

Particularly on rocky, well-travelled coast lines and in and around large harbours, lights are frequently mounted on towers, lighthouses, day beacons, etc. These lights, where practical, will be red to starboard when inbound. However their characteristics may be:

- Fixed or steady light
- Flashing in some other sequence than those listed above.
- Combination light: more than one colour or characteristic on one tower or lighthouse.
- Lights that may display a colour in one limited direction (arc of visibility), including sector lights.
- Lights of colours other than the three main colours of red, green and white.

There are exceptions to denote special circumstances. Range lights consisting of 2 lights in line denote a safe channel in the direction of their alignment. Sector lights denote either a safe or a hazardous area within the arc of visibility. Interpretation of safe passage areas is made by study of the chart.

The lateral buoyage system in North America consists of red or black buoys with "red right returning." In addition to the cardinal system of buoyage used in other areas of the world, including the Caribbean, some nations combine the cardinal with a lateral system except that the black or green is on the right when returning. The International Association of Lighthouse Authorities (IALA) has developed a universal system of buoyage combining both the cardinal and lateral systems and adopting a standardized colour and light system, though one significant variation still exists. There are two areas agreed upon by the IALA nations: Area A consists of all navigable waters in other than Area B. Area B consists of the Western Hemisphere, including North and South America, the Caribbean, Hawaii, Japan, the Republic of Korea and the Philippines. The new IALA maritime system of buoyage for Area B is reproduced on the end papers of this book. All aspects of the Area A system are identical except for the reversal of colours of the red and green buoys and lights.

Canada will be adopting the IALA system in 1983 and 1984. The United States will also adopt this system, probably in the latter part of the 1980's. The IALA system will not significantly affect the recreational boater because most inland waterways will be relatively unchanged except that the colours of fairway buoys will be changed to red and white and the black buoys will be painted green. The cardinal system aspect will principally prevail at landfalls and off the coasts. The benefits will be enormous in terms of standardization.

SUMMARY

There are various buoyage systems in different countries. In the U.S.A. and Canada, the lateral system of buoyage is used: "Red Right Returning." Keep all red buoys, beacons and lights on your right hand side when:

- Going upstream
- Against the ebb tide
- Into port
- Southbound on an East coast
- Northbound on a West coast

Always obtain a current issue chart of your area and interpret the buoys relative to the location of hazards. Keep your charts up-to-date through the use of the weekly *Notices to Mariners*.

3. Introduction to Charts

"To avoid getting lost, don't go anywhere."
SAUNDERS' LAW OF NAVIGATION *#3*

Charts are produced in Canada by the Canadian Hydrographic Services and in the U.S. by the Defense Mapping Agency or by the National Ocean Survey. These and foreign charts are available for virtually all navigable waters and may be obtained at most marine supply stores, many marinas and yacht clubs, as well as various authorized chart dealers.

Charts are the mariner's equivalent of a road map, except that they provide much more information and are far more vital to a mariner's safety than a map is to a motorist. They are a representation of the geographic and physical characteristics of a portion of the earth's surface — an aerial picture.

Charts provide information, location, size, colour or other pertinent data about the items listed below. The symbols used on charts are illustrated in U.S. and Canadian Charts #1.

- Aids — Buoys, Lights
- Conspicuous Objects
- Hazards — Magnetic
          — Storms
- Gunnery Ranges
- Rocks
- Shoals
- Anchorages
- Overhead Cables
- Submarine Cables
- Bridges
- Directions
- Ports/Harbours
- Services — Food/Fuel
- Marinas — Repairs
- Seaplane Bases
- Points of Local Interest
- Distance
- Location
- Shipping Lanes
- Waterfalls
- Dams
- Locks
- Tidal Rips
- Topography

REGULATORY REQUIREMENTS

In addition to being as important to safety as a life jacket, the "Small Vessel Regulations" require that all vessels, except rowboats and canoes, must carry on board appropriate charts of the area, unless the skipper or navigator can satisfy the authorities that he or she is totally familiar with *all* navigational aspects of the area. These charts must be updated to the latest issue of the weekly *Notices to Mariners*.

The regulations also require that in addition to charts all recreational vessels, except rowboats and canoes, must have on board the following publications:

Symbols and Abbreviations (Chart #1)   Contains data required to be able to interpret a chart.

Boating Handbook   A summary of the "Small Vessel Regulations."

Sailing Directions or, if appropriate, *Trent-Severn Waterways Guide* or *British Columbia Small Craft Guide*   These publications contain descriptions, sketches, aerial photographs of harbours, hazardous areas, prominent landmarks and coastlines.

List of Lights, Buoys and Fog Signals   Locations and characteristics of such aids to navigation.

Information Catalogue   Essentially a map listing the coverage and number of each of the charts of waterways.

Code of Navigating Practices and Procedures   Primarily appropriate to large commercial vessels.

The publications listed below may also be required as appropriate. Refer to Chapter 6 for a more detailed explanation of charts and their use.

Radio Aids to Marine Navigation   Location, frequency and characteristics of radio aids.

Tide and Current Tables   Available for the appropriate coastal area.

Canal Regulations   Required if using the Trent-Severn waterway or Rideau River locks.

Radio Telephone Operators Handbook   Required if the vessel is equipped with a VHF radio transmitter; both a radio station and operators licence are also required.

SUMMARY
The use of charts is:

- Vital to your safety.
- Required by regulation.

4. Basic Compass Knowledge

"If God had meant for us to travel in a fog, we would be magnets."
                                                                    A SAILOR

It is vital to your safety and the safety of your vessel that you know where you are at all times. Without such navigational aids as radar, Loran, Decca, Consolan or radio direction finders, the ship's compass is the only reliable source of knowledge. Few pleasure boats are equipped with sophisticated electronic devices, all of which are subject to equipment failure or failure of power to operate them. The compass, however, is a highly reliable device. In the writer's opinion it is more reliable than any more complex equipment for small craft use and well within the financial means of every boater.

Some boaters have a compass on their vessel either because it is expected of them, or because it was already installed when they purchased the boat. Some boaters have a compass as a means of satisfying their curiosity as to what approximate course they are steering, or to satisfy their curiosity that their cottage, marina or launch ramp is South-west of a funny red triangular sign on the tip of the island in the middle of the lake.

Far more practical, interesting and vital uses can be made of a properly installed and compensated compass. It may even spell the difference between a safe, enjoyable, interesting voyage and one that ends in disaster. For the boater who is sailing out of sight of land or familiar landmarks, or who is ever likely to be cruising in fog, rain, darkness — even in familiar waters — a compass is as necessary as a life jacket or a means of propulsion. However, equally as important as the compass itself is a complete understanding of its functions and uses.

USES OF A COMPASS
- Determining what course(s) to steer to get from where you are to where you want to be: plotting a course.
- Determining where you think you are: dead reckoning.
- Determining where you actually are: obtaining a fix.

© DANFORTH

FIG. 8

- Determining distance/direction to/from navigational hazards: distance off.
- Determining the direction and rate of leeway due to wind and/or drift due to current: difference between dead reckon position and fix.
- Estimating the time of day, from azimuth tables of the sun.
- Assisting in locating aids to navigation.
- Determining a specific location in the water in order to be able to return to it: good fishing, sunken treasure, wreck, etc.
- Navigating safely in reduced visibility: fog, rain, night, etc.
- Determining the most favoured tack to win sailing races (not a subject of this book).

THE THEORY OF MAGNETISM
The molecular structure of some materials is such that the molecules may line up in orderly rows. One end of a bar of iron, for example, will have a concentration of molecules that repel or oppose each other and

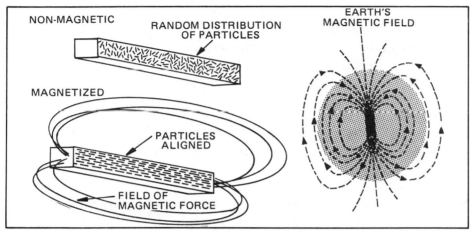

FIG. 9   FIG. 10

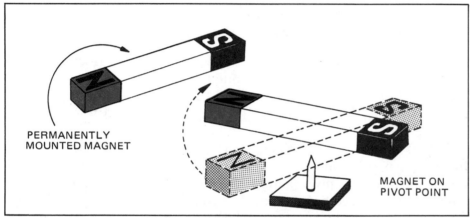

FIG. 11

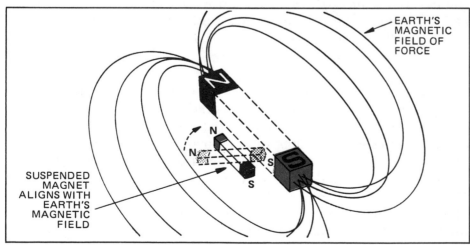

FIG. 12

try to move away from the concentration of molecules at the other end. One type of molecule (or concentration of molecules) is known as a North pole and the other as a South pole. (See Fig. 9.)

THE EARTH AS A MAGNET
The core of the earth is magnetic, and the molecules through its centre are lined up in such a way that one end of an imaginary bar through the centre of the earth is close to the Geographic North Pole and the other end is near the Geographic South Pole. (See Fig. 10.)

A MAGNET AS A COMPASS
When two magnets are placed close together and suspended so that they can rotate, the magnets will take positions where the South pole of one magnet will be close to the North pole of the other, because:

> Like Poles Repel Each Other, And
> Unlike Poles Attract Each Other.

Thus, if a magnet is suspended to rotate freely in the absence of any other magnets, it will rotate so that one end will be attracted toward the Magnetic North Pole of the earth, and the other end will be attracted toward the Magnetic South Pole. (See Figs. 11 and 12.)

COMPASS CONSTRUCTION
In a simple needle compass a small bar of magnetized iron is suspended on the top of a sharp pivot point so that the bar (needle) is free to rotate. One end of the needle will point toward the Magnetic North Pole, and the opposite end will point toward the Magnetic South Pole. The circular compass case is marked with directions such as East, West, North-east, South-east and so on. A ship's compass is built on the same theory as a simple needle compass, with some refinements to adapt it to easy use aboard a vessel. (See Fig. 8.)

Compass Card　The card of a ship's compass is a circular piece of non-magnetic material with markings on the upper surface in the form of a circular protractor. The circumference is marked with angles in a clockwise direction from 000° through 090°, 180°, 270° to 000° (360°). Marks are usually at 5° increments. (See Fig. 13.)

　　A magnet or pair of magnets is mounted on the under surface of the card so that the North-seeking pole is in line with the 000° mark on the upper side and the South-seeking pole is in line with the 180° mark on the upper side. (See Fig. 14.)

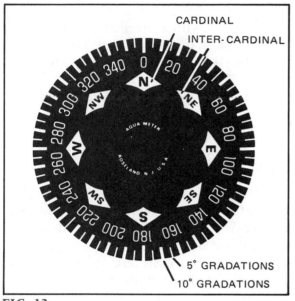

CARDINAL

INTER-CARDINAL

5° GRADATIONS

10° GRADATIONS

FIG. 13

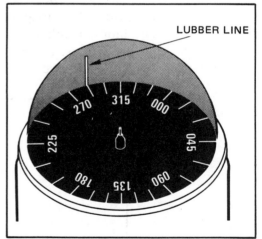

COMPASS CARD WITH MAGNETS MOUNTED ON UNDERSIDE OF CARD.

FIG. 14

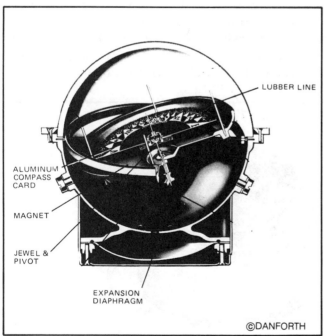

LUBBER LINE

ALUMINUM COMPASS CARD

MAGNET

JEWEL & PIVOT

EXPANSION DIAPHRAGM

©DANFORTH

FIG. 15

LUBBER LINE

FIG. 16

Suspension of the Compass Card   The card of a ship's compass is mounted on top of a sharp point, usually with a jewelled bearing, so the card is able to rotate freely and may tilt on top of the pivot. The card and pivot point are enclosed within a clear-topped case which is filled with a liquid such as kerosene. (See Fig. 15.)

The liquid serves to support part of the weight of the card, and because the card must move within the liquid, the card tends to move more slowly and does not "overshoot" the proper direction when rotating to align with the North and South Magnetic Poles. Thus, the movement of the card is damped and remains more steady.

Lubber Line and Compensators   A line (lubber line) is marked at one point on the circumference of the clear-topped housing. (See Fig. 16.) This line is used as a reference point enabling the helmsman to determine the direction in which the bow of the vessel is pointing. Below the container of liquid, inside the case, are mounted small magnets that can be rotated or positioned inside the case by means of small screws projecting through the case. (See Fig. 17.) These compensating magnets can be positioned by the adjustment screws to offset or nullify the magnetic effect of extraneous objects, such as the engine block or other iron parts of the vessel or items aboard the vessel. The entire case assembly is mounted within gimballed rings that permit the compass case to remain level as the vessel heels, rolls or pitches.

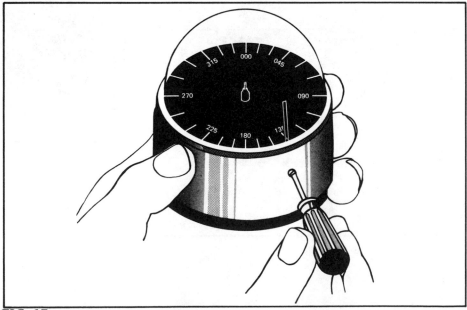

FIG. 17

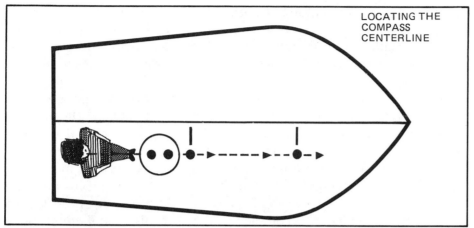

LOCATING THE COMPASS CENTERLINE

FIG. 18. *The line between the centre of the compass and the compass must be parallel to the keel.*

MOUNTING A COMPASS

Key factors to consider in mounting a compass are:

- Easy visibility for the helmsman.
- Keeping it as remote as possible from electrical, magnetic or electronic influence.
- Mounting it so that a horizontal line between the compass lubber line and the centre of the compass is parallel to the keel of the vessel. (See Fig. 18.)
- Positioning it so that it will not impede a clear view for the helmsman.
- To the extent possible, placing it so the maximum of the horizon is visible in all directions over the top of the compass to facilitate taking compass bearings.
- Positioning it to allow the compass to be self-levelling in the gimbals.
- Mounting it so that it will not be subject to damage: passengers or crew will not bump into it or be tempted to use it as a hand-hold.
- Pairs of electrical wires in the vicinity of the compass should be twisted together to minimize magnetic interference.
- Placing it adjacent to access to power if the compass is to be lighted.
- Securing it in a position to minimize theft from an unattended craft.

COMPASS COMPENSATION

Due to the magnetic properties of objects aboard a vessel, the compass may not align exactly with the earth's magnetic field. Most pleasure vessel compasses are equipped with a built-in means of correcting or compensating for these errors. A compass should be compensated when initially installed and subsequently any time that major equipment has been modified, moved or installed that may affect the magnetic properties of the boat.

A compass can only be compensated when mounted permanently in the vessel and with all switches and power, etc. in the normal operating position (either on or off) and with all normal gear installed and stowed. All iron, magnetic or electronic equipment should be stowed or installed as far from the compass as possible. The anchor, for example, should always be stowed the same way up and in the same position. The depth sounder and radios should be on or off as is your normal cruising practice. Do not leave lighters, tools, light meters, etc. in the vicinity of the compass. For a detailed compensation procedure, see Appendix A.

MAGNETIC COMPASSES

Flat Card Compass   The lubber line is on the forward edge of the compass case of a flat card compass. North (000°) will be marked on the card near the edge so that when the vessel is headed magnetic North, 000° will be on the forward edge of the card and will appear to be under the lubber line on the compass case. The markings will read clockwise from 000° through 090°, 180°, etc., to 000° (360°). When the vessel is headed magnetic West, 285° will be on the forward edge of the card and appear to be under the lubber line on the compass case. (See Fig. 16.)

Reverse Card Compass   The lubber line is on aft edge of the compass case. North (000°) will be marked on the card near the edge so that when the vessel is headed magnetic North, 000° will be on the aft edge of the card and will appear to be under the lubber line on the compass case. The markings read clockwise the same as stated above. All compass bearings taken in the usual manner on this style of compass will be reciprocal (reverse) bearings. (See Fig. 19.)

CAUTION: if the compass is designed for mounting with the lubber line forward, and, if you mount it lubber line aft, all courses will be reciprocal (reverse).

DRUM CARD COMPASS
This type is similar to automotive and aircraft compasses. The markings are printed on the outer surface of a drum and viewed through a window in the after side of the compass. The lubber line is aft. It is not

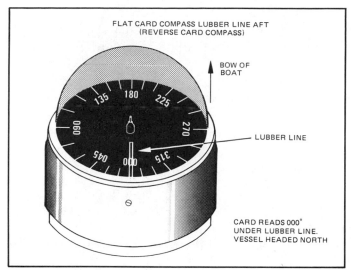

FLAT CARD COMPASS LUBBER LINE AFT
(REVERSE CARD COMPASS)

BOW OF
BOAT

LUBBER LINE

CARD READS 000°
UNDER LUBBER LINE.
VESSEL HEADED NORTH

FIG. 19

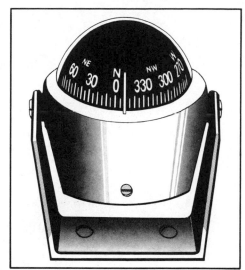

FIG. 20

practical to take bearings with this type of compass, although it is not un-common on sailboats and is usually "bulkhead-mounted." (See Fig. 20.)

HAND BEARING COMPASS

This is a portable, hand-held compass (usually drum type) with a viewfinder and reticule. (See Fig. 21.) It is designed to take bearings from your vessel to other objects. It is not practical to be used as a steering compass but it may be used as such in the event of failure of the main compass. Do not store or use a hand-bearing compass adjacent to the ship's compass.

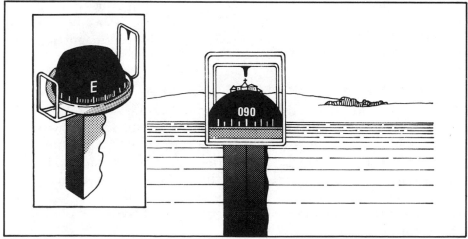

FIG. 21

HOW TO READ A COMPASS

In this section it is assumed that you have a regular boat or ship's compass: a flat card compass with the lubber line on the forward surface of the compass case.

From your position at the helm (aft of the compass), note the point on the compass card immediately below or in line with the lubber line. The numerical value of this point is the angle between your course line (ship's heading) and a line between your vessel and the Magnetic North Pole. For example, the compass in Figure 16 indicates that the boat is headed in a direction of 285°, which is a bit North of West.

Examples

1. **Your compass reads 000°.**

   You are headed along the line toward the Magnetic North Pole. Your ship's heading is 000° magnetic. (See Fig. 22.) We will discuss true courses and compass courses in Chapter 5.

2. **Your compass reads 090°.**

   You are headed along a line at 90° to the right (clockwise) of the line toward the Magnetic North Pole. Your ship's heading is 090° magnetic. You are headed East (magnetic). (See Fig. 23.)

3. **Your compass reads 135°.**

   You are headed along a line at 135° to the right (clockwise) of the line toward the Magnetic North Pole. Your ship's heading is 135° magnetic. You are headed South-east (magnetic). (See Fig. 24.)

4. **Your compass reads 285°.**

   You are headed along a line at 285° to the right (clockwise) of the line toward the Magnetic North Pole. Your ship's heading is 285° magnetic. You are headed somewhat North of West (magnetic). (See Fig. 25.)

HELMSMANSHIP AND THE COMPASS

The compass card is mounted on a precision bearing so that it is free to rotate. However, your compass card does not rotate! The compass case rotates under the compass card! On the card, 000° is continuously pointed toward the Magnetic North Pole. The compass case and vessel are fastened together and the lubber line is a permanent part of the compass case. Therefore, the vessel and lubber line rotate under the compass card! A total and clear understanding of these facts is vital to good helmsmanship.

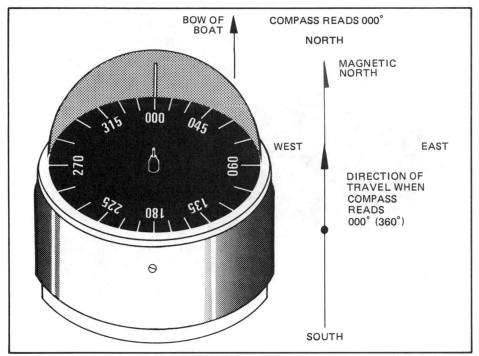

FIG. 22

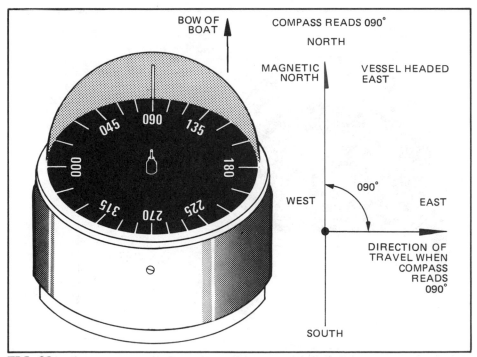

FIG. 23

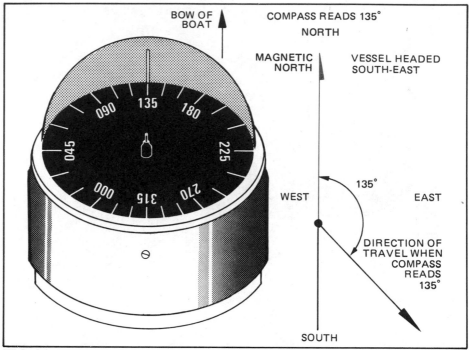

FIG. 24

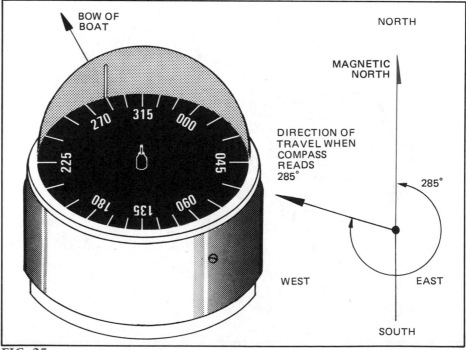

FIG. 25

If the lubber line is to the right of your intended heading, you must steer left — to port — to correct your heading. If the lubber line is to the left of your intended heading, you must steer right — to starboard — to correct your heading. These instructions (port and starboard) are reversed if your compass is the drum type or a flat card type with the lubber line aft.

Steer to move the lubber line. Do *not* steer to rotate the compass card.

SUMMARY

- A magnetic compass is the primary means of navigation for pleasure boats. As such, it is an instrument vital to safe boating.
- Magnetic compasses seek out the North (and South) Magnetic Poles (except for the deviation explained in the next chapter.)
- Magnetic compasses may require correction (compensation) after installation.
- Magnetic compasses are affected by outside magnetic influences, such as camera light meters, electrical current, iron and steel objects.
- Magnetic vessel compasses indicate direction of travel as an angle of direction relative to the North Magnetic Pole (except for deviation).

5. Compass Errors – Variation and Deviation

"If there is more than one possible destination (and there nearly always is), you will most assuredly arrive at the wrong one."

SAUNDERS' LAW OF NAVIGATION #4

TRUE NORTH AND ITS LOCATION

The earth rotates on its axis at the rate of one revolution every 24 hours. The axis of rotation of the earth can be compared to an axle. This axle (axis) intersects the earth's surface at two locations. One location is termed the True North Pole and the other is the True South Pole. This can be readily visualized by looking at a common globe of the earth. The two points of suspension are the True North Pole and the True South Pole. The globe rotates about the axis between these two points. (See Fig. 26.)

MERIDIANS OF LONGITUDE

If you stretch a string taut between the True North Pole and the True South Pole, it will represent the shortest distance between the two poles. This is called a meridian of longitude. If you are on the surface of the earth, you are somewhere on such a line, and if you look along this line in one direction, you will be looking directly toward one of the two true poles. Assume that it is the True North Pole. Then, if you reverse your direction 180°, you will be looking directly toward the True South Pole. (See Fig. 27.)

As you look toward the True North (or South) Pole, any object directly in your line of sight will be directly true North (or South) of you and will be on the same meridian of longitude as you are.

The equator is a line around the surface of the earth connecting all the points on all meridians of longitude that are equidistant from the

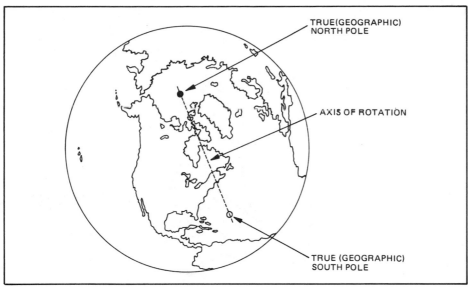

FIG. 26

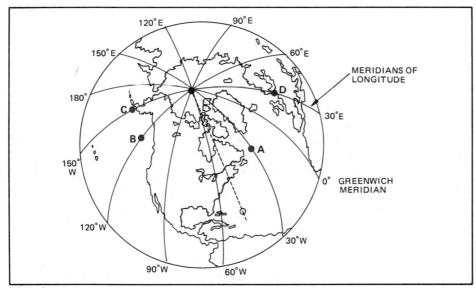

FIG. 27

Point A is on meridian 30°W. True North from Point A is directly along the 30°W meridian.

Point B is on meridian 120°W. True North from Point B is directly along the 120°W meridian.

Point C is on meridian 150°W. Any point on meridian 150°W between C and the True North Pole bears (lies) due North (true) of Point C.

Point D is on meridian 30°E. Any point on meridian 30°E between D and the True South Pole bears (lies) due South (true) of Point D.

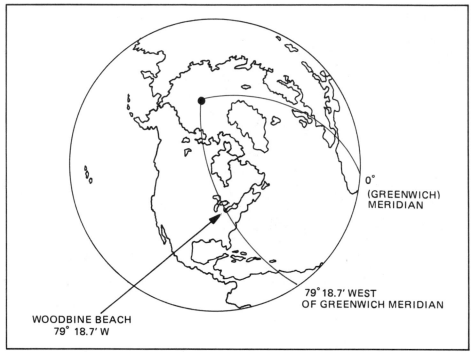

0°
(GREENWICH)
MERIDIAN

79° 18.7' WEST
OF GREENWICH MERIDIAN

WOODBINE BEACH
79° 18.7' W

FIG. 28

two poles. Just as there are an infinite number of points on the surface of the earth at the equator, then so are there an infinite number of meridians of longitude. By convention, most globes have the meridians of longitude marked on them at 15° increments.

The earth is 360° in diameter, as is every circle or sphere. Therefore, 24 meridians, each 15° apart, are marked on the globe. But, every point on earth falls on some meridian even though that meridian is not marked on the globe (or chart). As an example, a location on Woodbine Beach adjacent to the Coatsworth Cut at Ashbridges Bay in Toronto, Ontario, is on a meridian 79° 18.7' West of the meridian on which Greenwich, England, is located. By definition, the meridian of Greenwich is the Prime Meridian (0°) from which all other meridians are measured, either East or West. (See Fig. 28).

MAGNETIC NORTH AND ITS LOCATION
The theoretical bar magnet running through the centre of the earth and actuating your compass is not located on the axis of rotation of the earth, and so the Magnetic North Pole and Magnetic South Pole are not located at the same point on earth as the True North Pole and True

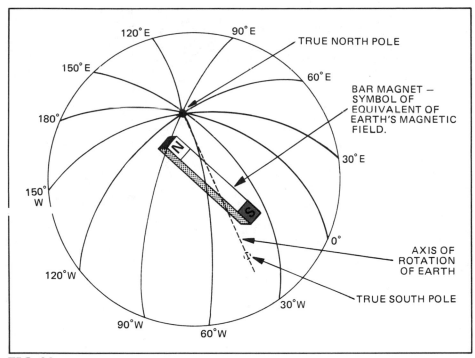

FIG. 29

Notice that the Magnetic North Pole of the earth's magnetic field is on approximately 90°W meridian in the Northwest Territories on Prince of Wales Island.
Similarly, the Magnetic South Pole is not located at the True (Geographic) South Pole.

South Pole. (see Fig. 29.) As a result, a magnetic compass does not seek out or point to the true poles but does seek out and point to the magnetic poles.

The compass card will *not* point along your meridian to the True North Pole. Because it points to the Magnetic North Pole, it will point along a line that makes an angle to your meridian.

VARIATION

This angular difference between the line toward the True North Pole (your meridian) and the line toward the Magnetic North Pole is called variation. The difference (*variation*) *will be a different amount* and in a *different direction depending on your location on earth.* (See Figs. 30, 31, 32 and 33.)

The Magnetic North Pole is located near Prince of Wales Island in Canada about 800 miles from the True North Pole. If you are on a meridian of longitude that passes through the location of the North

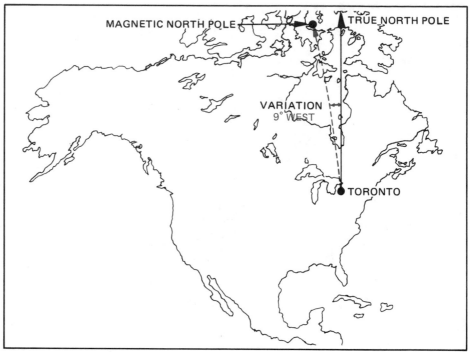

FIG. 30

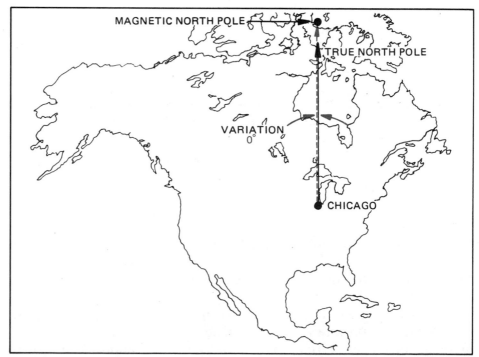

FIG. 31

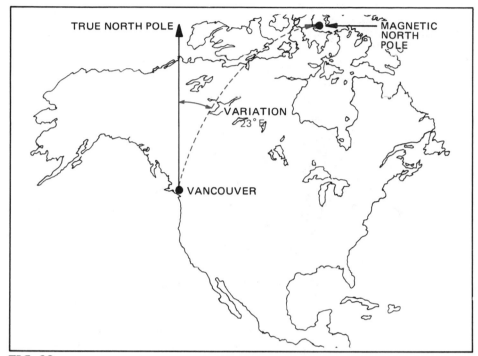

FIG. 32

Magnetic Pole, and if you are South of the Magnetic North Pole (say Chicago, Illinois), then variation will be 0°. (See Fig. 33.) This is so because your compass card is pointing along a line toward the Magnetic North Pole. The Magnetic North Pole and True North Pole are in line when you are in Chicago. Your compass card is then coincidentally pointing toward the True North as well as the Magnetic North Pole. No angular difference exists between the two lines, therefore there is no variation (0°).

Assuming that you are due East of the Magnetic North Pole, the compass card will, when pointing to the Magnetic North Pole, be pointing in a direction due West of you and variation will be 90° West. (See Fig. 33.)

Due to irregularities in the earth's magnetic field, the only way for the pleasure boater to determine variation for his locality is by consulting a chart. Within each compass rose on the chart there are two compass cards printed. The outer ring shows true directions, and the inner ring shows magnetic directions. The actual variation *for that locality* is also printed within the compass rose. Note that the variation may change slightly from year to year. (See Fig. 34.)

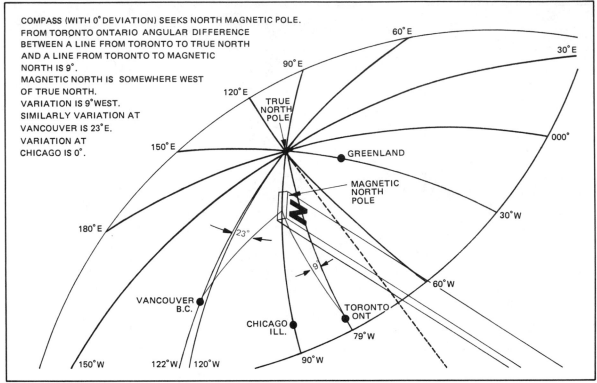

COMPASS (WITH 0° DEVIATION) SEEKS NORTH MAGNETIC POLE.
FROM TORONTO ONTARIO ANGULAR DIFFERENCE
BETWEEN A LINE FROM TORONTO TO TRUE NORTH
AND A LINE FROM TORONTO TO MAGNETIC
NORTH IS 9°.
MAGNETIC NORTH IS SOMEWHERE WEST
OF TRUE NORTH.
VARIATION IS 9° WEST.
SIMILARLY VARIATION AT
VANCOUVER IS 23° E.
VARIATION AT
CHICAGO IS 0°.

FIG. 33

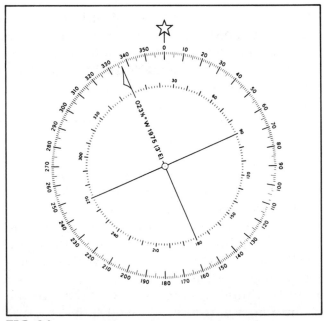

FIG. 34

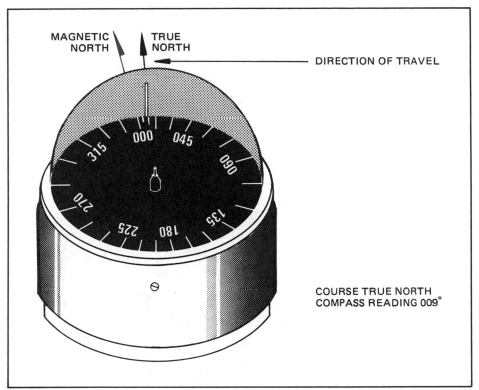

MAGNETIC NORTH

TRUE NORTH

DIRECTION OF TRAVEL

000 045 315 060 270 135 225 180

COURSE TRUE NORTH
COMPASS READING 009°

FIG. 35

Converting — True to Magnetic, Magnetic to True   *All directions on a chart are true directions*. Therefore, all courses and bearings must be plotted as true, even though the compass rose (inner) would allow the plotting of magnetic directions.

Consistency is important. Always plot true directions. Remember, variation differs depending where we are on the earth's surface. On some charts the variation at extreme sides of the chart may differ. Always use the compass rose closest to your location and *plot true directions only*.

Variation Examples   In determining how to convert magnetic to true (and vice versa), let us examine what happens to a compass card when we are in an area where variation is not 0°, say, Toronto, Ontario.

Assume that your vessel is headed true North (000°). By reference to a globe you will note that a line (meridian) from Toronto to the True North Pole does not pass through Prince of Wales Island, the location of the Magnetic North Pole. (See Fig. 33.) Prince of Wales Island is West of your meridian. On your compass card 000° will point to the Magnetic

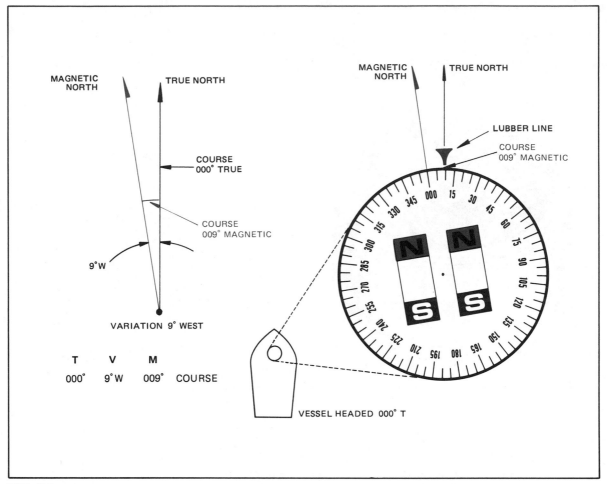

FIG. 36

North Pole and read 009°, assuming no other errors in your compass. (See Fig. 35.)

On your compass card, 000° will be rotated slightly counter-clockwise pointing West of true North. Referring to a chart of Toronto Harbour, you will note that variation is 9° West (approx.). Your compass card will be pointing 9° West of true North, even though you are headed true North, and thus your compass lubber line will give you a reading of 009°. (See Fig. 36.)

True Heading	000°
Variation	9° West
Magnetic Heading	009°

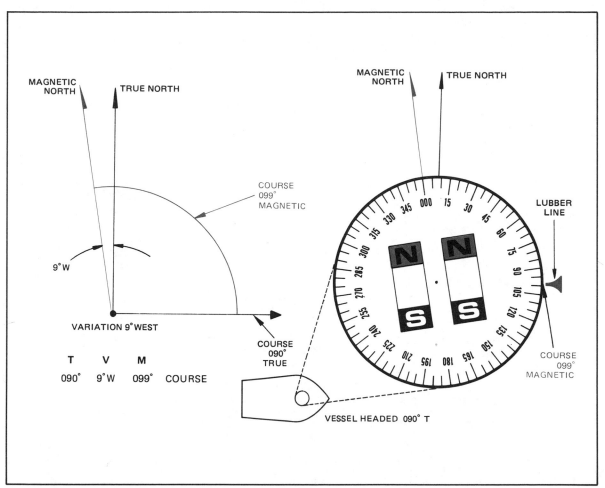

FIG. 37

Similarly, if your vessel is heading true East (090°), and you are in Toronto Harbour, your compass reading will be 099°, because the card is rotated 9° to the West of true North. (See Fig. 37.)

True Heading	090°
Variation	9° West
Magnetic Heading	099°

Therefore, if variation is West, *add* variation to the true heading to obtain your magnetic heading. (See Table I on page 48.)

Consider now that you are on the West Coast of Canada, say, Point Roberts, near Vancouver, British Columbia. Assume that your vessel

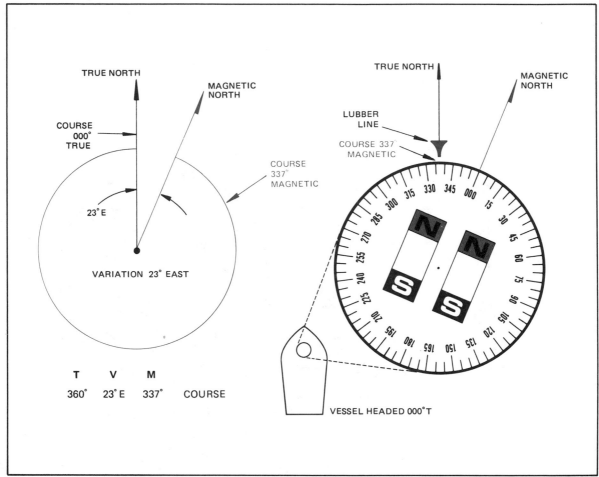

FIG. 38

is again headed true North (000°). Again, refer to the globe and you will note that Prince of Wales Island (Magnetic North Pole) lies East of your meridian. (See Fig. 33.) On the compass card 000° will be rotated clockwise pointing East of true North. Refer to Chart T-3450 and you will see that variation is 23° East (approx.). Even though you are headed true North, your compass lubber line will read 337° (See Fig. 38.)

True Heading	000° (360°)
Variation	23° East
Magnetic Heading	337°

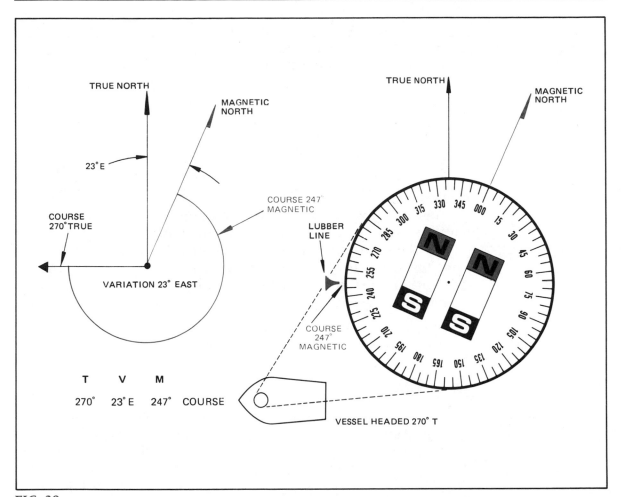

FIG. 39

Similarly, if you are headed true West, and you are near Point Roberts, your compass reading will be 247°, because the card is rotated 23° to the East of North. (See Fig. 39.)

True Heading	270°
Variation	23° East
Magnetic Heading	247°

Therefore, if Variation is East, *subtract* variation from the true heading to obtain your magnetic heading. (See Table I on page 48.)

TABLE I TVMDC		
True Direction	**Variation (from chart)**	**Magnetic Direction**
000°	9° West (Add)	= 009° Magnetic Greater (Best)
090°	9° West (Add)	= 099° Magnetic Greater (Best)
000° (360°)	23° East (Subtract)	= 337° Magnetic Lesser (Least)
090°	23° East (Subtract)	= 067° Magnetic Lesser (Least)
180°	23° East (Subtract)	= 157° Magnetic Lesser (Least)
270°	23° East (Subtract)	= 247° Magnetic Lesser (Least)

From Table I we can see that, in converting true to magnetic, variation West requires the addition of variation to true, while variation East requires the subtraction of variation from true. On the other hand, in converting magnetic to true, variation West requires the subtraction of variation from magnetic, while variation East requires the addition of variation to magnetic. These rules are easily remembered by the rhyme:

Variation East — Magnetic Least
Variation West — Magnetic Best

DEVIATION

Practically every vessel will have a magnetic field peculiar to that particular vessel due to iron objects or electrical circuits aboard. The engine block, anchor, galley stove, icebox or refrigerator, and iron fittings (including some types of stainless steel) all affect the magnetic field. Such fields result in the equivalent of a magnet being carried somewhere aboard. (See Fig. 40.) This "magnet" will have an effect on the compass, and *its effect will be peculiar to that particular vessel and equipment*. This magnetic effect will result in compass error. This error is called *deviation*, the angular difference between a line from the vessel to the Magnetic North Pole and the line along which 000° on the compass card is pointing. (See Fig. 41.) In other words, *deviation* is the angular *difference between magnetic North and compass North*; whereas *variation* is the angular *difference between true North and magnetic North*.

Compensating the compass as discussed earlier will nullify a great portion of this error. However, most small craft compasses cannot be compensated sufficiently to completely eliminate it.

How to determine the deviation of the compass on your boat is described fully in Appendix B. Remember that deviation must be determined on a series of different headings and is peculiar to your particular boat.

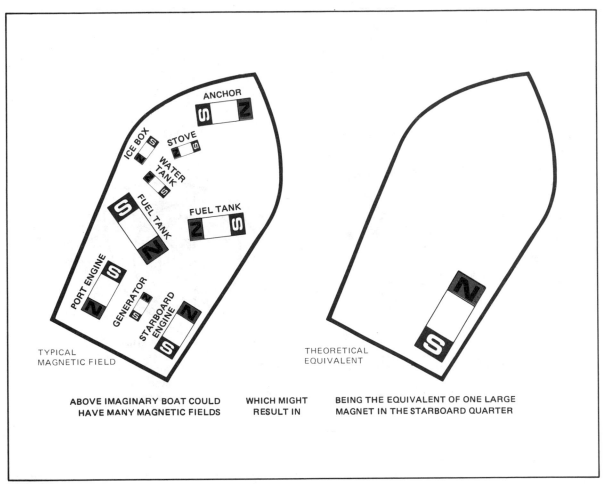

ANCHOR

ICE BOX

STOVE

WATER
TANK

FUEL TANK

FUEL TANK

PORT ENGINE

GENERATOR

STARBOARD
ENGINE

TYPICAL
MAGNETIC FIELD

THEORETICAL
EQUIVALENT

ABOVE IMAGINARY BOAT COULD
HAVE MANY MAGNETIC FIELDS

WHICH MIGHT
RESULT IN

BEING THE EQUIVALENT OF ONE LARGE
MAGNET IN THE STARBOARD QUARTER

FIG. 40

The amount of error (deviation) must be considered when determining a course, steering a course or taking bearings. Deviation is added to or subtracted from a magnetic direction to determine a compass direction. Similarly, deviation is subtracted from or added to a compass direction to determine a magnetic direction.

The consequences of not knowing how to determine the deviation of your compass or to apply the correction for this error can be extremely serious. An error of only 1° will result in your being 1 mile away from your calculated position every 60 miles of travel. A 5° error in a 30 mile trip will result in a position error of 2½ miles. On such a trip (across an inland lake or between coastal or offshore islands) you will experience an error in position of 2½ miles. You may be so far off course that you are unable to see your

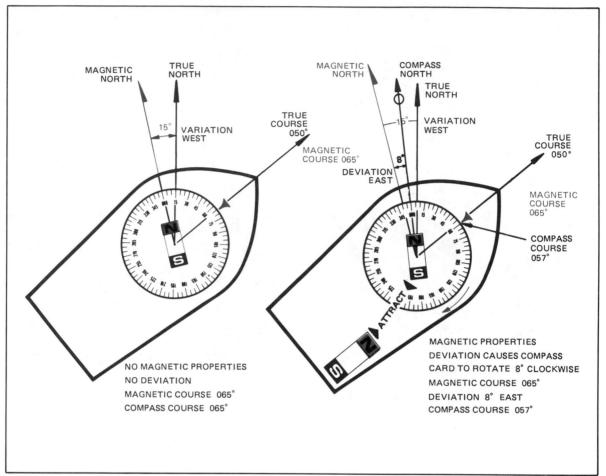

FIG. 41

destination or you may stray into a shoal area or some other hazardous condition.

Converting — True, Magnetic, Compass Consider now the magnetic field aboard a typical pleasure craft and its effect (deviation on the compass). This craft has a plywood or fibreglass hull with built-in steel fuel and water tanks, inboard engine, two anchors stowed forward, and a stove and icebox in the galley. Let us assume, for this example, that the magnetic properties are the same as though the imaginary magnet caused by these objects were stowed in an after starboard locker with the North-seeking pole at the forward end of the magnet. The vessel is located in Toronto Harbour; variation 9° West. Follow Figures 42 through 46 and the accompanying text.

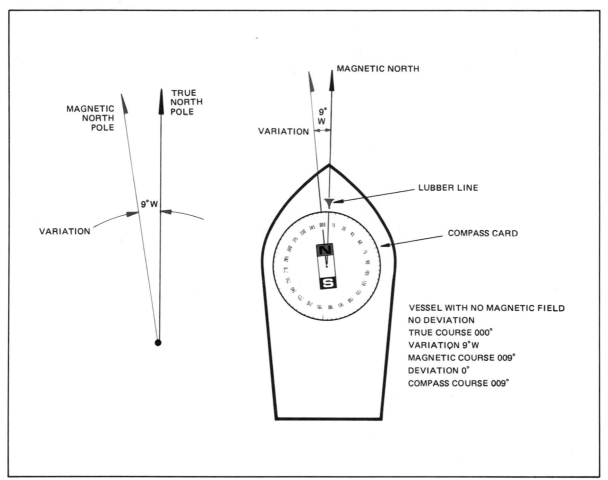

FIG. 42

To refresh our understanding of variation, consider a vessel with *no* magnetic field aboard.

Vessel headed true North (000°).

No magnetic field.

No deviation.

Compass points to compass North, which, due to no deviation, is the same as magnetic North.

Compass reads 009° due to variation of 9° West in Toronto, Canada:

True	Variation	Magnetic
000°	9° W	009°

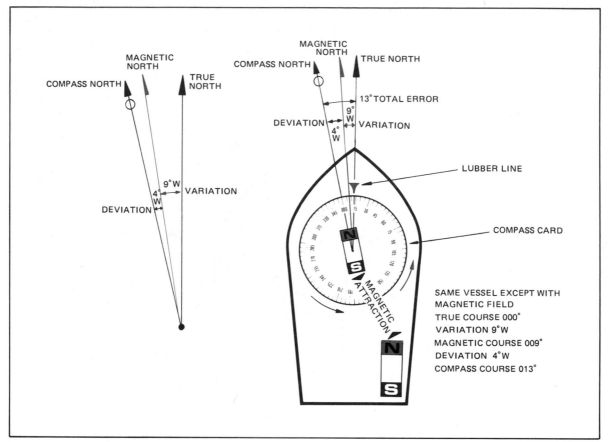

FIG. 43

Vessel headed true North (000°).

Theoretical vessel with magnetic field described above. Unlike poles of the compass card magnet and the vessel's magnetic field attract each other. This causes the compass card to rotate counter-clockwise and point to compass North, which, due to deviation, is no longer the same as magnetic North. In this example, the card was already rotated 9° counter-clockwise due to 9° West variation in Toronto and has been rotated a further 4° counter-clockwise due to the magnetic field (deviation).

The compass card reads 013° due to:

True course 000°

Variation 9° West

Deviation 4° West.

True	Variation	Magnetic	Deviation	Compass
000°	9° W	009°	4° W	013°

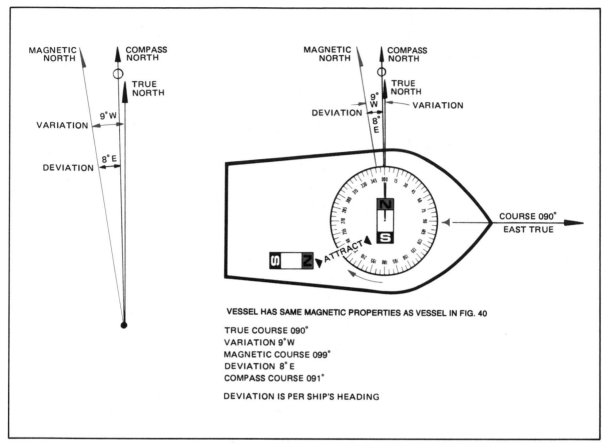

VESSEL HAS SAME MAGNETIC PROPERTIES AS VESSEL IN FIG. 40

TRUE COURSE 090°
VARIATION 9° W
MAGNETIC COURSE 099°
DEVIATION 8° E
COMPASS COURSE 091°

DEVIATION IS PER SHIP'S HEADING

FIG. 44

Vessel headed true East (090°).

Unlike poles of the compass and the vessel's field attract each other, causing the compass card to rotate clockwise and point to compass North. In this example, the card was already rotated 9° counter-clockwise due to variation. Deviation caused a clockwise rotation of 8°.

The compass card reads 091° due to:

True course 090°

Variation 9° West

Deviation 8° East

True	Variation	Magnetic	Deviation	Compass
090°	9° W	099°	8° E	091°

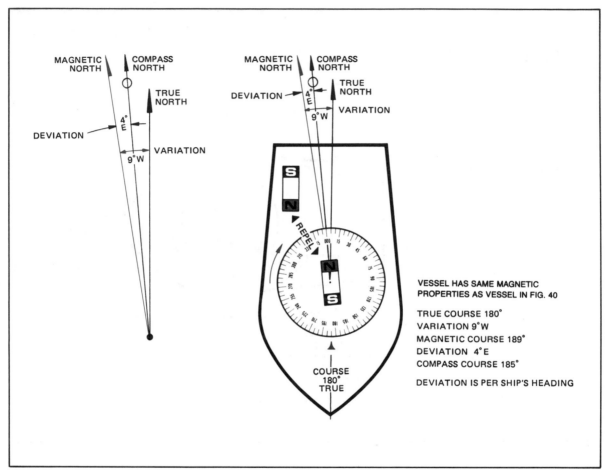

FIG. 45

Vessel headed true South (180°).

Like poles of compass and vessel repel, causing the compass card to rotate clockwise and point to compass North. In this example, the card was already rotated counter-clockwise 9° due to variation. Deviation caused a clockwise rotation of 4°. Compass card reads 185° due to:

True course 180°
Variation 9° West
Deviation 4° East

True	Variation	Magnetic	Deviation	Compass
180°	9° W	189°	4°E	185°

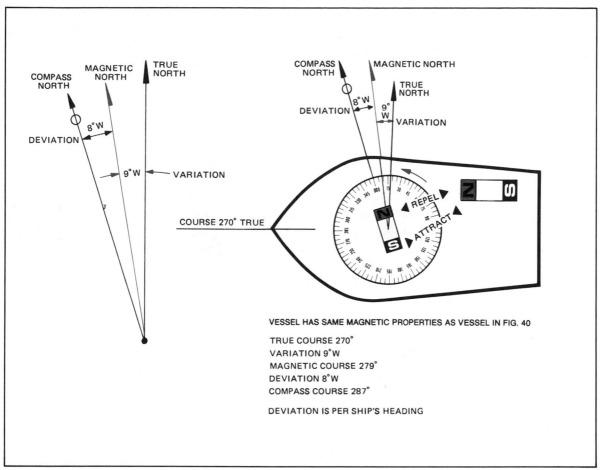

FIG. 46

Vessel headed true West (270°).

Like poles of compass and vessel repel, causing the compass card to rotate counter-clockwise and point to compass West. In this example, the card was already rotated counter-clockwise due to variation. Deviation caused a further counter-clockwise rotation of 8°. The compass card reads 287° due to:

True course 270°

Variation 9° West

Deviation 8° West

True	Variation	Magnetic	Deviation	Compass
270°	9° W	279°	8° W	287°

It is *extremely important* to note that *the amount of deviation and the direction of deviation* (E or W) varies *depending upon* the *direction* in which *the vessel is heading* at any time. It is imperative for a later understanding of bearings and fixes, as well as determining proper courses, that we appreciate that the *deviation varies with the ship's heading* (direction of travel). This point will be more fully explored in Chapter 9.

Deviation Examples   All of the examples used in this book are based on our theoretical boat having a deviation as in the Deviation Table, Appendix C. TVMDC figures for these illustrations are listed in Table II. Remember, though, that deviation for your boat is peculiar to your boat only. Developing a deviation table for your vessel is covered in Appendix B. Do not use the Deviation Table in Appendix C except for problems and examples in this book. (See page 259.) Do not interpolate for intermediate results until Chapter 12.

Although the theoretical table on page 61 appears to be extreme, is is important to realize the significant effect deviation may have on your safety. The writer has been aboard many pleasure vessels with this amount of deviation.

Note that converting a magnetic direction to a compass direction or vice versa follows a similar rule to that which we learned when converting from true to magnetic or vice versa:

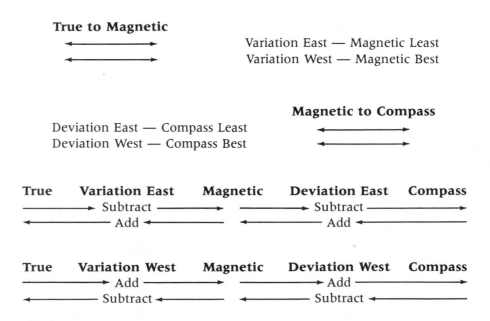

True to Magnetic

Variation East — Magnetic Least
Variation West — Magnetic Best

Magnetic to Compass

Deviation East — Compass Least
Deviation West — Compass Best

True	Variation East	Magnetic	Deviation East	Compass
→ Subtract →	→ Subtract →
← Add ←	← Add ←

True	Variation West	Magnetic	Deviation West	Compass
→ Add →	→ Add →
← Subtract ←	← Subtract ←

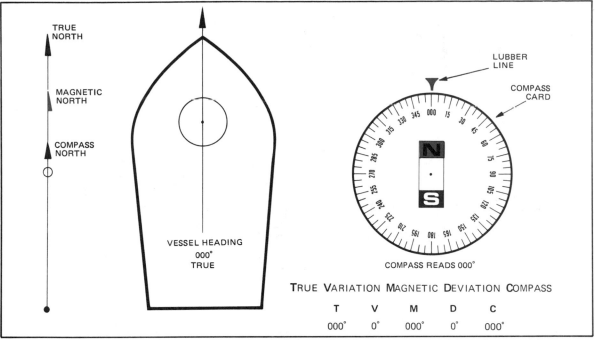

TRUE VARIATION MAGNETIC DEVIATION COMPASS

T	V	M	D	C
000°	0°	000°	0°	000°

FIG. 47 *Rubber dinghy with no metallic or electrical/electronic objects on board – no deviation. Cruising on southern Lake Michigan – no variation.*

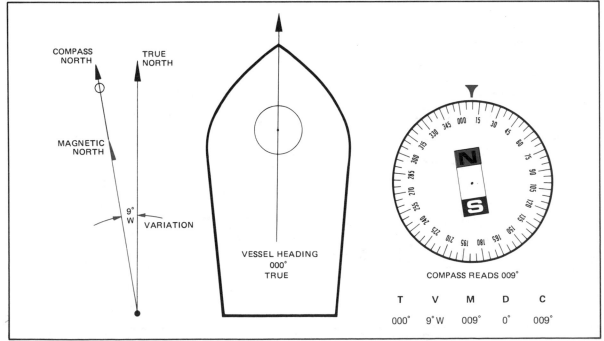

T	V	M	D	C
000°	9° W	009°	0°	009°

FIG. 48 *Same rubber dinghy – no deviation. Lake Ontario, Toronto, 9° West variation.*

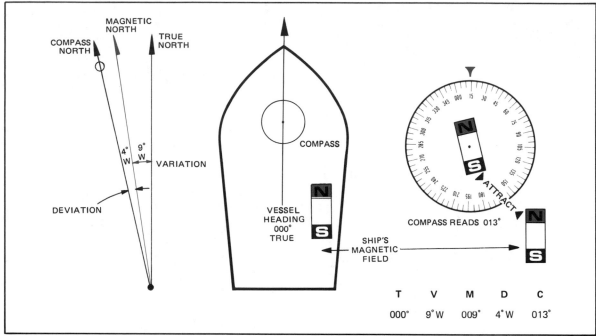

FIG. 49 *Theoretical Vessel – deviation as in Deviation Table, Appendix C. Lake Ontario, Toronto, 9° West variation.*

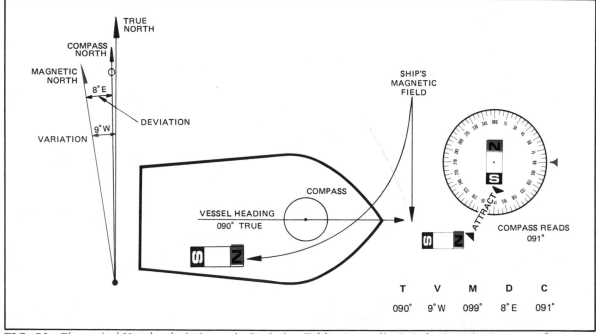

FIG. 50 *Theoretical Vessel – deviation as in Deviation Table, Appendix C. Lake Ontario, Toronto, 9° West variation.*

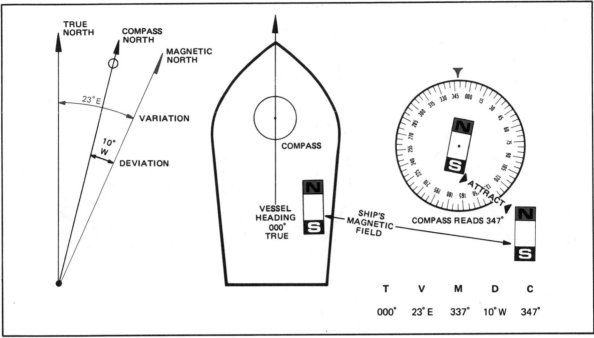

	T	V	M	D	C
	000°	23° E	337°	10° W	347°

FIG. 51 *Theoretical Vessel – deviation as in Appendix C. Point Roberts, B.C., 23° East variation.*

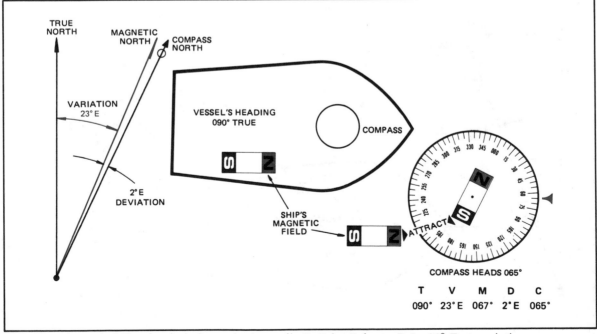

	T	V	M	D	C
	090°	23° E	067°	2° E	065°

FIG. 52 *Theoretical Vessel – deviation as in Appendix C. Point Roberts, B.C., 23° East variation.*

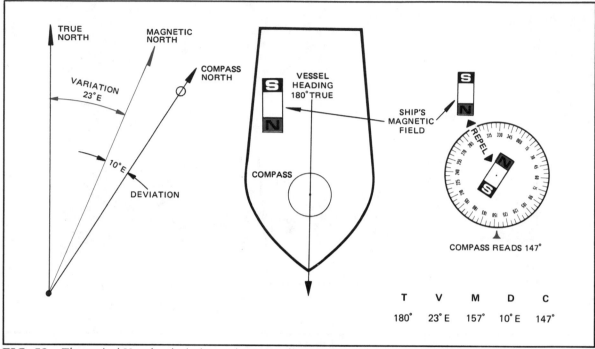

FIG. 53 *Theoretical Vessel – deviation as in Appendix C. Point Roberts, B.C., 23° East variation.*

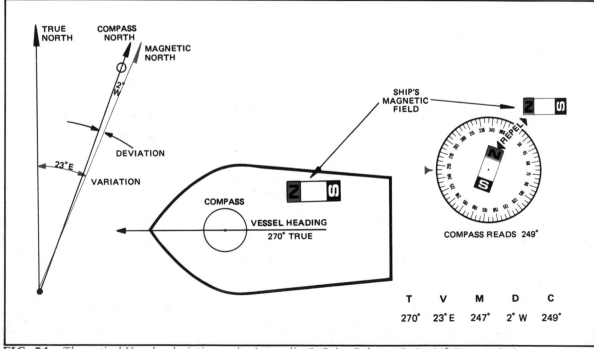

FIG. 54 *Theoretical Vessel – deviation as in Appendix C. Point Roberts, B.C., 23° East variation.*

			TABLE II TVMDC			
Fig.	T	Variation		M	Deviation	C
47	000°	0°	(from chart)	000°	0° (rubber dinghy)	000°
48	000°	9° W	″	009°	0° ″	009°
49	000°	9° W	″	009°	4° W (from Appendix C)	013°
50	090°	9° W	″	099°	8° E ″	091°
51	000°	23° E	″	337°	10° W ″	347°
52	090°	23° E	″	067°	2° E ″	065°
53	180°	23° E	″	157°	10° E ″	147°
54	270°	23° E	″	247°	2° W ″	249°

APPLICATION OF COMPASS (VARIATION AND DEVIATION)

There are three general uses for a compass:

1. To steer a course to arrive at a predetermined destination or to avoid hazards.

2. To plot a course which you have been steering.

3. To take bearings in order to determine your position.

Item 3 will be discussed in detail in Chapter 9. Let us examine the importance and application of variation and deviation to the first two items.

Purchase a copy of "Chart T-3450" (Canada West Coast) from your chart dealer in order to better follow the examples. In Canada you may be able to obtain this chart from your local Canadian Power Squadron. The method of measuring distances and directions will be described in Chapter 6.

Example I You are at Point Roberts light, near the right-centre of Chart T-3450, and wish to travel to Alden Point light, near the right-bottom of Chart T-3450. (See Fig. 55.) What course must you steer to arrive at your destination aboard the theoretical vessel with deviation on various headings being as in the Deviation Table in Appendix C?

- On Chart T-3450, draw a line from Point Roberts to Alden Point and determine from the outer compass rose that you must steer a course of 158° true.
- From the same chart determine that variation is 23° East. Therefore, the magnetic course is 135°.
- From the Deviation Table, Appendix C, you determine that deviation is 12° E for a magnetic course of 135°.

- To determine your compass course, the course to steer according to the ship's compass:

T	V	M	D	C
158°	23°E	135°	12°E	123°

True course 158°.

Variation 23° East: Variation East — Magnetic Least.

Therefore, subtract 23° East variation from true to obtain a magnetic course of 135°.

- Look in the Deviation Table, Appendix C, under the magnetic heading of 135° and determine that the *deviation on this heading* is 12° east: Deviation East — Compass Least.
- Therefore, subtract 12° East deviation from magnetic to obtain a compass course of 123°.

ANSWER: To reach Alden Point from Point Roberts, you must steer a course of 123° according to your vessel's compass. (See Fig. 55.) Consider the results if you had failed to account for deviation and variation on this 11.8 mile cruise. (See Fig. 56.)

You would have steered a course of 158°C (compass) which would result in a true course of 189°:

T	V	M	D	C
189°	23°E	166°	8°E	158°

Had you sailed that course (158° on your compass), *you would have run hard aground* off Saturna Island when you thought that you were still 1.2 miles from reaching the Alden Point light: that is, if you missed the rock lying approximately 0.5 miles offshore! *You would have been 6.1 miles off course* at the moment you ran aground! In somewhat limited visibility you would never have seen a landmark or aid to navigation before you ran aground after leaving Point Roberts.

You will be able to plot the result of this and the example that follows on your chart after completing Chapter 7.

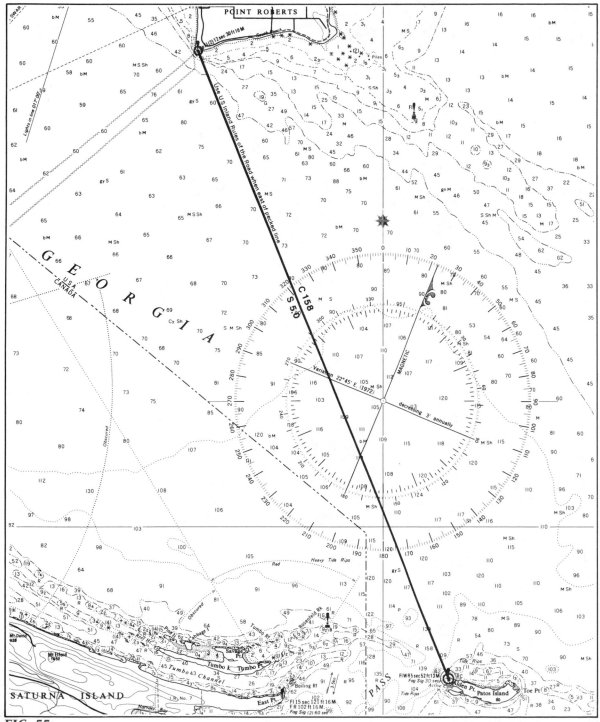

FIG. 55

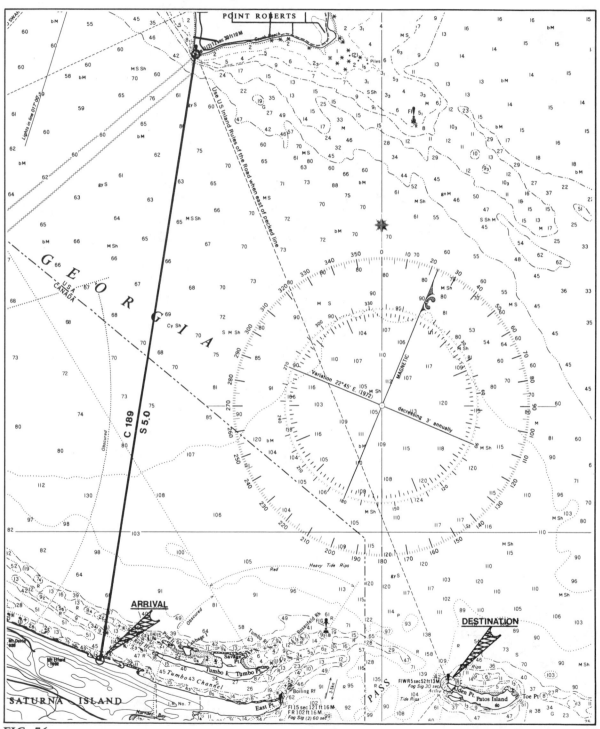

FIG. 56

Example 2 Assume that you left Point Roberts (Chart T-3450) on a compass course of 150°. After travelling 4.0 miles, you changed course to 103° on your compass, and you travelled another 6.0 miles. At this point in time, you may wish to know your location for any of a number of reasons:

- A storm is approaching, and you wish to run for the closest safe harbour.
- Fog descends, and you must know your position to avoid hazards while you continue your voyage.
- You receive a radio call for help, and must know your position to steer a course to find the vessel in trouble.
- Your vessel is in trouble, and you must know your position to radio for aid.

Assuming that you cannot accurately fix your position by visually sighting on charted objects, you have only one solution: plot your course and establish your position by dead reckoning.

To do this you must convert compass courses to true courses and plot them point by point as in the following steps. (See Fig. 57.)

1. Convert your compass courses to true courses:

T	V	M	D	C
181°	23°E	158°	8°E	150°
134°	23°E	111°	8°E	103°

2. Plot your course of 181° from Point Roberts. Draw a line at an angle of 181°, *using the outer compass rose*, through Point Roberts.
3. Measure along that line a distance of 4.0 miles.
4. From that point on the line, draw a line at an angle of 134° (the new true course).
5. Measure along that line a distance of 6.0 miles and mark that point.
6. The marked point is your dead reckoning position.
7. Latitude (L) 48° 50.1′N; Longitude (λ) 122° 58.5′W

Had you not converted your compass courses to true courses before plotting, you would have come up with a dead reckoning position approximately 4.9 miles North-east of your correct dead reckoning position as shown. You would be out of sight of your would-be rescuers. They may never find you — alive! (See Fig. 58.) Remember, to determine the deviation of *your* ship's compass, see Appendix B.

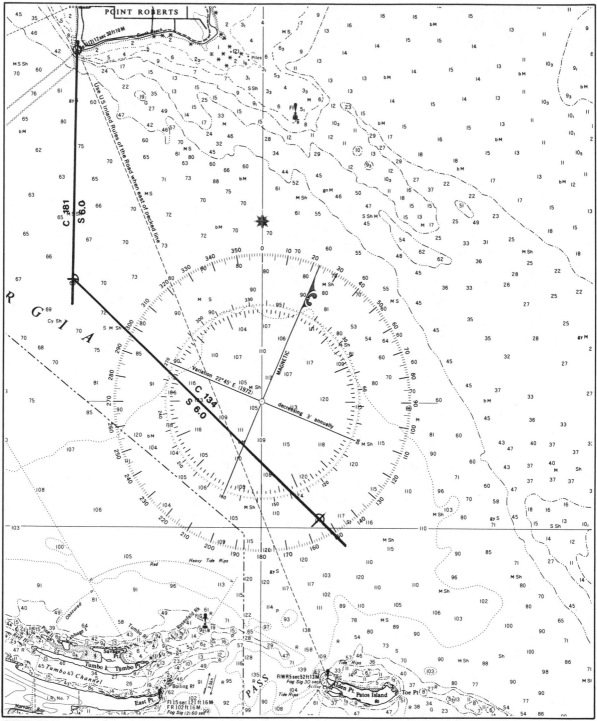

FIG. 57

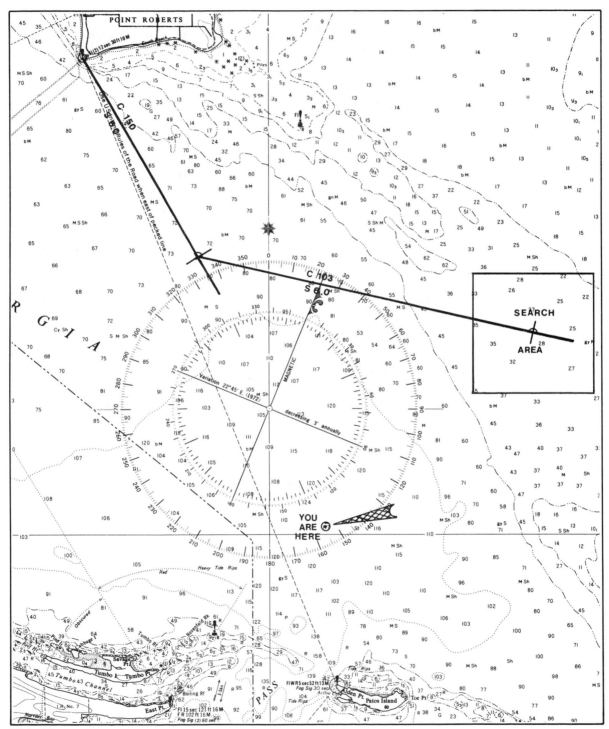

FIG. 58

SUMMARY

- Variation is the angular (direction) error due to the difference in location of the Geographic North (True) Pole and the Magnetic North Pole. The amount and direction of variation is dependent upon the location of the vessel.
- Deviation is the angular (direction) error due to the magnetic properties of the boat in which the compass is located. The amount and direction of deviation is dependent upon the magnetic properties of the specific boat.
- The amount and direction of variation is shown on the compass rose printed on a chart.
- The amount and direction of deviation is established for a particular boat and is kept as a deviation table for that vessel.
- To correct for compass errors, keep these letters and rhymes in mind:

True	Variation	Magnetic	Deviation	Compass
T	**V**	**V**	**D**	**C**
True	Virgins	Make	Dull	Company

TVM
Variation East — Magnetic Least
Variation West — Magnetic Best

MDC
Deviation East — Compass Least
Deviation West — Compass Best

- *Remember*, deviation is according to the ship's heading; it is affected by the compass course.

6. Charts and Time/Speed/Distance Calculations

"One accurate measurement is worth a thousand expert opinions."
SAUNDERS' LAW OF NAVIGATION **#5**

CHARTS

As stated earlier, a chart is simply the equivalent of a road map. It is a pictorial representation of the surface of the earth on a flat sheet of paper. In producing the surface of a sphere on a flat surface, certain distortions will occur. Various methods of projection to minimize this distortion have been developed. The detailed methods of projection are outside the scope of this book, but suffice it to say that the average pleasure boater will generally be using either a Mercator Projection (coastal charts), or a Polyconic Projection (Great Lakes charts). For all practical purposes, the two chart types are the same. All measurements, plotting and information in this book apply equally to both types of chart projections. The term "chartlet" as used here refers to a section of a chart.

When using any chart for the first time, check the title block (or elsewhere on the chart) for such information as:

- Distances — miles, kilometres.
- Depths — fathoms, feet, metres.
- Type of projection — for inland or coastal trips use only Mercator or Polyconic.
- Clearances — feet, metres.
- Date of issue and latest update.
- Special notes and cautions.
- Scale — 1-10,000 — large scale harbour charts with good detail.
  1-40,000 — smaller scale for short coastal or inland lake trips.
  1-100,000 — small scale coastal or planning charts.

Make certain that your chart is the latest possible issue. To ensure that you keep the chart updated, subscribe to the *Notices to Mariners* (no charge from Canadian Hydrographic Services) which will advise you of all revisions, additions, deletions of aids to navigation and other pertinent changes to Canadian charts. This publication is mailed to subscribers weekly. A similar publication is available in the U.S.A.

ABBREVIATIONS AND SYMBOLS

Obtain a copy of "Symbols and Abbreviations" from your chart dealer. Refer to the illustrations of the more common symbols and learn them thoroughly. Also learn to recognize their actual shape, colour, size and characteristics when seen on the waterway.

MERIDIANS OF LONGITUDE

Meridians of longitude were discussed briefly in Chapter 5. In order to visualize meridians of longitude and their measurements, cut halfway through an orange with a sharp knife so that the slit runs from pole to pole (from stem to bud end) at the centre. Rotate the orange counter-clockwise approximately 75° when viewed from the top and make a second knife slit from the outer edge to the centre. (See Fig. 59.)

The first cut represents 0°, or Greenwich Meridian. Greenwich, England, is located on that slit (meridian) on the surface of the orange (earth) somewhere between the stem (North Pole) and the bud (South Pole). The second cut represents the 75° West meridian. Ottawa, Ontario, is located approximately on that slit (meridian on the surface of the orange — earth) somewhere between the stem (North Pole) and the bud (South Pole).

Now remove the wedge of orange and note that the surfaces of the cuts (meridians) intersect at the core (axis) at an angle of 75°. (See Fig. 59.) The meridians of 0° and 75° subtend an arc of 75° at the axis of the earth. We could continue to make an infinite number of slits to produce an infinite number of meridians and find that each point on the surface of the earth is located on only one meridian and that all points on earth can be located by only one meridian of longitude. All meridians of longitude are measured and numbered from 0° at Greenwich either eastward or westward to 180°. (See Fig. 60.)

The width of the wedge at the outer surface is greater in the centre (equator) than at the ends (poles), even though the meridians are the same angular distance apart. (See Fig. 59.) Similarly, on the surface of the earth, one degree of longitude is longer at the equator than one degree of longitude halfway to the pole (45° latitude), and this distance continues to lessen as you approach the pole. Therefore, for purposes of

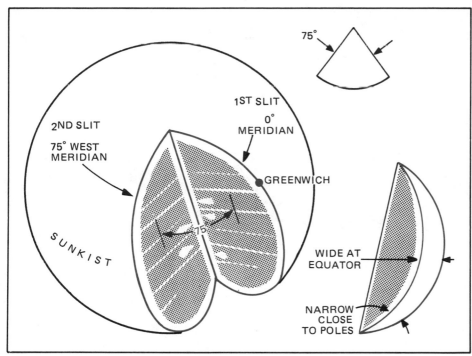

FIG. 59

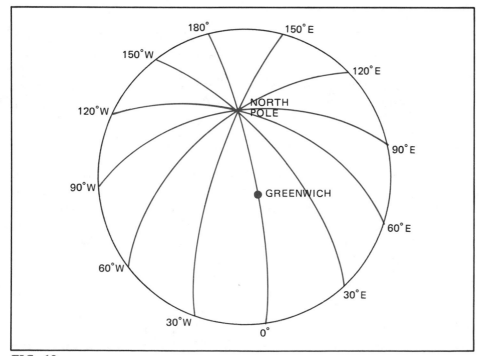

FIG. 60

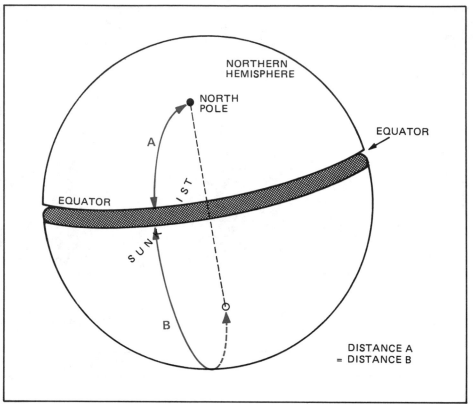

FIG. 61

pleasure craft piloting there is no relationship between a degree of longitude and a measurement of lineal distance (miles or nautical miles).

PARALLELS OF LATITUDE

Using a new orange and holding it with the stem up (North Pole) and bud end down (South Pole), slice the orange laterally into two halves to represent the Northern Hemisphere and Southern Hemisphere. (See Fig. 61.) You have sliced the orange (earth) into two pieces at the equator. Take the top half, Northern Hemisphere, lay it flat on a table on its equator, draw a line from the stem (North Pole) through the shortest possible distance to any point on the equator. This is a meridian (upper half only). Label it as 0°, Greenwich Meridian. Rotate the hemisphere 75° counter-clockwise and draw another meridian (75°West). Along the 75° West meridian and 0° meridian locate points midway between the North Pole and the equator. (See Fig. 62.) Draw a line around the

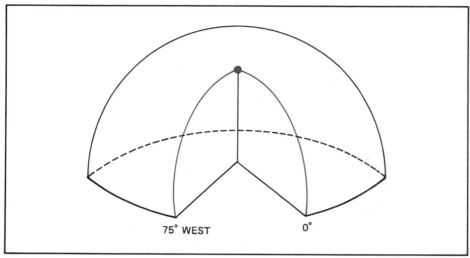

75° WEST   0°

FIG. 62

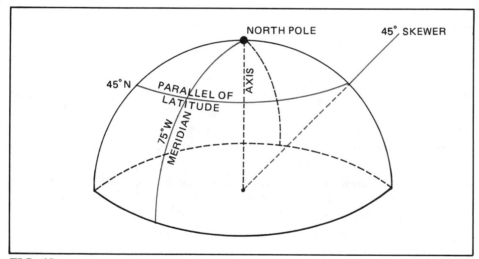

NORTH POLE   45° SKEWER

45° N   PARALLEL OF
LATITUDE   AXIS

75° W
MERIDIAN

FIG. 63

surface through that point parallel to (equidistant from) the equator. This is a parallel of latitude. At any point on that latitude insert a pin or skewer in such a way that the skewer intersects the core (axis) at the equator. (See Fig. 63.) Measure the angle that the skewer makes with the equator; in this case 45°. The parallel you have drawn is 45° North. An infinite number of parallels can be drawn at every possible angle from 0° to 90°.

Every point on earth is located on only one of the parallels of latitude, and as stated on page 70 will be located on only one of the

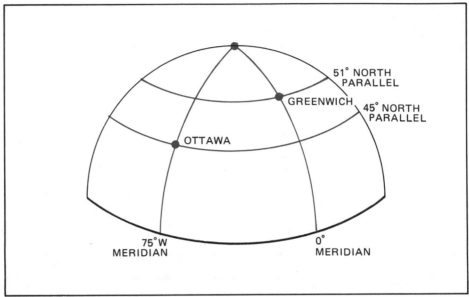

FIG. 64

meridians of longitude. The CN Tower in Toronto, Ontario, is located approximately at the intersection of meridian 79° West longitude and parallel 44° North latitude, because it lies on both that meridian (and only that meridian) and that parallel (and only that parallel). If "L" equals latitude and "λ" equals longitude, then Toronto, Ontario, is located at L 43° 39.0' N, λ 79° 23.0' W. Similarly, Greenwich, England, lies on 0° meridian and approximately on the 51° parallel (North of the equator); it is located at L 51° 28.0'N, λ 00° 00.0' W. (See Fig. 64.)

In defining the location of an object on the surface of a sphere, an angular form of measurement (degrees) has been used. If we must be more precise, we subdivide the degree into 60 divisions — minutes. Minutes are indicated by the symbol '. Each minute may be further subdivided into 10 parts (tenths), recorded as decimal parts of a minute. Conventionally, in navigation we "zero-fill" or specify the minutes or tenths, even though the quantity might be zero. We do not normally subdivide angular minutes into angular seconds.

You will observe that the distance on the surface of the earth between any two parallels is constant around the earth's surface. Note also that the distance on the surface of the earth between any two parallels 1° (or 10' or 30', etc.) apart is the same as the distance on the surface of the earth between any two other parallels 1° (or 10' or 30', etc.) apart.

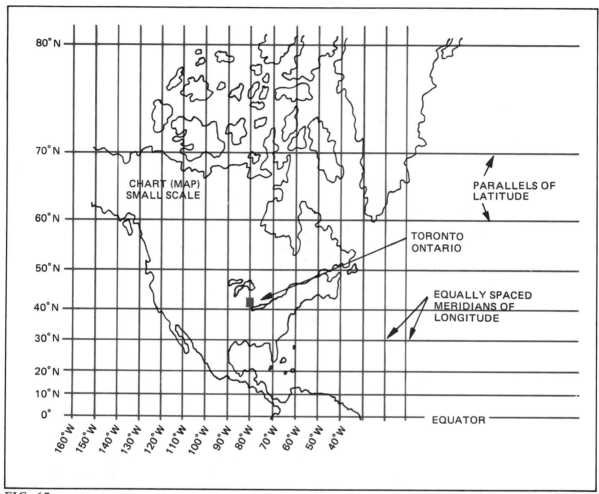

FIG. 65

DETERMINING DISTANCE ON A CHART

By definition, 1 nautical mile is the distance on the earth's surface between any two parallels of latitude $\frac{1}{60}$ of 1° apart = (00° 01.0'). This distance equals approximately 6080 feet.

1 statute mile   = 5280 feet
1 nautical mile = 1.15 statute miles = 1' of latitude = 1852 metres

As we saw earlier, meridians of longitude converge to meet at the poles. However, in order to "stretch" the earth's curved surface flat onto a chart some distortion occurs. The meridians of longitude become vertical, parallel lines. (See Fig. 65.)

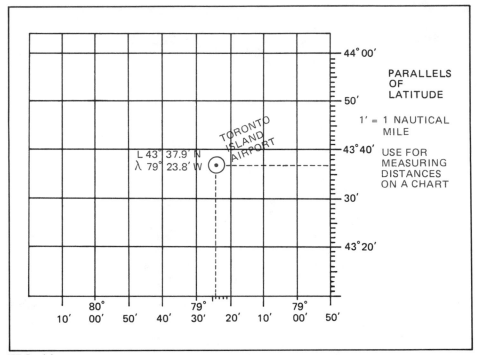

FIG. 66

Other distortions also occur in order to minimize the amount of distortion in any one area. Generally, parallels of latitude are undistorted, but on a chart they appear successively further apart as you move further from the equator, either North or South. The parallels are marked and numbered at the right and left edges of the chart, generally in increments of $1/10$ of 1 minute of latitude. (See Fig. 66.)

Because 1 minute of latitude equals 1 nautical mile (by definition), we may use the latitude scale to measure distances in nautical miles. However, *do not use the longitude scale at the top and bottom of the chart, because the distance between meridians is not constant as we go North or South away from the equator.* Use dividers to transfer the distances between the latitude scale at the side of the chart and the objects on the chart between which the distance is being measured. (See Figs. 67 and 68.)

DETERMINING DIRECTIONS ON A CHART
There are two principal reasons for determining directions on a chart. First, to determine the direction (course or bearing) from one location or object to another, that are already plotted on the chart. Second, to draw a line on the chart for the purpose of plotting an object or position

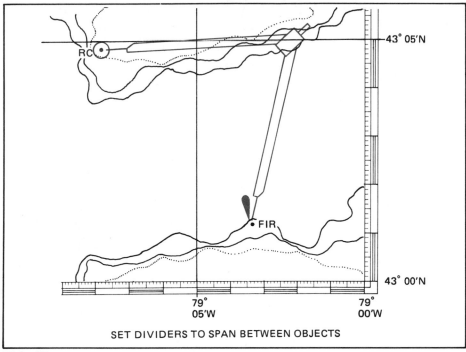

43° 05'N

43° 00'N

79°
05'W

79°
00'W

SET DIVIDERS TO SPAN BETWEEN OBJECTS

FIG. 67

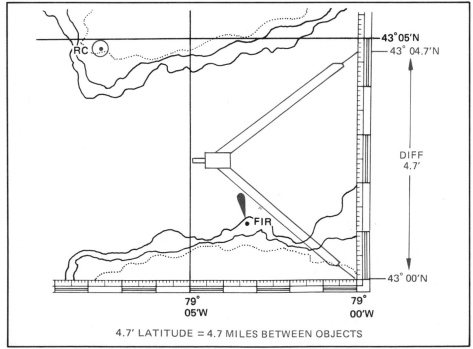

43° 05'N
43° 04.7'N

DIFF
4.7'

43° 00'N

79°
05'W

79°
00'W

4.7' LATITUDE = 4.7 MILES BETWEEN OBJECTS

FIG. 68

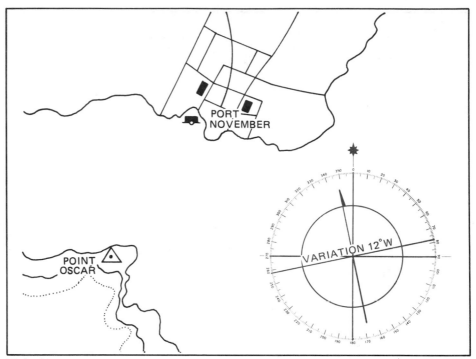

FIG. 69

when the direction is known: plotting a dead reckoning course or bearing.

All parallels of latitude run true East and West. All meridians of longitude run true North and South. The outer compass rose on the chart (usually more than one on a large chart) indicates all true directions in increments of 1°. (See Fig. 69.)

A parallel ruler is used to transfer directions from a location on the chart to the compass rose, or from the compass rose to a location on the chart. See Figures 70 and 71 for the use of the parallel ruler. To determine the direction between two objects, line up one outer edge of the ruler between them. (See Fig. 70.) Hold that edge firmly against the paper and open the rulers. Now hold the other edge firmly and close the ruler. Continue this sequence to "walk" the ruler to the closest compass rose so that one edge runs through the centre point of the compass rose. At least one of the two ruler sections must be held firmly against the paper at all times to prevent slippage. Run your eye from the centre of the rose along the edge of the ruler in your intended direction (see Fig. 71) until you reach the outer scale on the rose. At that point you read your intended direction. If you run your eye in the opposite direction from

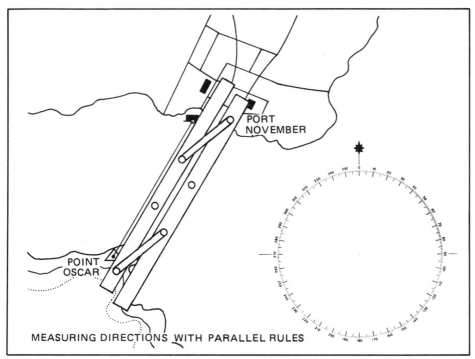

MEASURING DIRECTIONS WITH PARALLEL RULES

FIG. 70

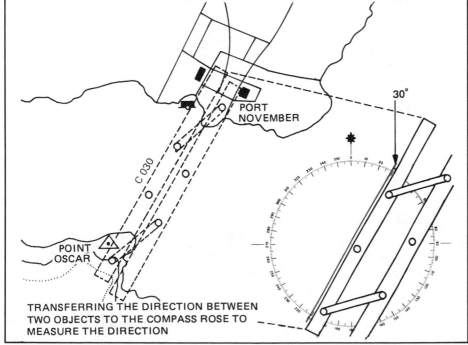

TRANSFERRING THE DIRECTION BETWEEN
TWO OBJECTS TO THE COMPASS ROSE TO
MEASURE THE DIRECTION

FIG. 71

the centre of the rose to the outer scale, you will have read the reverse (or reciprocal) direction.

Convert all compass directions to true before plotting (TVMDC).
or
After determining a true direction from the chart, convert to compass for steering (TVMDC).

ESTABLISHING YOUR INTENDED COURSE
See Figure 70 and Figure 71 and preceding dialogue. Your true course from Point Oscar to Port November is 030°.

PLOTTING YOUR COURSE (POSITION) OR A BEARING
Example: You are travelling on course 045° true from Sierra Harbour to Tango Bay. Will you miss the Uniform Shoals? (See Figs. 72 and 73.)

DETERMINING LATITUDE AND LONGITUDE ON A CHART
There are two principal reasons for determining latitude and longitude on a chart. First, to determine and be able to convey to someone else the latitude and longitude of an object or position which is plotted on your chart. For example, you may have your position plotted on the chart and wish to radio your location to someone else so that the other person will be able to meet you or come to your assistance. Second, you have been given the latitude and longitude of some object or position which is not plotted on your chart, and you wish to plot that object or position on your chart and be able to determine its direction and distance from you. For example, you may have received a radio message of distress, and the skipper of the vessel in trouble has transmitted his position in terms of latitude and longitude.

   To determine the latitude and longitude of an object (or position) which is plotted on your chart:

1. Put one point of the dividers on the object and with the other point sweep an arc to just reach the closest parallel of latitude. (See Fig. 74.)
2. Transfer the dividers to the *side* of the chart, placing one point on the same parallel of latitude as in (1.) above and place the other point (not changing the setting) on the latitude scale in the same direction from the parallel line as the desired location is. (See Fig. 75.)
3. Read the desired latitude from the scale. (See Fig. 76.)
4. Perform a similar process to a meridian of longitude and read the desired longitude from the upper or lower scale. (See Fig. 77 and 78.)

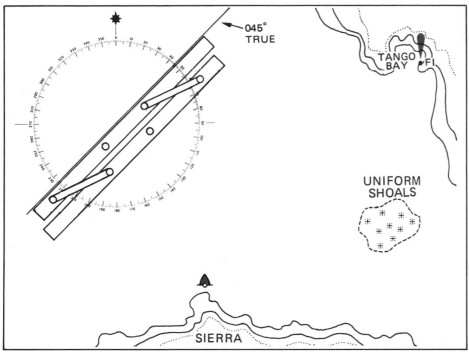

FIG. 72

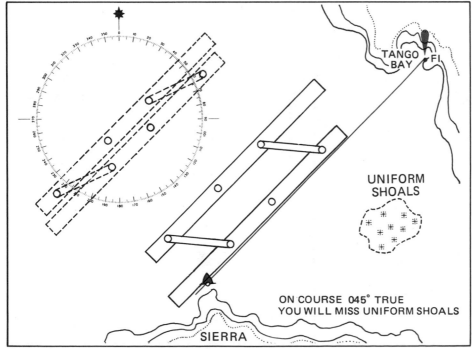

FIG. 73

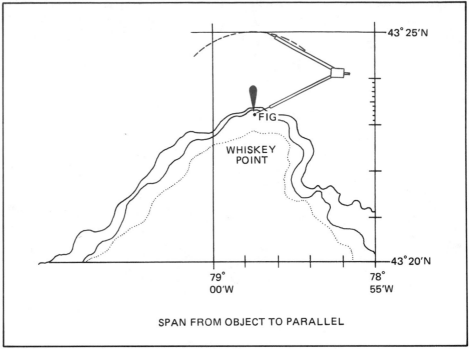

SPAN FROM OBJECT TO PARALLEL

FIG. 74

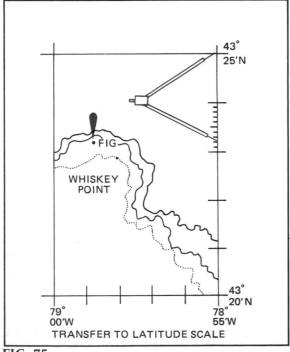

TRANSFER TO LATITUDE SCALE

FIG. 75

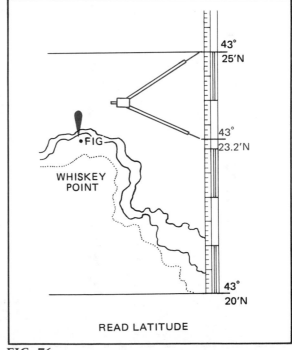

READ LATITUDE

FIG. 76

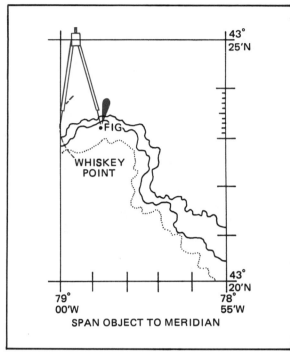

FIG. 77

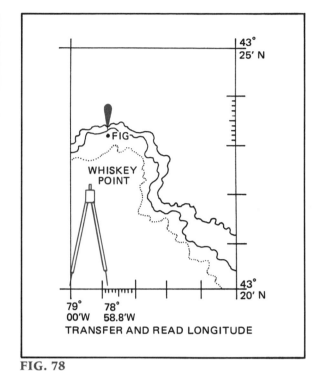

FIG. 78

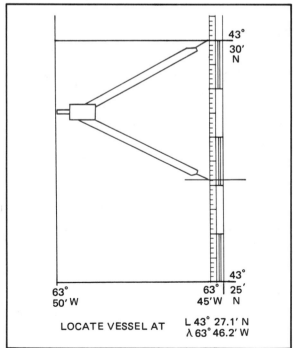

FIG. 79

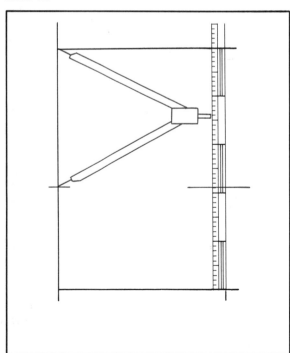

FIG. 80

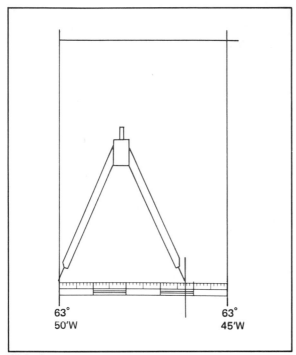

63°
50'W

63°
45'W

FIG. 81

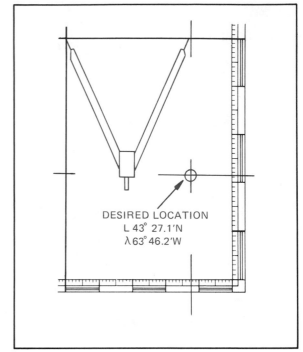

DESIRED LOCATION
L 43° 27.1'N
λ 63° 46.2'W

FIG. 82

To plot an object (or position) on your chart whose latitude and longitude are known:

1. Place one point of the dividers on the desired latitude on the scale at one side of the chart and the other point on the closest printed line of latitude. (See Fig. 79.)
2. Preserving this setting, transfer the dividers to a place along the printed parallel as in (1.) above where a printed meridian of longitude intersects it. The meridian should be close to the approximate site of the desired location.
3. Place the other point on that meridian and mark the location. (See Fig. 80.)
4. Similarly, mark a meridian on the other side of the approximate place of the desired location.
5. Connect these points with a light line.
6. Perform a similar series of operations for longitude, except that your operations will be vertical rather than horizontal. (See Fig. 81.)
7. The intersection of these two lines is the desired latitude and longitude. (See Fig. 82.)

STRIP CHARTS

Some charts for the use of recreational boaters are supplied as strip charts. Strip charts are the mariner's equivalent of a strip map supplied by auto clubs or petroleum companies that mark out a preferred route within a fairly narrow "aisle" or band of terrain. Strip charts are particularly common through much of Ontario's Trent and Rideau waterways and the East side of Georgian Bay. Somewhat like strip maps, true North is not always toward the top of the strip chart. True North on various sheets or different sections of the same sheet may be oriented in almost any direction. Meridians and parallels will not be marked along each side, top or bottom. Rather, they will be marked centrally within the chart, and a section of each will be subdivided into minutes and tenths of minutes of arc. Use only the latitude scale that is marked along a meridian for measuring nautical miles. Otherwise, everything else said about charts in this book applies equally to strip charts.

TIME

Conventional hours and minutes are used in nautical calculations and notations. There are three primary differences between nautical and civil time:

1. For basic piloting (not celestial navigation), seconds are usually converted to decimals of minutes and (after calculations are complete) are rounded off to the closest full minute. For example, 28 minutes, 42 seconds becomes 28.7 minutes which is rounded off to 29 minutes.
2. The 24 hour clock system is used aboard ship. All time is measured, noted or communicated each day as from midnight each day:
   1:28 A.M. civil time is 1 hour and 28 minutes after midnight; this is equivalent to 0128 nautical time.
   10:30 A.M. civil time is 10 hours and 30 minutes after midnight; this is equivalent to 1030 nautical time.
   1:15 P.M. civil time is 1 hour and 15 minutes after noon; this is equivalent to 1315 nautical time (13 hours and 15 minutes after midnight).
   10:45 P.M. civil time is 10 hours and 45 minutes after noon; this is equivalent to 2245 nautical time (22 hours and 45 minutes after midnight).
3. Nautical time is always written in four digits. The first two digits always indicate hours; the second two digits always indicate minutes to the closest whole minute. Although written as four digits, we

must remember that time is hours and minutes. Counting is to the base 60. *It is not a decimal base*:

0158 = 1 hour 58 minutes after midnight
0159 = 1 hour 59 minutes after midnight
0160 = 0200 = 2 hours after midnight (*not* 1 hour 60 minutes)

Addition and Subtraction   The following practices will reduce mathematical errors to a minimum when performing calculations in units of time.

While performing calculations segregate hours and minutes as in the following examples:

Time 1058 equals 10 hours and 58 minutes after midnight.
Write as 10   58.
Elapsed time (time between events) — 1 hour and 01 minute.
Write as 1   01.

When adding, add the hours, then separately add the minutes and then simplify. Add 4 hours and 15 minutes to a time of 1012.

SOLUTION: 4   15
                  + 10   12
                  ──────────
                   14   27
ANSWER: 1427

Add 4 hours and 38 minutes to a time of 1047.

SOLUTION: 4   38
                  + 10   47
                  ──────────
                   14   85
Simplify: Minutes exceed 60
           Deduct 60 minutes and add 1 hour
                   14   85
                  ──────────
                   15   25
ANSWER: 1525

When subtracting, if necessary create a situation where the number of minutes in the time from which you are subtracting is greater than the number of minutes in the time being subtracted. Deduct a time of 4 hours and 12 minutes from a time of 0831.

SOLUTION: 08   31
                  − 04   12
                  ──────────
                    4   19
ANSWER: 4 hours and 19 minutes

Deduct a time of 0541 from a time of 1026.

SOLUTION: 10   26   =   09   86
              − 05   41   − 05   41
              ───────────   ───────────
                                      4   45

ANSWER: 4 hours and 45 minutes

Multiplication and Division   Sequence of operations:
1. Convert hours and minutes to minutes
2. Multiply or divide.
3. Convert minutes to hours and minutes.

   For example, 4 hours and 16 minutes multiplied by 3.

SOLUTION: 4 hours = 4 × 60 minutes = 240 minutes
             16 minutes   =   16 minutes
                                        ───────────────
                                        256 Minutes

        256 minutes × 3 = 768 minutes

ANSWER: 768 ÷ 60 minutes = 12 hours and 48 minutes or $12^{48}/_{60}$

Caution: *not* 12.48 hours; *not* 12.8 hours;
        but 768 ÷ 60 = $12^{48}/_{60}$ = 12 hours and 48 minutes

   Follow the same procedure for division. For example, 5 hours and
37 minutes divided by 3.

SOLUTION: 5 hours = 5 × 60 = 300 minutes
                              =   37 minutes
                             ───────────────
                              337 minutes

        337 ÷ 3 = 112 minutes

ANSWER: 112 ÷ 60 = $1^{52}/_{60}$ = 1 hour and 52 minutes

Caution: *not* 1.52 hours; *not* 1.86 or 1.9 hours;
        but 112 ÷ 60 = $1^{52}/_{60}$ = 1 hour and 52 minutes

DISTANCE

Consult page 75 for a definition of nautical and statute miles and the
method to measure and plot nautical miles on a chart. Use the latitude
scale at the sides of the chart, *not* the longitude scale. For consistency
and to minimize error, do *not* use the scale of miles on the chart title
block if (as is sometimes the case) such a scale is printed on it. Always
perform calculations in nautical miles. Unless otherwise specified as
statute miles, the word miles is understood to mean nautical miles.

   Some small craft waterways' charts, such as strip charts of the Trent
waterways, have markings at each mile from some reference location.
These are statute miles and are so specified in the title block or chart
notes. The locations of these markings will be revised on new issue
charts when they are reissued in metric format. The distance will then
be in kilometres.

TIME/SPEED/DISTANCE CALCULATIONS

Remember this address: 60 D St. If you know the amount of time it took you to travel a known distance, you can determine at what speed you were travelling. If you know at what speed you will be travelling and what distance you will travel, you can determine how long it will take for the trip. If you know at what time you will depart, you can then determine your estimated time of arrival (ETA). If you know the speed at which you are travelling, you can determine what distance you will travel in any given amount of time.

To travel 1 statute mile in 1 hour, your rate of speed will be 1 statute mile per hour. To travel 1 nautical mile in 1 hour, your rate of speed will be 1 nautical mile per hour. By definition 1 nautical mile per hour is 1 knot. However, the term knot(s) per hour does not apply to nautical navigation. It is a scientific term involving a rate of acceleration.

To convert time and speed to distance, time and distance to speed or speed and distance to time, use the address 60 D Street, meaning 60 × distance (nautical miles) = S (knots) × t (minutes), or 60 D = St. In this formula, distance is measured in nautical miles, speed in knots and time in minutes; 60 is a constant, because time is always in minutes. Therefore:

$$D = \frac{St}{60} \qquad\qquad S = \frac{60D}{t} \qquad\qquad t = \frac{60D}{S}$$

A simple tip for those unfamiliar with algebraic conversion: remember 60D = St., then circle the unknown item (the one you are trying to determine) and put the other item which is on the same side of the equal sign underneath the two items on the opposite side of the equal sign.

Examples

1. You know the speed and time. You want to know the distance:

   $60D = St \qquad\qquad 60\,ⓓ = St$

   $$D = \frac{St}{60}$$

2. You know the speed and distance. You want to know the time.

   $60D = St \qquad 60D = S\,ⓣ$

   $$\frac{60D}{S} = t \qquad \text{or} \qquad t = \frac{60D}{S}$$

3. You know the time and distance. You want to know the speed.

   $60D = St \qquad 60D = ⓢt$

   $$\frac{60D}{t} = S \qquad \text{or} \qquad S = \frac{60D}{t}$$

Bear in mind that D = distance in nautical miles, S = speed in knots, t = time in minutes

Problems

1. You have been travelling 3 hours and 17 minutes at 7 knots since you departed from the dock. How far have you travelled?

$$60\,\textcircled{D} = St$$

$$D = \frac{St}{60}$$

S is 7 knots

t is 3 hours 17 minutes

$$3 \text{ hours} \times 60 = \quad 180 \text{ minutes}$$
$$\underline{+\ 17 \text{ minutes}}$$
$$t \text{ is} \quad 197 \text{ minutes}$$

$$D = \frac{St}{60} \qquad D = \frac{7 \times 197}{60} = \frac{1379}{60} = 22.98$$

Distance travelled is 23.0 nautical miles.

2. You have travelled from A to B, a distance of 11.6 miles in 1 hour and 54 minutes. At what speed were you travelling?

$$60D = \textcircled{S}t$$

$$\frac{60D}{t} = S \qquad \text{or} \qquad S = \frac{60D}{t}$$

D is 11.6 miles

t is 1 hour 54 minutes

$$1 \text{ hour} \times 60 = \quad 60 \text{ minutes}$$
$$\underline{+\ 54 \text{ minutes}}$$
$$t \text{ is} \quad 114 \text{ minutes}$$

$$S = \frac{60 \times 11.6}{114} = \frac{696}{114} = 6.10$$

Speed is 6.1 knots

3. How long will it take you to travel from A to B (a distance of 11.6 miles) if you travel at a speed of 6.0 knots? If you leave point A at 1155, at what time will you arrive at point B?

$$60D = S\,\textcircled{t}$$

$$\frac{60D}{S} = t \qquad \text{or } t = \frac{60D}{S}$$

D is 11.6 miles

S is 6.0 knots

$$t = \frac{60 \times 11.6}{6.0} = \frac{696}{6.0} = 116 \text{ minutes}$$

$116 \div 60 = 1^{56}/_{60} = 1$ hour 56 minutes

Departure time	11	55
Travel time	+ 1	56
Arrival time (ETA)	12	111

$111 - 60 = 51$

ETA is 1351

SUMMARY

The most common chart projections for small boat navigation are Mercator or Polyconic.

- On these charts, directions can be measured directly by means of the compass rose on the chart, and distances can be measured by use of the *latitude* scale. One minute of latitude equals 1 nautical mile of 6080 feet.
- Keep your charts updated by use of *Notices to Mariners*.
- North-South co-ordinates on a chart are meridians of longitude (λ) and are measured East or West from the Greenwich Meridian.
- East-West co-ordinates on a chart are parallels of latitude (L) and are measured North or South from the equator.

Location is specified by means of latitude, the distance North or South of the equator; and longitude, the meridian East or West of Greenwich, England. Woodbine Beach, Toronto, Canada, for example, is located at L 43° 39.5′ N (latitude), λ 79° 18.7′ W (longitude).

For time/speed/distance calculations, 60D = St (60D Street). The constant 60 multiplied by distance (in nautical miles) is equal to speed (in knots) multiplied by time (in minutes).

$$\text{Time} = \frac{60 \times \text{Distance}}{\text{Speed}}$$

$$\text{Speed} = \frac{60 \times \text{Distance}}{\text{Time}}$$

$$\text{Distance} = \frac{\text{Speed} \times \text{Time}}{60}$$

7. Elementary Plotting

"A series of mistakes, if cleverly done, will cancel each other out. But don't rely on it."　　　　SAUNDERS' LAW OF NAVIGATION *#6*

DEAD RECKONING

Dead reckoning is the continuous plotting of your course and position based on known facts: time, speed, distance, course, variation and deviation. Dead reckoning is a deduction of your position assuming *dead* air and *dead* water conditions. That is, no leeway due to wind, and no drift due to current. Leeway and drift may be estimated but are not generally exactly known. Advanced piloting methods, described in Section II of this book, take into account these two factors to arrive at estimated positions. However, dead reckoning plots are maintained on the chart by the most experienced and advanced navigators and are therefore applicable to all small craft skippers.

Some of the reasons that you should maintain a plot of your dead reckoned (DR) position are:

- Immediate or very rapid determination of your approximate position so that you may be quickly located in the event of an emergency aboard your boat.
- Knowledge of your position so that you can quickly go to another vessel's assistance in the event of an emergency.
- To be able to plot a course, knowing where you are at any time, to a desired destination by the safest, shortest, and/or most economical course(s).
- To be able to make important decisions as to the proper action in the event of adverse conditions: fog, wind, storm, equipment failure, and so on.

Dead reckoned plots should be based on true courses and should be clearly labelled for future reference. A common standard of plotting and labelling is recommended so that, if necessary, others will be able to quickly take over and clearly understand the situation. Although more than one standard or "convention" exists, if you follow the method of plotting and labelling in this book, your results will conform closely to most current, generally accepted standards.

The following exercise using Chart T-3450, obtainable from Canadian Hydrographic Services or your local chart dealer, will give you an opportunity to put into practice all that you have learned thus far and to learn to determine and label a DR plot. Although your copy of Chart T-3450 may be a later issue than the one used here, the differences should not be significant, and I strongly urge that you obtain the chart and work the problem through step by step.

On the chart (T-3450), Point Roberts light is located at L 48° 58.3′ N, λ 123° 04.9′ W. For this example consider variation to be 23° E. Now plot the cruise listed below.

1. You leave Point Roberts light at 1016 on compass course 204° at 6.0 knots.
2. At 1117 you change course to 092° according to the ship's compass and maintain speed at 6.0 knots.
3. At 1156 you change speed to 8.0 knots and continue on course 092° compass.
4. At 1234 you change course to 045° compass and maintain your speed of 8.0 knots.
5. After travelling 6.1 miles you note that your watch has stopped.
   What time is it?
   Where are you?
   What course do you steer to return to Point Roberts light?
   What is your ETA at Point Roberts if you travel at 8.0 knots?
6. You immediately proceed on this course toward Point Roberts at 8.0 knots.
7. Twenty minutes later you note that a storm is approaching and increase your speed. However, at the same time your RPM indicator has failed and you do not know your speed.
8. You arrive at Point Roberts light at 1429.
   What was your speed from the time that your RPM indicator failed?
   What total distance did you travel?
   What was the total time of your voyage?

Solution Plotting and Labelling   The following chartlets are the progressive plotting of the voyage in the problem. Chartlet IV represents what your chart should look like on return to Point Roberts. The text will take you progressively through the four legs of your journey.

Chartlet I

1. Circle your point of departure and note the time of departure (1016). Because you are alongside a charted aid to navigation (Point Roberts light), no other notation is required.

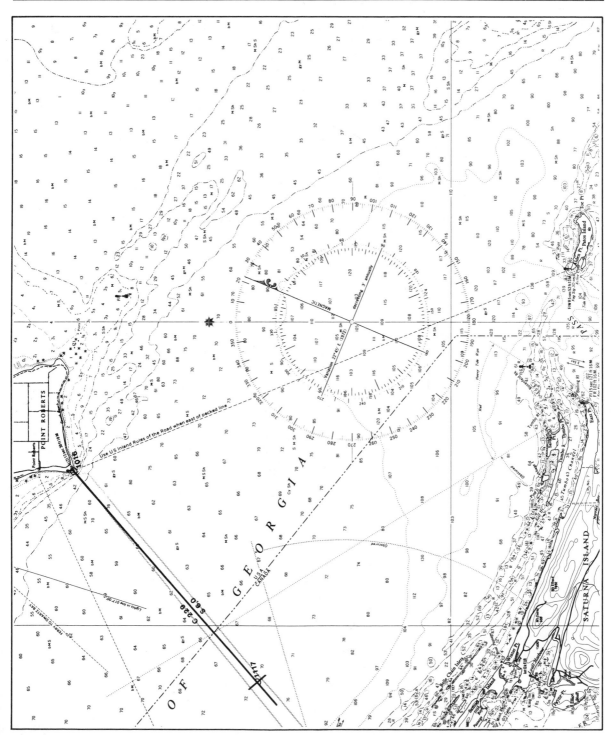

Chartlet I

2. Plot your true course equivalent of the initial compass course of 204°.

T	**V**	**M**	**D**	**C**
229°	23°E	206°	2°E	204°

This must be plotted as 229° true. Using your parallel rule and outer compass rose, "walk" the direction of 229° over to Point Roberts light and draw a line at 229° through the locating point of the light. Label this course line with the true course above the line and the speed below the line.

3. Calculate how far along this course you travelled.

$60D = St$　　S is 6.0 knots

t is the difference between 1117 and 1016 which is 61 minutes.

$$\begin{array}{r} 11 \quad 17 \\ - \ 10 \quad 16 \\ \hline 1 \quad 01 \end{array} = 1 \text{ hour and 1 minute}$$

$$1 \text{ hour} \times 60 = 60 \text{ minutes}$$
$$+ \quad 1 \text{ minute}$$
$$\text{t is} \quad \overline{\quad 61 \text{ minutes}}$$

$$60D = St \qquad D = \frac{St}{60} = \frac{6.0 \times 61}{60} = \quad 6.1 \text{ miles}$$

4. With your dividers set at 6.1 miles from the latitude scale (say one point on 50′ and the other point on 56.1′), measure along the course line a distance of 6.1 miles in direction 229° from Point Roberts light.

5. Mark this point on the line. Label it as DR (dead reckon) and the time 1117.

Chartlet II

1. Plot your true course equivalent of the new compass course of 092°.

T	**V**	**M**	**D**	**C**
123°	23°E	100°	8°E	092°

This must be plotted as 123° true.

2. Draw a line through your 1117 DR position in a direction of 123° true. Label this course line with course and speed. Note that you must plot your DR position each time you change your course or speed.

3. Now plot your 1156 position, at which time you changed speed to 8.0 knots.

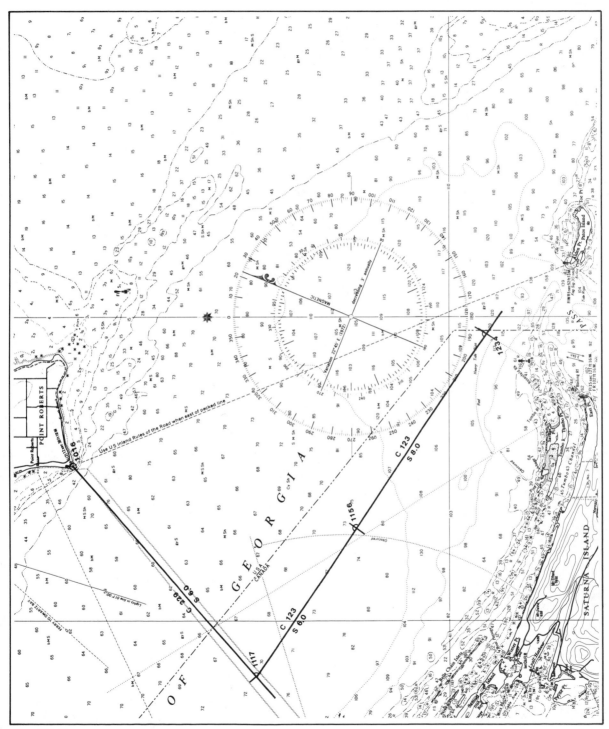

Chartlet II

$$60D = St \quad S \text{ is 6.0 knots}$$
$$t \text{ is } 1156 - 1117 = 39 \text{ minutes}$$
$$D = \frac{6.0 \times 39}{60} = 3.9 \text{ miles}$$

4. Measure along direction 123° from your 1117 DR a distance of 3.9 miles and plot and label your 1156 DR.

5. Continue your course line in direction 123° and label your course and new speed at 8.0 knots.

6. Plot your 1234 DR position
$$60D = St \quad S \text{ is 8.0 knots}$$
$$t \text{ is } 1234 - 1156 = 38 \text{ minutes}$$
$$D \text{ is } \frac{8.0 \times 38}{60} = 5.1 \text{ miles}$$

7. Measure 5.1 miles from your 1156 DR along your 123° course line and mark this point.

8. Plot and label this point as your 1234 DR.

Chartlet III

1. Plot and label your new course.

T	V	M	D	C
068°	23°E	045°	0°	045°

Draw and label this true course line of 068° from your 1234 DR.

2. Measure along this course line a distance of 6.1 miles.

3. Plot and label your DR. For the time of this DR, see the answer to the question in 4 below.

4. What time is it?
$$60D = St \quad D = 6.1 \text{ Miles}$$
$$S = 8.0 \text{ Knots}$$
$$t = \frac{60D}{S} = \frac{60 \times 6.1}{8.0} = 46 \text{ minutes elapsed time from 1234.}$$

$$\begin{array}{r} 12 \quad 34 \\ + \quad 46 \\ \hline 12 \quad 80 = 1320 \end{array}$$

Time is 1320.

5. Where are you?
We can answer this question in two different ways, either as distance and direction from a charted object (A), or by latitude and longitude (B).

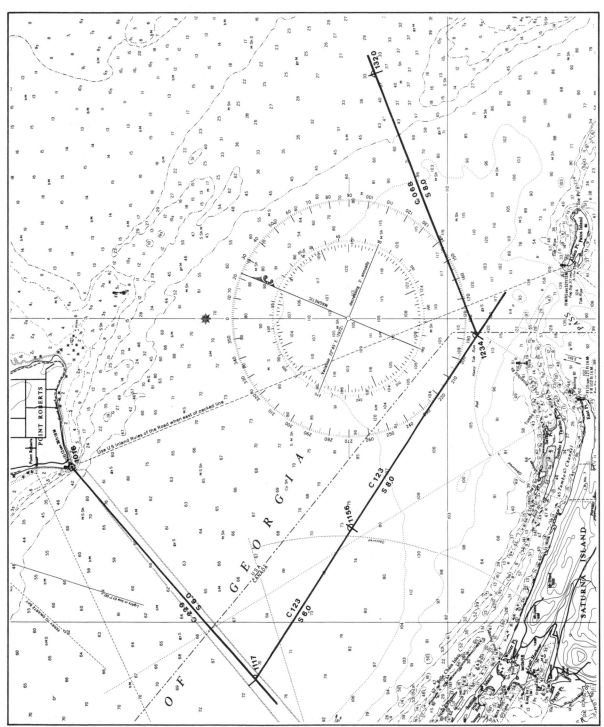

Chartlet III

A. Place parallel rules between Point Roberts light and your 1320 DR. "Walk" rules to the compass rose and read direction from the outer rose. Note that you must consider the centre point of the compass rose as the "from" point (in this case Point Roberts light). You must go to the point on the outer rose in the same general direction as the DR is from the light, in this case 128°. With your dividers, measure the distance from Point Roberts light to your 1234 DR: 10.8 miles. You are located 10.8 miles from Point Roberts light on a true bearing (angle) of 128°, that is, in a direction of 128° from Point Roberts light.

B. Using your dividers and the latitude and longitude scales, determine your latitude and longitude.

   L 48° 51.6′ N
   λ 122° 51.9′ W
Label your 1320 DR.

6. What course do you steer to return to Point Roberts light? Using parallel rules, transfer the direction between your 1320 DR and the light to the compass rose to obtain the correct course.

T	**V**	**M**	**D**	**C**
308°	23°E	285°	8°W	293°

Steer compass course 293°.

7. At 8.0 knots what is your ETA at Point Roberts light?

60D = St   D = 10.8 miles (answer to 5A)
               S = 8.0 knots

$$t = \frac{60D}{S} = \frac{60 \times 10.8}{8.0} = 81 \text{ minutes}$$

Elapsed time = 1 hour 21 minutes

```
    13   20
 +   1   21
 ──────────
    14   41
```

ETA 1441

Chartlet IV

1. Plot and label your 308° course line and speed.

2. Plot and label your DR 20 minutes later when you change speed at 1340. This DR is 2.7 miles from the 1320 DR.

3. Label your course line after the 1340 DR with course and new speed. At this point in time your speed is unknown.

4. What was your speed between 1340 DR and arrival at Point Roberts light at 1429?

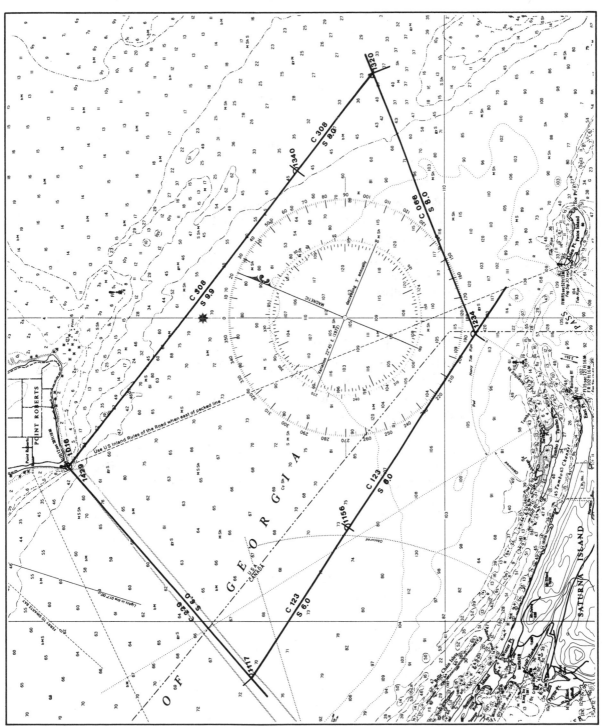

Chartlet IV

$$60D = St \quad D = 10.8 - 2.7 = 8.1 \text{ miles}$$
$$t = 1429 - 1340 = 49 \text{ minutes}$$

$$\begin{array}{r} 13 \quad 89 \\ - \; 13 \quad 40 \\ \hline 0 \quad 49 \end{array}$$

$$S = \frac{60D}{T} = \frac{60 \times 8.1}{49} = 9.9 \text{ knots}$$

Speed is 9.9 knots

5. What total distance did you travel?
From your log (see Ch. 8):
6.1 + 3.9 + 5.1 + 6.1 + 2.7 + 8.1 = 32.0 miles

6. What was the total time of the voyage?
From your log: started 1016, ended 1429; elapsed time 4 hours and 13 minutes.

NOTE: In addition to plotting your DR at each change of course and/or speed, you should also plot your DR each hour on the hour. This has not been done on these chartlets only in the interest of simplicity and clarity.

RPM/SPEED CURVE

If your power boat does not have an accurate speedometer (statute miles per hour), or, preferably, a knot meter (nautical miles per hour), then you must develop a relationship (curve or chart) between your RPM indicator and vessel speed.

In any event, most small power-craft knotmeters are not dependable and somewhat inaccurate over the whole range of the vessel's speed, and you should therefore have an RPM/Speed curve for your vessel. Appendix E explains a method for developing such a curve.

STANDARDS OF ACCURACY

All problems should result in answers that are within:

Time   ± 1 minute
Distance   ± 0.1 nautical mile
Speed   ± 0.1 knot

Latitude   ± 00° 00.1′
Longitude   ± 00° 00.1′
Courses (directions)   ± 1°

Recognizing that under actual conditions aboard a small vessel you may not be able to steer a course, maintain a speed or plot to that degree of accuracy, you must, nonetheless, strive to attain it.

PLOTTING AND LABELLING SYMBOLS AND PRACTICES

The conventional standards and symbols for labelling vary from country to country and change through time. Different standards also prevail between naval and mercantile mariners within the same country. A generally accepted standard of symbols and practices is included in Appendix F and is used throughout this book.

SUMMARY

Dead reckon (DR) position is determined by calculating your speed and plotting your position based on this calculated speed and the course steered according to your compass (corrected for variation and deviation). Remember to *plot true courses and directions only on your chart*. Correct compass courses and directions for variation and deviation of the course steered.

8. Maintaining a Log

"Where you have been is what determines where you are."
SAUNDERS' LAW OF NAVIGATION #7

A log is a record of actions or incidents aboard a vessel. A deck log is a record of incidents pertinent to the movement and navigation of the ship. I strongly recommend that you maintain a deck log similar to the example below. The log will provide an orderly way of noting all data that you will require to maintain a dead reckoning plot. Future practice cruises and major examples will include the appropriate log entries.

LOG OF THE _____   DATE _____

| TIME | LOCATION L λ | DIST n.m. | SPEED Knots | SHIP'S HEADING OR BEARING | | | | | RPM | CALCULATIONS/COMMENTS |
				True	V	Mag.	D	Comp		

VARIATION EAST MAGNETIC LEAST
VARIATION WEST MAGNETIC BEST
DEVIATION EAST COMPASS LEAST
DEVIATION WEST COMPASS BEST

$60D = St$

$S = \dfrac{60D}{t}$

$t = \dfrac{60D}{S}$

Log books or sheets can be purchased commercially at marine supply stores or chart dealers. You may prefer to lay out a log sheet format to meet your own personal preferences and have it duplicated by photocopying or inexpensive "instant" printing.

Log entries should be made:
- At the beginning of each voyage.
- Each time the course (heading) is changed.
- At each change of RPM or speed. If under sail, use estimated averages over half-hour periods or calculate the speed periodically from time and distance.
- Each time a bearing is taken.
- On passing close (100 yards) to an aid to navigation.
- Every hour on the hour.
- At the end of each voyage.
- At the time of any particularly noteworthy event.

READING A LOG
These example lines are taken from the sample log pages given on the following pages.

Time of 1320 is the time of the occurrence about which you are writing. In this example at 1320 you wound and reset watch, determined your L and λ from your DR plot, determined what course to steer to reach Point Roberts light and estimated your time of arrival at Point Roberts light.

Location should be noted if it has significant consequences. In this case, you used your location to determine the future course to steer and ETA.

Distance travelled since the last entry should be entered; this may be the accumulated distance.

Speed travelled should be noted after changing speed.

Ship's heading or bearing should be recorded on which you are going to steer (or were steering when you took a bearing).

RPM and Comments are self-explanatory and optional.

LOG OF THE _Alzarc_ _____   DATE _July 15, 198–_

TIME	LOCATION L λ	DIST n.m.	SPEED Knots	SHIP'S HEADING OR BEARING					RPM	CALCULATIONS/COMMENTS
				True	V	Mag.	D	Comp		
1016	Pt. Roberts Light	0.0	6.0					204°		Leave anchorage.
1117			6.0					092°		Changed course.
1156			8.0					092°		Increased speed.
1234			8.0					045°		Changed course.
1320		6.1	8.0							Wound and reset watch.

VARIATION EAST MAGNETIC LEAST   60D = St
VARIATION WEST MAGNETIC BEST
DEVIATION EAST COMPASS LEAST $S = \frac{60D}{t}$
DEVIATION WEST COMPASS BEST $t = \frac{60D}{S}$

SUMMARY

Maintain a log of all pertinent details of your trip.

Record time and date of:
- Each course or change of course.
- Each speed or change of speed.
- Location of your position each time that you determine it.
- Any other data pertinent to the navigation or safe operation of your vessel.

LOG OF THE _Alzarc_   DATE July 15, 198–

TIME	LOCATION L λ	DIST n.m.	SPEED Knots	SHIP'S HEADING OR BEARING					RPM	CALCULATIONS/COMMENTS
				True	V	Mag.	D	Comp		
1016	Pt. Roberts Light	0.0	6.0	229°	23°E	206°	2°E	204°		Leave anchorage.
1117		6.1	6.0	123°	23°E	100°	8°E	092°		Changed course.
1156		3.9	8.0	123°	23°E	100°	8°E	092°		Increased speed.
1234		5.1	8.0	068°	23°E	045°	0°	045°		Changed course.
1320	48° 51.6'N 122° 51.9'W	6.1	8.0	308°	23°E	285°	8°W	293°		Wound and reset watch. ETA Point Roberts 1441.
1340		2.7	9.9	308°	23°E	285°	8°W	293°		Storm warnings. Increased speed.
1429		8.1	—							Moored.

VARIATION EAST MAGNETIC LEAST   60D = St
VARIATION WEST MAGNETIC BEST
DEVIATION EAST COMPASS LEAST $S = \frac{60D}{t}$
DEVIATION WEST COMPASS BEST $t = \frac{60D}{S}$

9. Bearings and Fixes

"Any bit of information most needed will be least available."
SAUNDERS' LAW OF NAVIGATION *#8*

FIXES

A fix is an accurate determination of the vessel's location. This location is usually obtained by determining the location of the vessel relative to two or more charted, visible objects.

However, only one object is required in some circumstances; for example: when right alongside a charted object, or when using the advanced methods of obtaining a fix as outlined in Section II of this book.

A fix is the point of intersection of two or more lines of position. A line of position (LOP) is a line on which the vessel is located and which can be accurately plotted on a chart. It can be obtained by taking a bearing on a visible, charted object.

Let's take the confusion out of these new terms by examining the process of obtaining a fix in the proper sequence. First, you must take a bearing on a visible, charted object.

BEARINGS

A bearing is an angle between two lines. To take a bearing is to measure an angle between these two lines. There are several types of bearings: true, magnetic, compass and relative.

True Bearing: an angle between two lines. One line is between the vessel and the True North Pole (your meridian of longitude). The second line is between the vessel and a charted, visible object (your line of sight to a charted, visible object). (See Fig. 83.)

Magnetic Bearing: an angle between two lines. One line is between the vessel and the Magnetic North Pole (same as true North except for variation). The second is a line of sight to a charted, visible object. (See Fig. 84.)

Compass Bearing: an angle between two lines. One line is between the vessel and compass North (same as true North except for variation

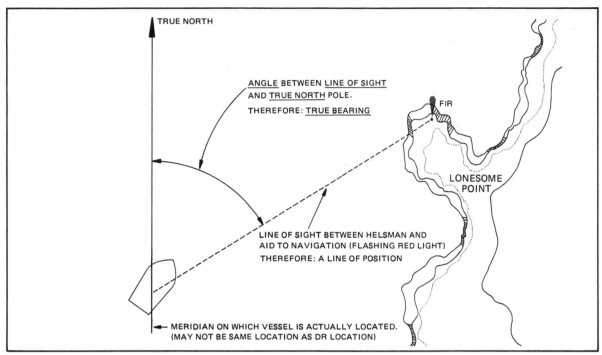

TRUE NORTH

ANGLE BETWEEN LINE OF SIGHT AND TRUE NORTH POLE.

THEREFORE: TRUE BEARING

FIR

LONESOME POINT

LINE OF SIGHT BETWEEN HELSMAN AND AID TO NAVIGATION (FLASHING RED LIGHT)

THEREFORE: A LINE OF POSITION

← MERIDIAN ON WHICH VESSEL IS ACTUALLY LOCATED. (MAY NOT BE SAME LOCATION AS DR LOCATION)

FIG. 83

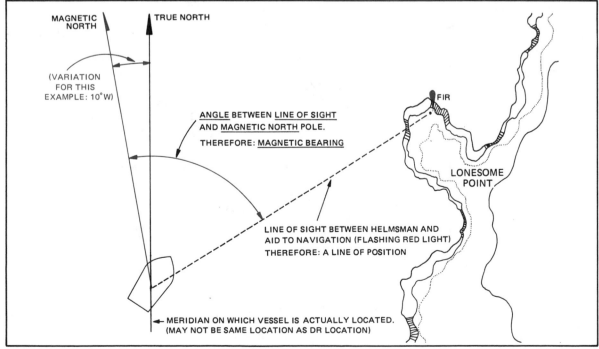

MAGNETIC NORTH

TRUE NORTH

(VARIATION FOR THIS EXAMPLE: 10°W)

ANGLE BETWEEN LINE OF SIGHT AND MAGNETIC NORTH POLE.

THEREFORE: MAGNETIC BEARING

FIR

LONESOME POINT

LINE OF SIGHT BETWEEN HELMSMAN AND AID TO NAVIGATION (FLASHING RED LIGHT)

THEREFORE: A LINE OF POSITION

← MERIDIAN ON WHICH VESSEL IS ACTUALLY LOCATED. (MAY NOT BE SAME LOCATION AS DR LOCATION)

FIG. 84

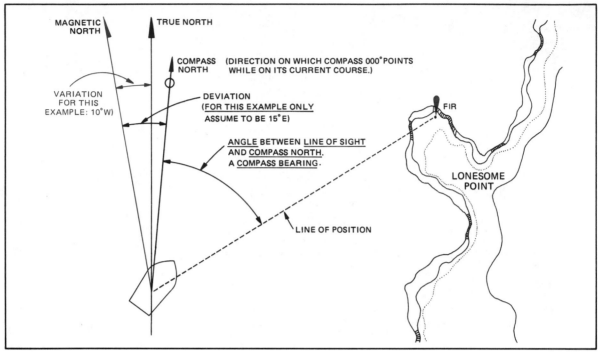

FIG. 85

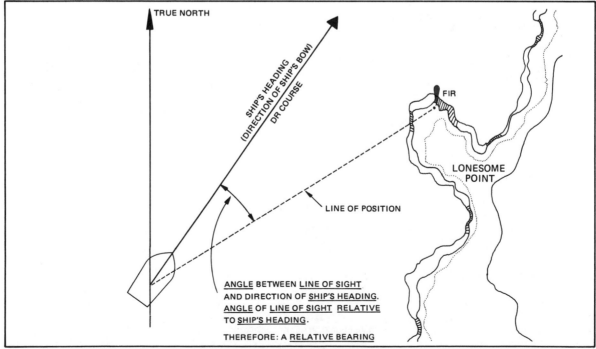

FIG. 86

and deviation). The second is a line of sight to a charted, visible object. (See Fig. 85.)

Relative Bearing: an angle between two lines. One line is between the vessel and the direction that the bow of the vessel is headed. The second is a line of sight to the object on which the bearing is taken. (See Fig. 86.)

Taking a Bearing To take a bearing (to measure an angle) you need some type of angle measuring device such as a protractor. The card in your ship's compass is a 360° protractor. On this protractor 000° is always pointing along the line between your vessel and compass North. If you stand with the compass between you and some charted, visible object, you can determine where your line of sight (between the centre of the compass card and the object — your line of position) intersects the edge of the card. This point of intersection is your measurement of the angle between compass North and your line of position. The angle is your compass bearing on that object. (See Fig. 87.)

Plotting the bearing You *cannot* plot this bearing on your chart. It is a *compass bearing* and *must be converted to* a *true bearing* by correcting for deviation and variation.

Before converting refer again to Figures 51, 52, 53 and 54 and bear in mind the letters TVMDC. You will recall that deviation is different on each ship's heading. The Deviation Table in Appendix C gives you the deviation according to ship's heading.

The compass card magnets have no way of knowing whether your eyes are open or closed. Even if your eyes are open, the compass card is not affected by whether you are looking forward or aft or whether you are looking at the charted buoy in Figure 87. We must determine and apply deviation according to ship's heading from the Deviation Table when converting the compass bearing to a true bearing, as in the example shown in Figure 88.

T	**V**	**M**	**D**	**C**
038°	23°E	015°	4°W	019°
			(Deviation of the ship's heading)	(Ship's heading)

Then convert the compass bearing to true:

T	**V**	**M**	**D**	**C**
080°	23°E	057°	4°W	061°
			(per ship's heading)	(bearing on red, "RB," buoy)

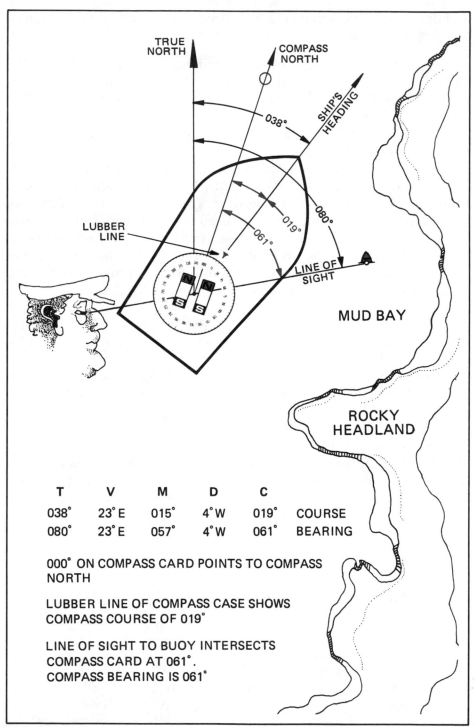

T	V	M	D	C	
038°	23°E	015°	4°W	019°	COURSE
080°	23°E	057°	4°W	061°	BEARING

000° ON COMPASS CARD POINTS TO COMPASS NORTH

LUBBER LINE OF COMPASS CASE SHOWS COMPASS COURSE OF 019°

LINE OF SIGHT TO BUOY INTERSECTS COMPASS CARD AT 061°.
COMPASS BEARING IS 061°

FIG. 87

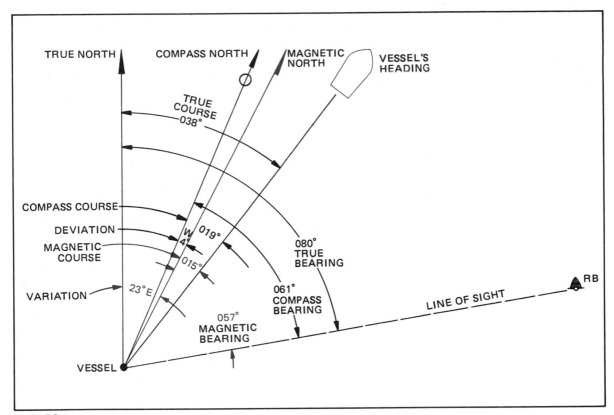

FIG. 88

If you had used deviation according to the 061° compass bearing, you would have applied 2°E deviation, an error of 6°. Remember, apply *deviation according to the ship's heading!* Refer again to Figure 88 and you will see the reason for and proof of this example.

You are headed 038° true. Due to variation, 000° on the compass card is rotated 23° clockwise of true North. The ship's magnetic heading is 015°. Due to deviation on that magnetic heading, 000° on the compass card is rotated 4° counter-clockwise of magnetic North. Your compass heading reads 019°; This is the compass heading or ship's heading according to the compass.

Your line of sight to the buoy intersects the compass card at 061°. If you measure the angle between true North and the line of sight to the "RB" buoy, the result is 080° which agrees with your TVMDC calculation of 080°.

The value of maintaining a log as suggested in Chapter 8 will now become apparent. We logged our course and speed at the time that we last changed either course or speed. Study the following example.

Time	Course or Bearing					Speed (knots)	Remarks
	T	**V**	**M**	**D**	**C**		
1220	038°	23°E	015°	4°W	019°	8.0	Changed speed
1242	080°	23°E	057°	4°W	061°		Took bearing on RB

When you took the bearing on the RB buoy, you noted it in the log. Of course, you entered the compass bearing, because you took the bearing over the compass. You can refer to the last course entry in the log and enter the same deviation and variation on the bearing line as appear on the course line. Now you merely "fill in the blanks" of magnetic and then true bearing directions, using the rules in the summary of Chapter 5.

You now have the true direction of a charted object from your boat. This line of direction is your line of sight, a line on which you must be located. This is a line of position (LOP) which you can plot on your chart.

Plotting a Line of Position   To plot the true bearing 080° *to* buoy "RB," set your parallel rules at 080° on the outer compass rose and transfer this angle to draw a line *toward* the buoy. (See Fig. 89.) Because this is a line of sight, you must be located on that line. This plotted true bearing is one line of position. Label the line with the time the bearing was taken above and the true direction below. See Figure 89 and Appendix F.

Establishing a Fix   To fix your position you must plot two or more lines of position; that is, you must take bearings on two (or more) visible, charted objects at the same time. Two bearings taken within two or three minutes of each other are considered simultaneous in view of the speed of travel of the average pleasure craft. Plot these two bearings (lines of position) on the chart. The intersection of the two lines of position is where you are; it is your fix.

Plotting and Labelling a Two-Bearing Fix   Refer again to Figure 87. You wish to fix your position accurately in order to avoid a hazard that may be on your course.

Take simultaneous bearings on the "RB" buoy and the "FlR" light. Plot these two lines of position and establish your fix.

1. Take a bearing over your compass on buoy "RB." Record the time and direction.
2. Record your compass course and maintain course.

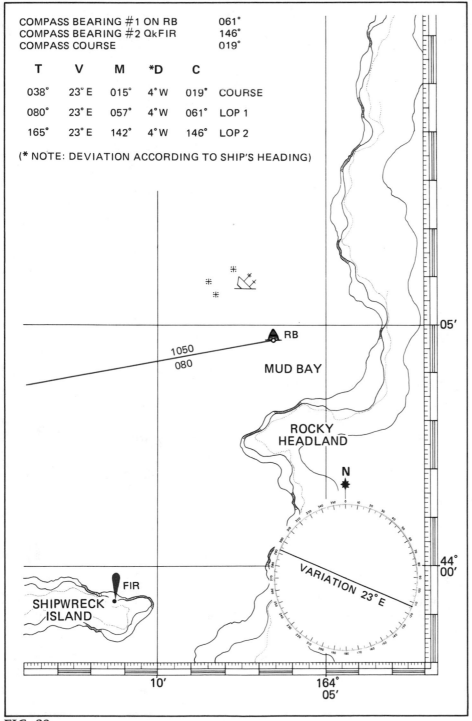

COMPASS BEARING #1 ON RB   061°
COMPASS BEARING #2 QkFlR   146°
COMPASS COURSE   019°

T	V	M	*D	C	
038°	23° E	015°	4° W	019°	COURSE
080°	23° E	057°	4° W	061°	LOP 1
165°	23° E	142°	4° W	146°	LOP 2

(* NOTE: DEVIATION ACCORDING TO SHIP'S HEADING)

1050
080

RB

MUD BAY

ROCKY
HEADLAND

N

VARIATION 23° E

FIR

SHIPWRECK
ISLAND

05'

44°
00'

10'

164°
05'

FIG. 89

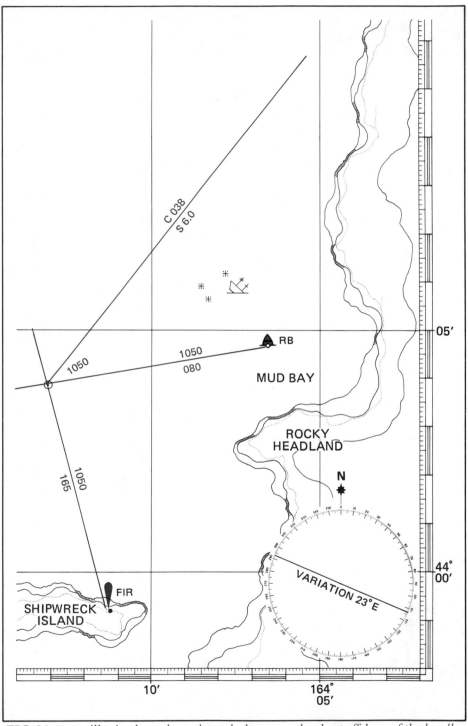

FIG. 90. *You will miss the rocks and wreck shown on the chart offshore of the headland.*

3. Take a bearing over your compass on light, "QkFlR." Record the time and position.
4. Convert compass bearings to true bearings, using deviation according to your ship's heading.
5. Plot the true bearings.
6. The intersection of the LOPs is your position.
7. Determine the latitude and longitude of your fix.

See Figures 89 and 90 for the complete solution and plot. *Remember deviation according to your ship's heading – always!*

Continuing a DR Course   Your fix is an accurate position, whereas your dead-reckon position (DR) is subject to the accuracy of your helmsmanship, the measurement of your speed and your leeway and drift. A plotted DR course is a calculation of where you think you are based on known courses and speeds. The fix is a positive determination of your position based on the bearings you have taken. Once you have a fix, you continue DR plotting from that fix and *not* from your DR position taken at the same time. Abandon your previous DR plot and start a new DR plot *every* time you establish a fix.

This practice is also true for running fixes which we will learn about in Chapter 12. Although not as accurate as a fix, the running fix will be more accurate than your DR plot. Plot a DR course from fix (or running fix) to fix (or running fix). Do not continue a DR plot from a previous DR if you have subsequently obtained a fix or running fix.

BEARINGS — OTHER METHODS

There are three other ways to obtain bearings: by the use of an azimuth ring for compass bearings, a pelorus for relative bearings, or by employing a hand-bearing compass.

Azimuth Ring   As you can appreciate, it is somewhat difficult to obtain accurate compass bearings by sighting over a compass and reading where the compass card is intersected by the imaginary line of sight to an object. Generally, it is sufficiently accurate for small craft piloting, but an azimuth ring will significantly increase this accuracy. (See Fig. 91.)

An azimuth ring is a sighting device that sits atop your compass and is free to rotate on the compass case through 360°. It is similar to the sighting vane of a pelorus. (See Fig. 92.) You sight the object through the vane just like aiming a camera view-finder, and when the object is lined up on the sighting post, you hold the ring from moving and quickly read your compass card at the mark on the ring. (See Fig. 91.)

You can easily build such an azimuth ring to fit your own compass. Be certain to use non-magnetic materials!

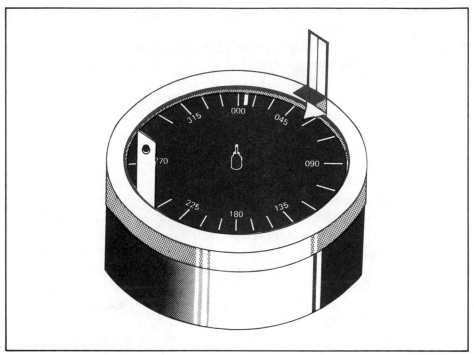

FIG. 91

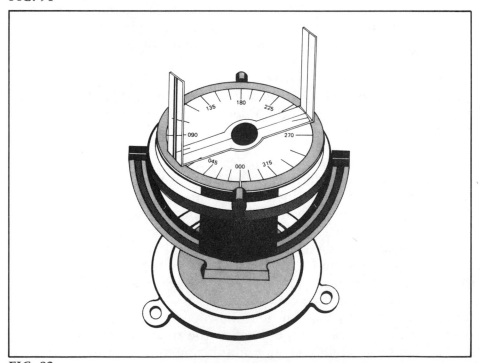

FIG. 92

The Pelorus — Compass and Relative Bearings A pelorus is merely a "dummy" compass with a sighting vane or azimuth ring. (See Fig. 92.) It is a "dummy" compass, because the Pelorus card, although somewhat free to rotate, has no magnets, and 000° will not seek out compass North. The base plate, like your compass case, has a lubber line which must be set parallel to the keel when positioning the pelorus for use. Conventionally the lubber line mark is forward. The flat pelorus card is marked in the same way as a flat compass card. A sighting vane is mounted on top of the pelorus card just like an azimuth ring on a compass.

The pelorus card can be rotated on the base plate and locked at any desired position, or it can be built to rotate but quite stiffly so that it will remain at any desired setting. The sighting vane is free to rotate independently but on the same axis as the Pelorus card, so that rotation of the sighting vane will not cause rotation of the card.

In constructing a pelorus, if the "peep hole" is kept sufficiently small (approx. $3/4$ to $1^1/4$ mm in diameter), the sighting vane or wire will be brought into adequately sharp focus while the sighted object is still in focus.

To take a compass bearing with a pelorus:

1. Rotate the pelorus card so that it reads the same as your compass card while steering a course during the time that you will take a bearing. You may find that it is difficult to safely operate the boat and at the same time set the pelorus, sight on the object and read the pelorus. These instructions assume that you have two people involved: the helmsman (vessel operator) and the observer (the bearing taker or pelorus reader and operator). Refer now to Figure 93.

2. Maintain your compass course to the pelorus reading. Call to the observer "Mark" at every instant that your ship's compass reads exactly your pre-determined course as set on the pelorus.

3. The observer sights the object through the sighting vane.

4. At any point in time that the observer simultaneously sights the object and hears the helmsman call "Mark," the observer holds the vane stationary to the pelorus card and reads the compass bearing on the pelorus card at the sighting vane mark.

5. The observer also notes the time of the bearing.

6. Because this is a compass bearing, convert it to a true bearing in exactly the same manner as you convert compass bearings to true: TVMDC. Again, *deviation is according to ship's heading*.

7. Plot the true bearing on the chart as previously discussed.

CAUTION: You must reset the Pelorus card to your ship's heading (compass) each time you change course. The observer should re-check

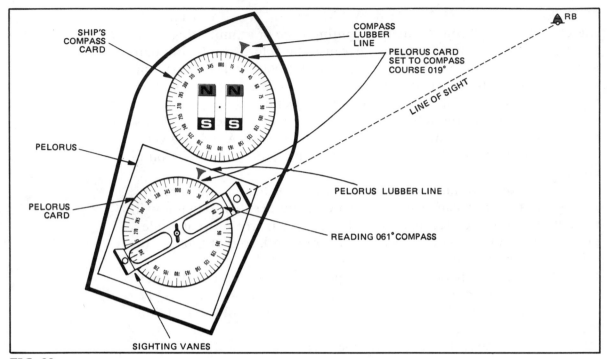

FIG. 93

with the helmsman before and after each bearing to be certain that the pelorus card was properly set.

In the case of relative bearings taken with a pelorus, recall that you have already learned that a relative bearing is one taken relative to the direction that the bow of the vessel is pointed; that is, relative to the ship's heading. (See Fig. 86.) If you set 000° of the pelorus card at the lubber line of the pelorus, any reading on the pelorus card sighted through the vanes will be a reading relative to the ship's heading.

Converting Relative Bearings to True Bearings

A pelorus relative bearing, is the angle between object and heading.

The compass course is the angle between heading and compass North.

The relative bearing plus the compass course equals the compass bearing.

True course is the angle between heading and true North.

The relative bearing plus true course equals the true bearing.

(See Fig. 94.)

The addition of a course angle plus a relative bearing angle may

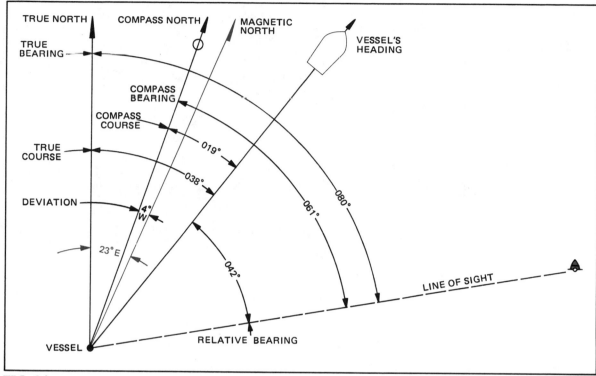

FIG. 94.

Pelorus reads angle from vessel heading to Line of sight.
Pelorus reads 042°.
Relative bearing is 042°.
Compass reads angle from compass North to vessel heading.
Compass reads 019°.
Compass bearing is compass course plus relative bearing:

> 019° *Compass course*
> + 042° *Relative bearing*
> ─────────────────────
> 061° *Compass bearing*

Convert compass bearing to true bearing:

T	V	M	*D	C	
038°	23°E	015°	4°W	019°	Course
080°	23°E	057°	4°W	061°	Bearing

*(Note: deviation according to ship's heading!)
> *Or:*
True course plus relative bearing equals true bearing:

T	V	M	D	C	
038°	23°E	015°	4°W	019°	Course

> 038° *True course*
> + 042° *Relative bearing*
> ─────────────────────
> 080° *True bearing*

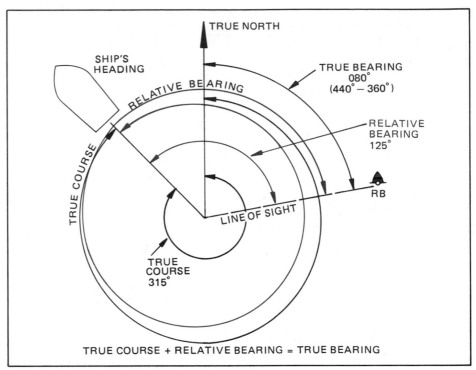

FIG. 95.
True course   315°
Relative bearing + 125°
                  ──────
                  440° True bearing
                  − 360°
                  ──────
                  080° True bearing

The measurement of angles 440° and 080° both start and end at the same line. The 440° angle goes one extra revolution (360°). Therefore, deduct 360°.

exceed 360°. If the answer exceeds 360°, deduct 360° in order to simplify to a correct answer. (See Fig. 95.)

For taking relative bearings the pelorus has several distinct advantages. It can be permanently set on 000° and fastened down so that visitors cannot inadvertently reset it. You will not forget to reset it if you change course. After converting course to true and automatically using the correct deviation, you need not worry about deviation again while on that course; just add the relative bearing to the true course to get a true bearing.

Hand-bearing Compass   A hand-bearing compass is a portable compass with a drum card, built-in viewing window and sighting vane. The viewing window has a split image. One image is of a sighted object seen through the vane. The other image is of the compass drum card and lubber line. Aim the sighting vane at the visible, charted object and simultaneously read the compass card. (See Fig. 21.) The result is a compass bearing of the object.

Convert the compass bearing to a true bearing, as in Figure 21. The result is 61°. However, we have no deviation table for a hand-bearing compass! Generally, no such table is developed, because the hand-bearing compass will not always be used from *exactly* the same location in the vessel. Therefore, use the hand-bearing compass from a location aboard as remote as possible from major potential magnetic influences, such as the engine, ship's compass, etc. Assume deviation to be 0° in the example, and your figures should read:

T	V	M	D	C
084°	23°E	061°	0°	061°

Of course, the hand-bearing compass would probably not read exactly 061°, because the error may be greater or less than 4°. But the hand-bearing compass, particularly with an approximate deviation table, is still better than a guesstimate.

Although the compass is used to arrive at a plotted course line, caution should be exercised not to treat this course line as a line of position. It is seldom true that the course line (DR track) is also a line of position. Only if the vessel is pointed directly toward a visible, charted object is the course line a line of position. In these rare instances the course direction is a bearing. If the compass course is used for the bearing, it will be a compass bearing; the relative bearing would be 000°.

THREE-BEARING FIX

Because a fix is the intersection of two or more lines of position, it is possible that you may have taken a bearing on three objects. This may have been done due to some level of doubt about the accuracy of one of the bearings. But all three lines of position may not intersect at one point. (See Fig. 96.) The resulting triangle is commonly referred to as a "cocked hat." Again, you are cautioned not to confuse the course line with a line of position. When you do have a cocked hat, your fix position is assumed to be the centre of the triangle, unless you are close to a hazard, in which case your fix is assumed to be that point in the triangle closest to the hazard.

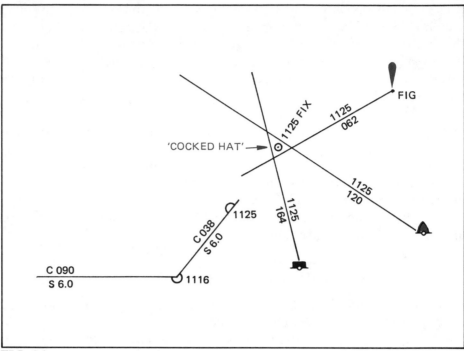

FIG. 96

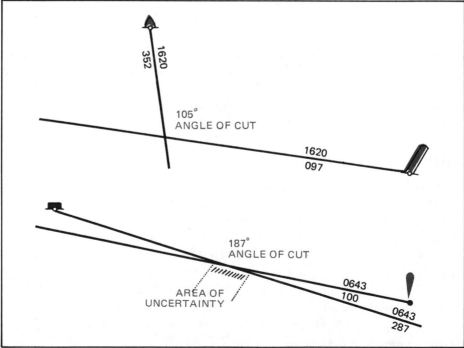

FIG. 97

ANGLE OF CUT

You will no doubt have noted that in the case of a two-bearing fix the closer the intersection of the LOPs is to 90°, the more accurate your fix will be. (See Fig. 97.) Similarly, in a three-bearing fix the accuracy will be increased as the "angle of cut" (the intersection of two LOPs) approaches 60° or 120°.

SUMMARY

- A bearing is the direction to an object from the boat.
- A line of position is a line plotted on a chart through an object in the direction of the bearing.
- A fix is the accurate determination of your position and is located at the intersection of two or more lines of position.
- The deviation to be used for converting a compass bearing to a true bearing (in order to plot a line of position on the chart) must be according to the ship's heading! Do *not* use the deviation of the compass bearing.
- Compass course plus a relative bearing is equal to the compass bearing.
- True course plus a relative bearing is equal to the true bearing.
- The use of a pelorus is strongly recommended.

10. Circular LOPs and Distance Off

"You have to do a thing to learn to do it." JACK TAR

The purpose of this chapter is to "clean up" some special cases and definitions before going on to Section II of this book which involves more advanced techniques of coastal piloting.

BEARINGS BY AIMING THE VESSEL

In the previous chapter you were cautioned that a course line or DR track is not a line of position and should be ignored when determining the intersecting point of plotted lines of position. However, when steering the plotted course if the vessel is pointed directly at a charted object, then, and only then, does the course line become a line of position.

If you do not have an azimuth ring or pelorus fitted to your compass, and if you do not have a hand-bearing compass, you can take accurate compass bearings as follows:

1. Slow your boat until you have bare steerage way.
2. Point the bow toward one charted object and note your compass reading under the lubber line. This will be both your compass course at the time of the bearing and your compass bearing.
3. Point the bow toward a second charted object and note your compass reading. This will again be both your compass course at the time of the second bearing and your second compass bearing.
4. Convert the compass bearings to true bearings and plot the LOPs.
5. The intersection of the LOPs is your fix.

But deviation will *not* be the same for both bearings, because the heading is not the same for both bearings. *Deviation must be according to the ship's heading.*

The value of the log will be evident once more if you entered the course at the time that you were lined up with the first object and then again entered the same data for the first bearing. You would then enter the new course when you lined up on the second object and enter the same data for the second bearing.

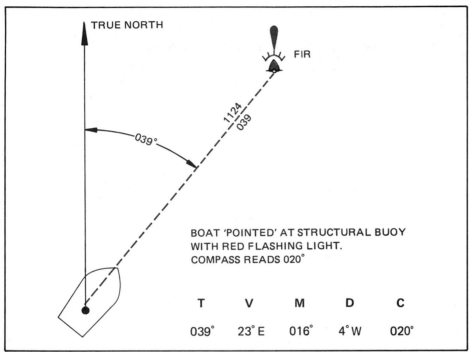

FIG. 98

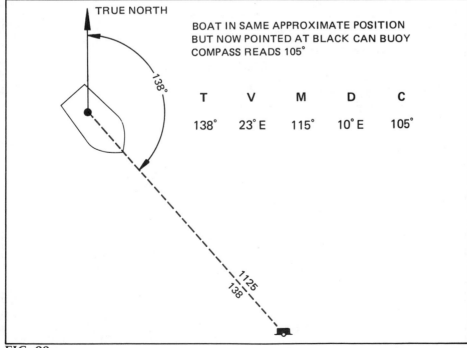

FIG. 99

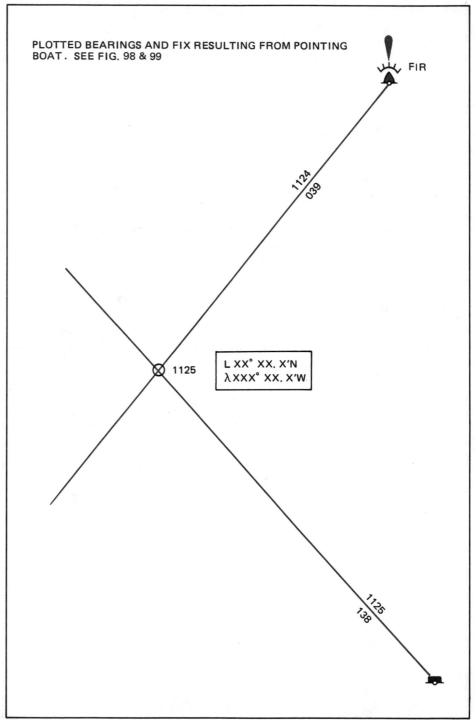

PLOTTED BEARINGS AND FIX RESULTING FROM POINTING BOAT. SEE FIG. 98 & 99

FIR

1124
039

⊗ 1125

L XX° XX. X'N
λ XXX° XX. X'W

1125
138

FIG. 100

TIME	COURSE OR BEARING					SPEED	REMARKS
	T	**V**	**M**	**D**	**C**		
XXXX	039°	23°E	016°	4°W	020°	x.x	Course to RB
XXXX	039°	23°E	016°	4°W	020°		Bearing to RB
YYYY	138°	23°E	115°	10°E	105°	x.x	Course to QkFlr
YYYY	138°	23°E	115°	10°E	105°		Bearing to QkFlr

Based on Figures 98 and 99, your log would look like the above: Plot the true bearings 039° and 138°; your position is the intersection of these two lines of position. (See Fig. 100.)

RECIPROCAL BEARINGS

A reciprocal bearing is a reverse bearing or a "bearing with opposite direction." In the case of the true bearing 039° above for example, 039° is the true direction or true bearing from the boat *to* the object. The reverse of this, the direction of the boat *from* the object, would be the reciprocal of 039° or 039° + 180° = 219°. The reciprocal of a true direction is that true direction plus 180°. If the result exceeds 360°, then subtract 360° from the result to obtain the answer. (See Fig. 101).

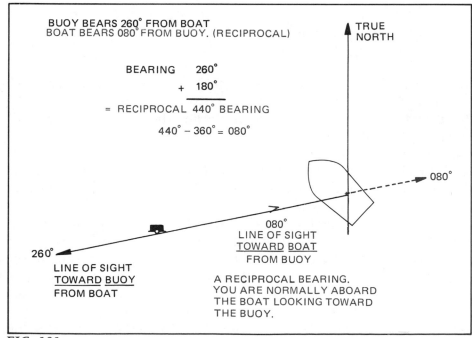

BUOY BEARS 260° FROM BOAT
BOAT BEARS 080° FROM BUOY. (RECIPROCAL)

TRUE NORTH

BEARING   260°
+   180°
= RECIPROCAL 440° BEARING
440° – 360° = 080°

080°

080°
LINE OF SIGHT
TOWARD BOAT
FROM BUOY

260°
LINE OF SIGHT
TOWARD BUOY
FROM BOAT

A RECIPROCAL BEARING.
YOU ARE NORMALLY ABOARD
THE BOAT LOOKING TOWARD
THE BUOY.

FIG. 101

RECIPROCAL COURSE

A reciprocal course is, similarly, the opposite direction, or course + 180°. Note that a compass course + 180°, if steered by your compass, will not result in sailing a reciprocal true course. You must first convert the compass course to the true course, add 180°, then convert this reciprocal true course to a compass course. You must do this because, as you will recall, deviation is according to the ship's heading.

For example:

Course steered = 090° (compass course).
Variation in the area is 12°W.
Deviation is 6°E according to Appendix C.

T	V	M	D	C
084°	12°W	096°	6°E	090°

Reciprocal True Course:

T	V	M	D	C		
084°					*not*	090°
+ 180°						+ 180°
264°	12°W	278°	8°W	286°	*not*	270°

The reciprocal heading or course steered is 286°. Using the incorrect method would result in an error of 16°.

RANGES

A range is the direction of a line (or the extension of a line) between any two charted objects. For example, two aids to navigation may be built on shore so that when they are in line the extension of this line out into the water represents an area of safe passage. The direction of this line or range is generally shown on charts when the objects were built for the primary purpose of being used in this manner. The direction will be the true direction when looking along the range toward shore.

Ranges are also used for such purposes as showing the location, direction or course to steer when entering a harbour or ferry slip. (See Fig. 102.) A back range is useful for navigation when travelling in the opposite direction, such as leaving the harbour. One simply steers a course so as to keep the objects in line when viewing them over the transom. The true direction of travel would then be the reciprocal of the range. "Running a range" is a method of checking your deviation *on that particular magnetic course.*

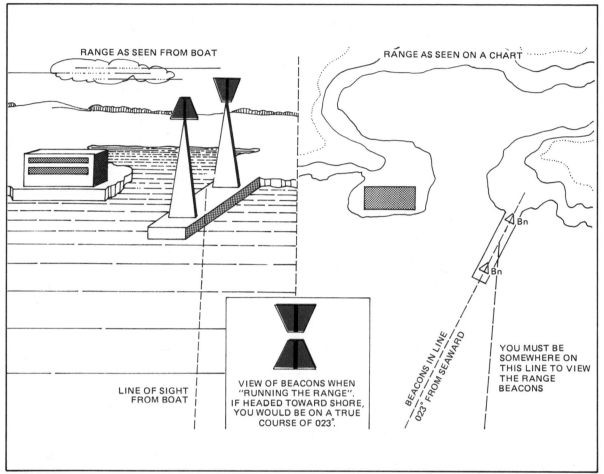

RANGE AS SEEN FROM BOAT

RANGE AS SEEN ON A CHART

Bn

Bn

VIEW OF BEACONS WHEN
"RUNNING THE RANGE".
IF HEADED TOWARD SHORE,
YOU WOULD BE ON A TRUE
COURSE OF 023°.

LINE OF SIGHT
FROM BOAT

BEACONS IN LINE
023° FROM SEAWARD

YOU MUST BE
SOMEWHERE ON
THIS LINE TO VIEW
THE RANGE
BEACONS

FIG. 102

COLLISION BEARINGS

Periodically checking the relative bearing of another vessel is a means of determining if you are on a collision course with it. If the relative bearing of another boat on a converging course remains constant, you are on a collision course with that boat. To check for potential collision bearings you do not require the accuracy of a pelorus. You need only see, for instance, that a vessel may be just ahead of the second stanchion abaft your bow. If, a little later, you see that it is still just ahead of the second stanchion abaft the bow, then you know that you are on a collision course. A collision will result if neither vessel changes its course or speed. Always be conscious of constant relative bearings on other objects that may represent a potential collision. Consult Figures 103 to 108 for examples.

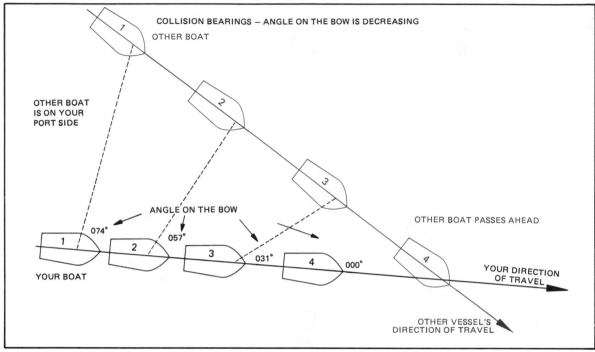

COLLISION BEARINGS — ANGLE ON THE BOW IS DECREASING

OTHER BOAT

OTHER BOAT IS ON YOUR PORT SIDE

ANGLE ON THE BOW

074°   057°   031°   000°

YOUR BOAT

OTHER BOAT PASSES AHEAD

YOUR DIRECTION OF TRAVEL

OTHER VESSEL'S DIRECTION OF TRAVEL

FIG. 103

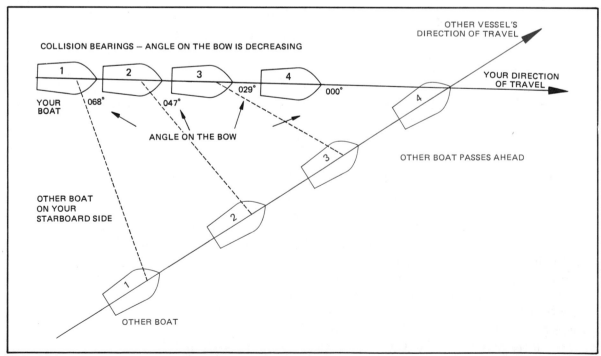

OTHER VESSEL'S DIRECTION OF TRAVEL

COLLISION BEARINGS — ANGLE ON THE BOW IS DECREASING

YOUR BOAT

YOUR DIRECTION OF TRAVEL

068°   047°   029°   000°

ANGLE ON THE BOW

OTHER BOAT ON YOUR STARBOARD SIDE

OTHER BOAT PASSES AHEAD

OTHER BOAT

FIG. 104

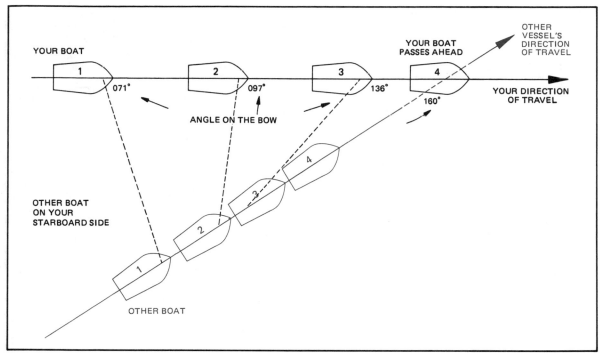

FIG. 105

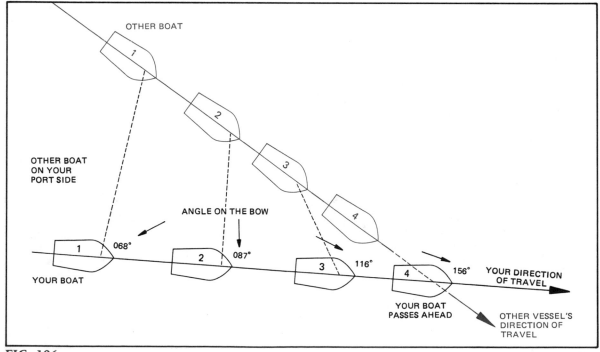

FIG. 106

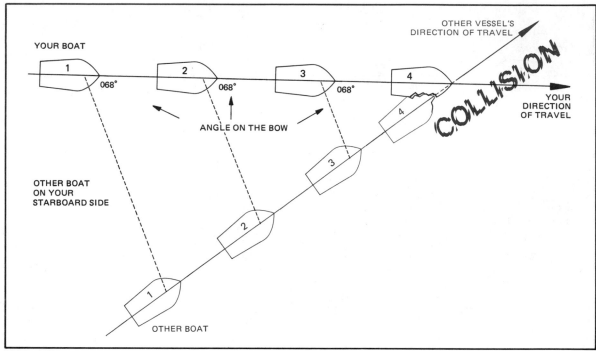

FIG. 107

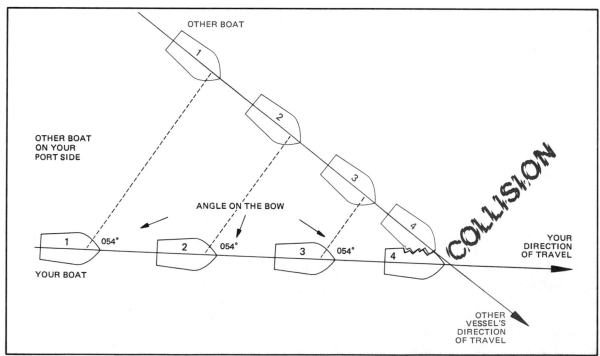

FIG. 108

CIRCULAR LINES OF POSITION

Although the special cases of establishing a fix by bow and beam bearings are thought by many to be advanced coastal piloting techniques, they have been included in this section of the book because these methods are easily grasped without learning any new principles or ideas. Occasionally, a skipper may find it necessary to obtain a fix when he has reference to or can only see one charted object or aid to navigation. For example, in the case of Figure 109 you may have been travelling for the last two or three hours without having obtained a fix. But you have, of course, been plotting your dead reckon position and have turned onto a northerly course after approaching the shore. According to your DR plot, you believe that you are approximately 1.5 miles offshore and will safely pass by the rocky shoal that lies about 0.8 miles offshore. The rocks are awash (just at the surface), and you will not see them until too late if they are on your course. You cannot fix your position by any method previously learned, because the only charted object you can see is the water tower on shore. Like most sailors you cannot estimate the distance offshore with sufficient accuracy to risk your life on it. You must determine your distance off (shore) with a reasonable degree of accuracy before reaching the shoal area. You can do this by means of obtaining a circular line of position. (See Fig. 109.)

If you know the distance away from some charted object, then you can draw a circle on the chart using your distance away from the object as the radius of the circle and the charted object as the center of the circle. All points on such a circle are equal to your distance from the object, and therefore you must be located somewhere on that circle. (See Fig. 110.) The idea, then, is to determine your distance away from the object, called "distance off."

Distance Off   You will recall that in a right-angled isosceles triangle one angle equals 90°, the other two angles equal 45° each and the sides opposite the 45° angles are equal in length to each other. (See Fig. 111.) In notation form: side BA = side CA if angle B = angle C, and angles B and C will both be 45° if angle A = 90°. Therefore, if you could determine the length of side AB, you would know the length of side AC.

In the example in Figure 111, think of line BA as being some portion of your direction of travel. BA is either on your course or parallel to it. Think of point C as being the visible, charted object. Line BC will be your line of sight toward the object at the instant that the object is 045° off your bow. That is, at 045° to your direction of travel. In this case it is 045° relative, because it is off your starboard bow.

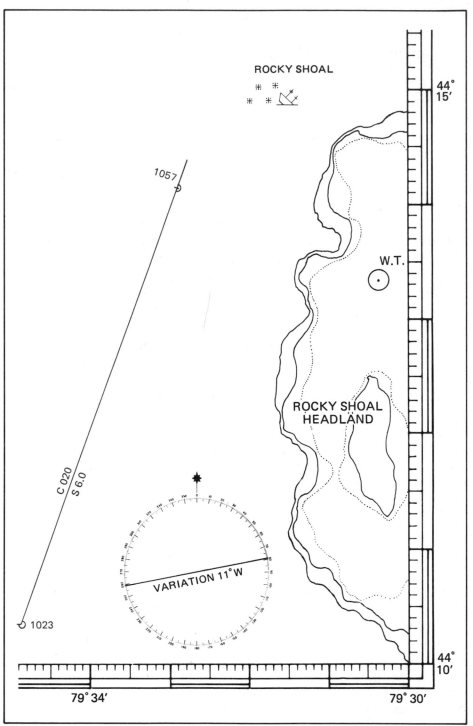

FIG. 109

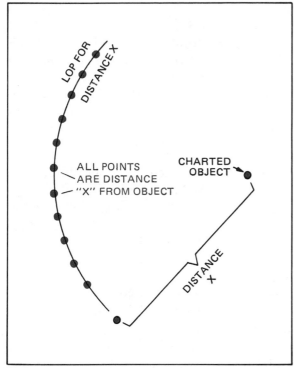

FIG. 110

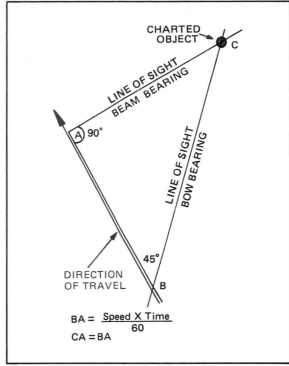

FIG. 111

Bow Bearing   When an object is 45° off the bow (either 045° relative if on the starboard side, or 315° relative if on the port side) the relative bearing is referred to as a bow bearing.

Beam Bearing   Let us consider, then, that you are travelling in direction BA (your true course). At some time in your travel the charted object (C) will be exactly 90° off your bow; that is, the object will be directly abeam. It would then be 090° relative. If it had been on your port side, it would be 270° relative. This type of relative bearing is referred to as a beam bearing.

Distance Travelled Equals Distance Off   In Figure 111, if you knew the distance that you had travelled between the time that the object was 45° off the bow (time of the bow bearing) and the time that the object was 90° off the bow (time of the beam bearing), you would know the distance BA. Because CA = BA, you would then know CA, which is the distance away from the object (distance off) at the time that the object was abeam. Simply stated, distance off equals distance travelled.

RUNNING FIX (R FIX)
FROM BOW AND BEAM BEARINGS

Let us apply this principle to the actual situation shown in Figure 109. After changing course at 1023 onto a true course of 020° you become concerned about the shoal area ahead. Because of wind or current, you may be closer to shore (further to the East) than your dead reckoning plot shows you to be. You therefore may be in danger of running aground on the rocks. You can see only one charted object, the water tower on Rocky Shoal Headland. Variation is 11°W.

1. Set your pelorus card to 000° under the pelorus lubber line.
2. Set your pelorus sighting vane on 045° relative.
3. Maintain your course of 020° true (033° compass) and speed at 6.0 knots.
4. Sight through the pelorus vane, and when the water tower is in line note the time of the bow bearing in your log.
5. Continue to maintain course and speed.
6. Reset your pelorus sighting vane to 090° relative.
7. Sight through the pelorus vane, and when the water tower is in line note the time of the beam bearing in your log.
8. Calculate the distance travelled between the first sighting (bow bearing) and the second sighting (beam bearing).
9. The calculated distance travelled is equal to your calculated distance off (distance away from) the tower when the tower was abeam (at the time of the beam bearing).
10. Plot the beam bearing. Draw a line through the water tower from seaward in the direction of its true bearing. Add the true course and the relative bearing to obtain the true bearing: true course plus 90°, or 20° + 90° = 110°. When the relative bearing is 90° or 270°, the resultant true bearing is the beam bearing.
11. Measure out to seaward (in the reciprocal direction of the bearing) 290° for a distance equal to the calculated distance travelled between bow and beam bearings.
12. Point 11 represents the intersection of the beam bearing LOP and the distance off circular LOP.
13. This intersection of two LOPs is, as we learned in Chapter 9, a fix. However, it is a fix or position determined over a period of time that you were running (moving), and hence it is called a running fix (RFix).
14. This running fix is plotted and labelled, and you must continue your DR plotting from this RFix.
15. See Figure 112.
16. You have determined that you are approximately 0.4 miles off

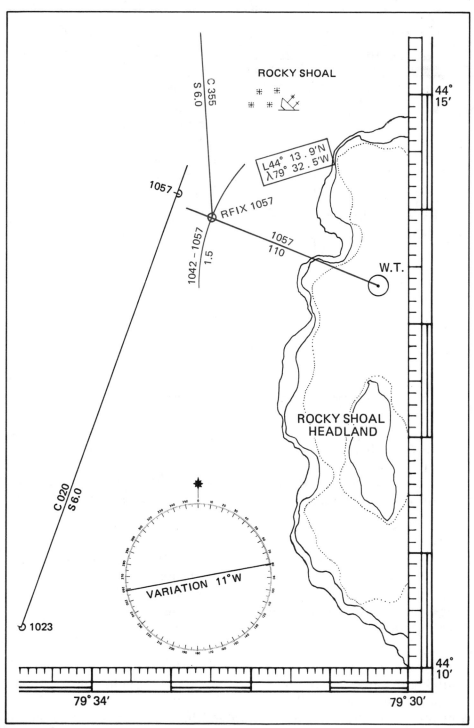

ROCKY SHOAL

L44° 13.9'N
λ79° 32.5'W

RFIX 1057

C 355
S 6.0

1057

1042 – 1057
1.5

1057
110

W.T.

C 020
S 6.0

1023

ROCKY SHOAL
HEADLAND

VARIATION 11°W

44°
15'

44°
10'

79° 34'   79° 30'

FIG. 112

LOG OF THE _Azare_   DATE _July 18, 198-_

TIME	LOCATION L λ	DIST n.m.	SPEED Knots	SHIP'S HEADING OR BEARING					RPM	CALCULATIONS/COMMENTS
				True	V	Mag.	D	Comp		
1000	See plot	36.0	6.0	085°	11°W	096°	6°E	090°		Steaming as before.
1023		38.3	6.0	020°	11°W	031°	2°W	033°		Changed course.
1030										Set pelorus for bow bearing.
1042		40.2		065°						045° bow bearing on water tower.
1045										Set pelorus for beam bearing.
1057		41.7		110°						090° beam bearing on water tower. Distance-off = $\frac{6.0 \times 15}{60}$ = 1.5 mi.
1057	See plot	41.7	6.0	355°	11°W	006°	6°W	012°		Changed course.

VARIATION EAST MAGNETIC LEAST
VARIATION WEST MAGNETIC BEST
DEVIATION EAST COMPASS LEAST
DEVIATION WEST COMPASS BEST

$60D = St$

$S = \frac{60D}{t}$

$t = \frac{60D}{S}$

course to the East, and if you continue your original course, you will run afoul of the rocks.

17. You elect to change course to a true course of 355° to continue your journey. See the log for entries between 1000 and 1100.

DOUBLE AND SPECIAL ANGLES

"Fine," you say, "but what if the rocks are between me and the water tower?" You cannot wait until you are abeam of the tower to determine your distance off. In such situations you can make use of certain other angles and, without the horror of trigonometry, pre-calculate your distance off.

Double Angle and 7/10ths Rule   To pre-calculate your distance off by doubling the angle off the bow and applying the 7/10ths rule, you may use almost any angle off the bow, although it should be close to 22½°. You then time the run until the second bearing is twice the angle of the first bearing (45° for the second if 22½° was used for the first). The distance run between the bearings will be the distance that you are away from the object at the time of the second bearing.

You may now apply the $^7/_{10}$ths rule to these calculations. Seven-tenths of the distance run (distance run multiplied by 0.7) equals the distance that you will be away from the object when it is abeam. Using the double angle and applying the $^7/_{10}$ths rule, follow these steps:

1. Set pelorus vane for $22^1/_2°$ off the bow.
   $022^1/_2°$ relative if the object is on the starboard side or
   $337^1/_2°$ relative if the object is on the port side.
2. Note time object is in line.
3. Maintain course and speed.
4. Set pelorus vane for 45° off the bow: 045° relative if the object is on the starboard side or 315° relative if the object is on the port side.
5. Note time object is in line.
6. Calculate distance run between the two bearings: 60D = st
7. Distance run equals distance off (radius of circular LOP) *at the time of second bearing*, and:
8. Distance run *multiplied by 0.7* equals the distance that you will be off *at the time that you are abeam of the object*.

You can now plot the second relative bearing after converting it to a true bearing by adding the true course. And you can measure the distance off (distance travelled) from the object along this line in order to plot your running fix. Continue your plot from this course in order to determine if you are steaming into danger by continuing your course. (See Fig. 113.)

Special Angles — 36° and 69° Off the Bow   There are combinations of angles off the bow or relative bearings that will give you a pre-determined distance off when abeam from the calculated distance run between bearings. The relative bearings or angles off the bow of 36° for the first and 69° for the second bearing are a good combination to use from the standpoint of accuracy. Using the special angles of 36° and 69°:

1. Set pelorus vane on 36° off the bow.
2. Note time object is in line.
3. Maintain course and speed.
4. Set pelorus vane on 69° off the bow.
5. Note time object is in line.
6. Calculate distance run between bearings.
7. Distance run equals distance that you will be off when abeam.
8. You can plot a beam bearing through the object and measure the calculated distance off along that line.

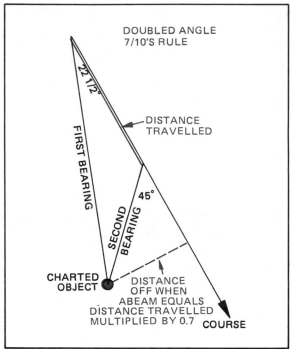

FIG. 113

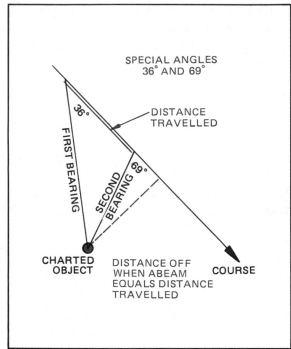

FIG. 114

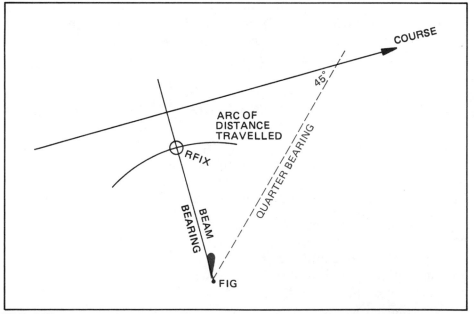

FIG. 115

9. This will be a Running Fix (RFix) plotted before you get there. (See Fig. 114.)

Beam and Quarter Bearings   If you wish to obtain a running fix on an object but were unable to obtain a bow bearing for some reason, proceed as follows:

1. Set pelorus vanes on 90° off the bow (090° or 270° relative).
2. Note time that object is in line.
3. Maintain course and speed.
4. Reset pelorus vanes to 45° off the stern to obtain a quarter bearing (135° or 225° relative).
5. Note time that object is in line.
6. Plot the *beam* bearing only.
7. Distance travelled between the beam bearing and quarter bearing is the calculated distance off when you were abeam.
8. This results in a delayed running fix of where you were when abeam. (See Fig. 115.)

SUMMARY
- The deviation of each bearing taken by aiming the vessel will be different, but deviation will still be according to the ship's heading.
- Reciprocal bearings are bearings in the opposite direction. The reciprocal of a bearing from a boat to an object is a bearing from the object to the boat. A reciprocal is obtained by adding 180° to the bearing.
- A constant relative bearing is a collision bearing.
- A range is the direction of two charted objects when in line.
- A circular line of position is the arc of a circle whose radius is equal to some known or determinable distance.
- The intersection of a circular line of position and some other line of position results in a fix.
- Bow and beam relative bearings may be used to calculate distance off which gives a circular line of position. The intersection of the beam bearing and the circular line of position will result in a running fix.
- Bow and beam bearings are taken 045° and 090° relative, or 315° and 270° relative.
- Distance travelled equals distance off.
- In the case of bow and beam bearings or beam and quarter bearings, *plot only the beam bearing and calculated distance off*. Do not plot the bow or quarter bearings or construct the triangle on your chart. Ignore

your DR course line. The RFix is the intersection of the beam bearing and the circular LOP of distance off.

- Special angles and the $^7/_{10}$ths rule of doubling angles will provide distance off that you will be when abeam before you are abeam of the object. *Plot only the beam bearing line and your pre-calculated distance off.* Do not plot your bow bearings or construct the triangle on your chart.

11. Practice Cruise

"Practice makes perfect — unless you practice the wrong way — then you are perfectly wrong."   TRUISM BY SAUNDERS.

This practice cruise has been constructed so that you may follow an example of each step in a theoretical cruise. In it you will apply each of the principles covered thus far.

For the purposes of the cruise it is suggested that you obtain "Chart T-3450" which happens to be of an area off the West Coast of Canada. The principles involved are universal. Except for minor differences in charting techniques and symbols in various countries, the practice cruise is applicable world-wide. The chart can be obtained through any chart dealer who handles Canadian Hydrographic Charts and publications. If not in stock, your dealer can place a special order or you may order it directly from the Canadian Hydrographic Service. In 1981, the cost of this chart in Canada was $2.00.

The answers to each question are provided in the diagrams and step-by-step solutions. However, it is strongly recommended that you work each section out on your own chart and compare your results to the answers in the text.

Although course lines, lines of position, etc. appear as bold lines here, in the interest of accuracy you should use sharp, fine, medium-hard (2H) lead for all your plotting.

We are in a 26 foot (8 m) cruiser with 32" (.8 m) draft. Sailors be patient, we will be under sail for the Final Cruise in Chapter 18. The deviation table used is in Appendix C *without interpolation*. See Appendix F for a review of plotting and labelling conventions. Variation on the chart's compass rose is 23°E.

CRUISE I, PART A

1. Depart Point Roberts, near Tumbo Island L 48° 58.3′N, λ123° 05.0′W, at 1430 and head for Alden Point.
   Compass course is 145° to end up heading on a generally southerly true course.
   Speed 5.0 knots.
   Make entry in log (line 1).
   Plot true course 178° from Point Roberts light.

Label DR course and speed.
Label departure time.

2. At 1615, as you approach the Tumbo Island area, you sight Alden Point light and head directly for it continuing at 5.0 knots.
   Assuming that you are on course:
   • What distance had you travelled when you changed course?
   • What will your ETA (Estimated Time of Arrival) at Alden Point be?
   • What is your true course to Alden Point?
   Make entry in log (line 2):
   Distance travelled (60D = St):

   $$D = \frac{St}{60} = \frac{5.0 \times 105}{60} = 8.75 = 8.8 \text{ n.m.}$$

   $$\begin{array}{rr} 16 & 15 \\ -14 & 30 \\ \hline \end{array} \qquad \begin{array}{rr} 15 & 75 \\ -14 & 30 \\ \hline 1 & 45 \end{array} = 105 \text{ minutes}$$

   Plot 1615 DR and Label.
   Draw DR course (118° true) to Alden Point and label.
   Calculate ETA at Alden Point:

   $$60D = St \qquad T = \frac{60D}{S} = \frac{60 \times 4.6}{5.0} = 55 \text{ minutes}$$

   $$\begin{array}{rr} 16 & 15 \\ + \; 0 & 55 \\ \hline 16 & 70 \\ - & 60 \\ + \; 1 & \\ \hline 17 & 10 \end{array} = \text{ETA } 1710$$

   Your compass will read 088° as you proceed to Alden Point.
   (See Chartlet II.)

3. You arrive at Alden Point and stay the night. Make entry in log (line 3).

CRUISE I, PART B

1. The following morning at 0930 you leave Alden Point for Turn Point WSW of you. You decide to travel at a speed of 5.5 knots.
   • What is your true course to Turn Point? (240°)
   • What compass course must you steer? (215°)
   • What is your ETA at Turn Point?
   Plot and label the course to Turn Point.
   Label your 0930 fix at Alden Point.

LOG OF THE Alzarc   DATE July 25, 198-

TIME	LOCATION L / λ	DIST n.m.	SPEED Knots	SHIP'S HEADING OR BEARING True	V	Mag.	D	Comp	RPM	CALCULATIONS/COMMENTS
	Part I Tuesday, July 25									
1430	Pt. Roberts Lt.	0.0	5.0	178°	23°E	155°	10°E	145°		Depart Pt. Roberts.
1615		8.8	5.0	117°	23°E	094°	6°E	088°		ETA Alden Pt. 1710. Changed course.
1710		13.4	—	—						Arr. Alden Pt.
	Part II Wednesday, July 26									
0930	Alden Pt.	13.4	5.5	240°	23°E	217°	2°E	215°		ETA Turn Pt. 1143.
1003		16.4		195°						Bow bearing 315° relative on Shipjack.
1014		17.4		150°						Beam bearing 270° relative on Shipjack.
1014	48°44.8'N 123°03.1'W	17.4	5.5	244°	23°E	221°	0°	221°		Running fix. Changed course.
1143		25.6	—	—						Arr. Turn Point.

VARIATION EAST MAGNETIC LEAST
VARIATION WEST MAGNETIC BEST
DEVIATION EAST COMPASS LEAST
DEVIATION WEST COMPASS BEST

$$60D = St$$
$$S = \frac{60D}{t}$$
$$t = \frac{60D}{S}$$

Log Cruise I, Part A and B

Measure the distance to Turn Point.
Calculate the ETA at Turn Point:

$$60D = St \qquad T = \frac{60D}{S} = \frac{60 \times 12.2}{5.5} = 133 \text{ min.} = 2 \text{ hrs., } 13 \text{ min.}$$

```
   09  30
 +  2  13
   11  43  = ETA, Turn Point, 1143
```

Make entry in log (line 4).

2. You decide to obtain bow and beam bearings on Skipjack Island light
   to check your course by using a distance off and a running fix:
   Set your pelorus vane at 315° relative (45° off your port bow).
   Note time in log (line 5) when the light is in line with the pelorus
   vanes.
   Maintain your course and speed.
   Reset your pelorus vane to 270° (90° off your port bow).
   Note time in log (line 6) when the light is again in line with the
   pelorus vane.

What is the distance off when abeam Skipjack?

$$\begin{array}{ll} 10 & 14 \\ -\,10 & 03 \\ \hline & 11 \text{ min.} \end{array} \qquad 60D = St \qquad D = \dfrac{5.5 \times 11}{60}$$

= distance off = 1.0 miles

What is true bearing of Skipjack Island when abeam? (150°).

Plot true beam bearing and label.

Plot circular LOP (distance off).

Label running fix.

Enter latitude and longitude in the log on line 7.

You are approximately 0.6 miles off your intended course.

(See Chartlet IV.)

3. From your RFix position of 1014, determine a new course to Turn Point.

Continue your cruise at 5.5 knots.

Plot and label new DR course.

Complete line 7 entry in the log.

Enter line 8 in the log on arrival at Turn Point.

CRUISE I, PART C

1. Depart Alden Point light at 0952 for a general cruise of the area.

Compass course 021°.

Speed 8.0 knots.

Make entry in the log on line 9.

Plot true course 040°.

Label DR course and speed.

Label departure time.

2. At 1021 you change course to leave Alden Bank light to port.

Compass Course 110°.

Speed continues at 8.0.

Make entry in the long on line 10.

3. You decide to practice taking bearings over the compass and at 1035 you take two compass bearings within one minute of each other, using the ship's compass and an azimuth ring.

Compass bearing on Alden Bank light, 091°.

Compass bearing on Clements Reef red buoy, 183°.

Make appropriate entries in the log (lines 11, 12, 13).

Plot and label true bearings.

Deviation according to ship's heading is 10°E.

Label fix and determine latitude and longitude.

(See Chartlet VIII.)

4. Continue compass course 110° until 1058 at a speed of 8.0 knots.

LOG OF THE _Alzare_   DATE _August 10, 198-_

TIME	LOCATION L λ	DIST n.m.	SPEED Knots	SHIP'S HEADING OR BEARING					RPM	CALCULATIONS/COMMENTS
				True	V	Mag.	D	Comp		
	Part III Saturday, August 10									
0952	Alden Pt.	0.0	8.0	040°	23°E	017°	4°W	021°		Depart Alden Pt.
1021		3.9	8.0	143°	23°E	120°	10°E	110°		Changed course.
1035		5.8		124°	23°E	101°	10°E	091°		Compass bearing Alden Bank.
1035		5.8		216°	23°E	193°	10°E	183°		Compass bearing Clements Reef.
1035	48°48.1'N 122°51.7'W	5.8	8.0	143°	23°E	120°	10°E	110°		Fix.
1058		8.9	8.0	115°	23°E	092°	6°W	086°		Changed course.
1111		10.6		021°						Lummi Is. 266° relative.
1111		10.6		278°						Puffin Is. 163° relative.
1111	48°44.1'N 122°44.1'W	10.6	8.0	—						End of cruise.

VARIATION EAST MAGNETIC LEAST   60D = St
VARIATION WEST MAGNETIC BEST $S = \frac{60D}{t}$
DEVIATION EAST COMPASS LEAST
DEVIATION WEST COMPASS BEST $t = \frac{60D}{S}$

Log Cruise I, Part C

Change course to 086° compass.

Continue speed at 8.0 knots.

Plot DR courses (start from fix at 1035 *not* 1035DR) and label.

Make entry in the log on line 15.

5. At 1111 take relative bearings within a couple of minutes using your pelorus on the lighted structural buoy off the North end of Lummi Island and the light on Puffin Island. To take the pelorus relative bearings, leave the pelorus card set at 000° on the pelorus lubber line as recommended in Chapter 9.

Make the entries in the log on lines 16 and 17.

Convert relative bearings to true bearings by adding them to the true course.

Plot and label the bearings.

Plot and label the fix.

Determine the latitude and longitude of your position.

(See Chartlet XI.)

6. If you were continuing the cruise you would continue plotting the DR course from the fix.

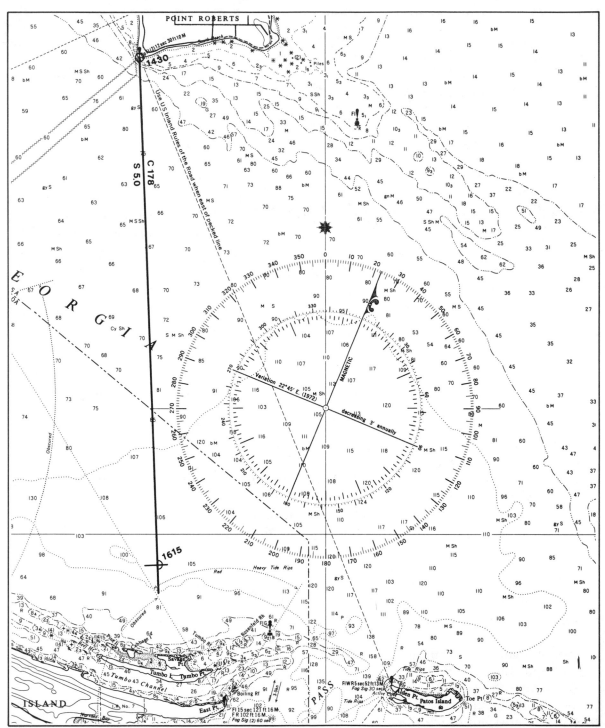

Chartlet I

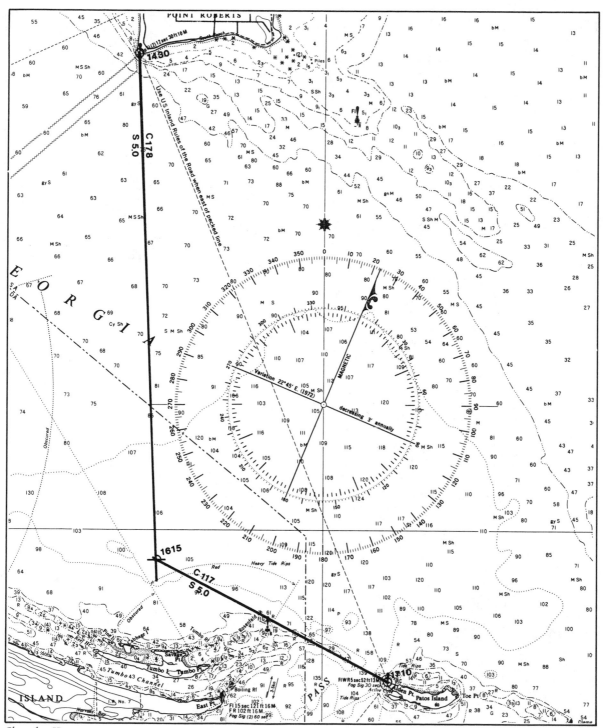

Chartlet II

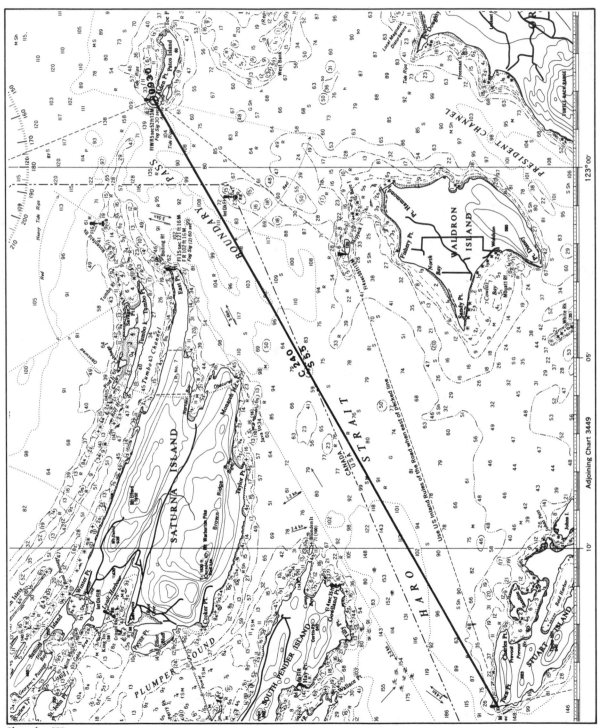

Chartlet III

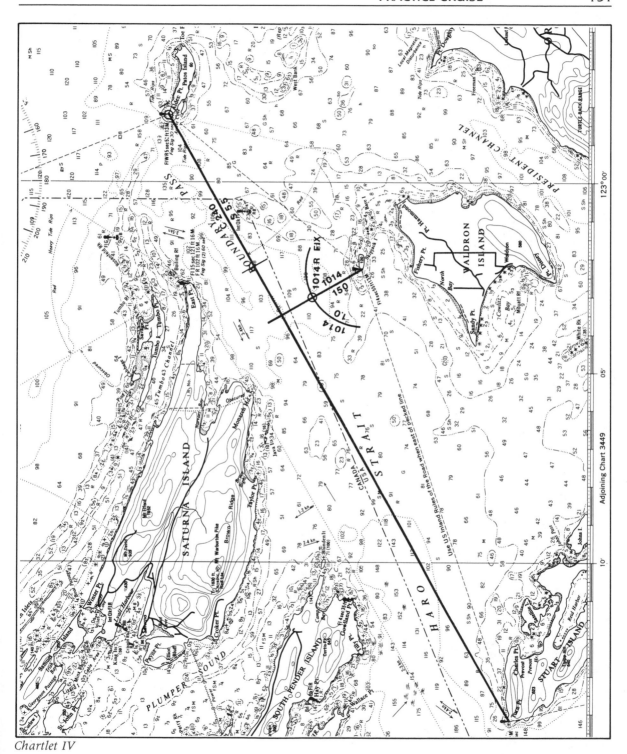

Chartlet IV

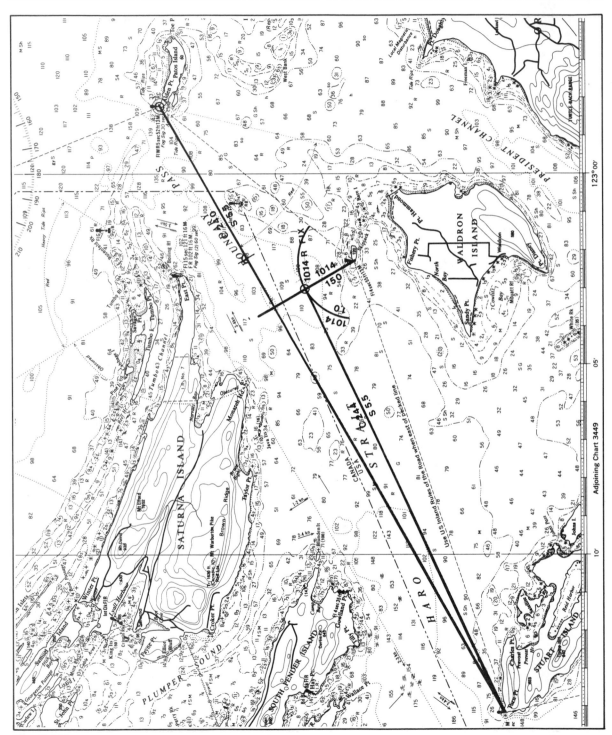

Chartlet V

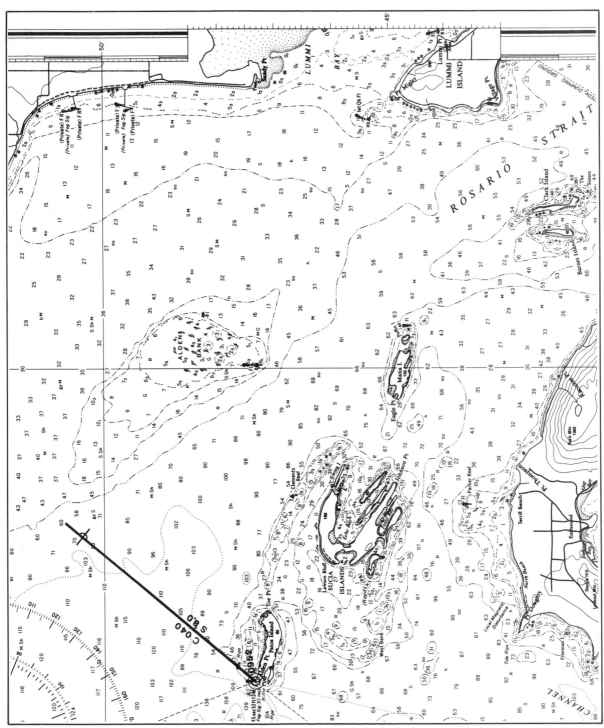

Chartlet VI

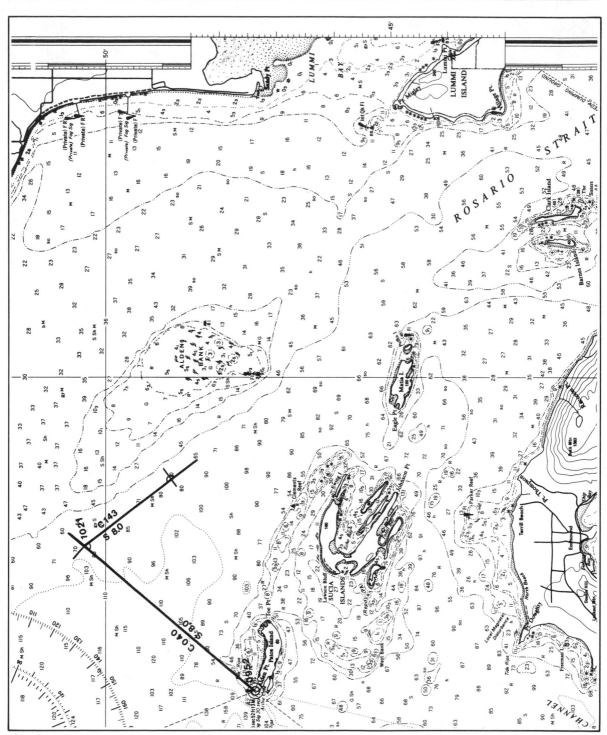

Chartlet VII

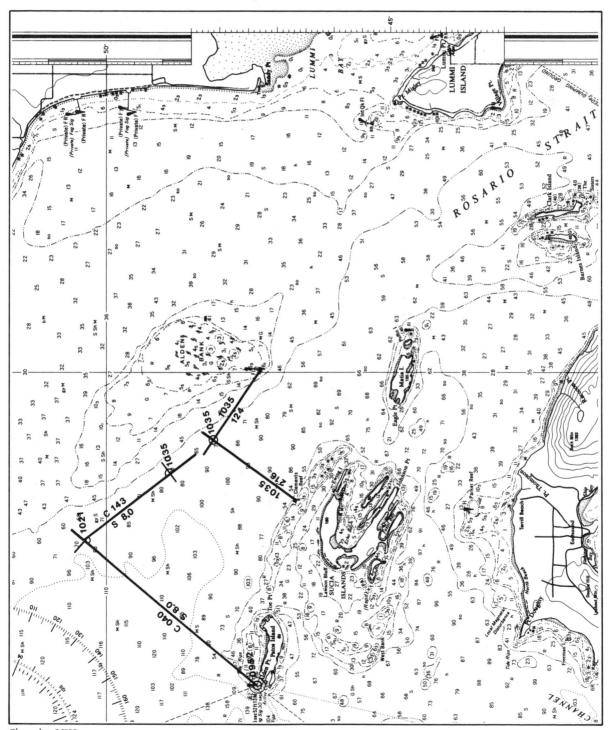

Chartlet VIII

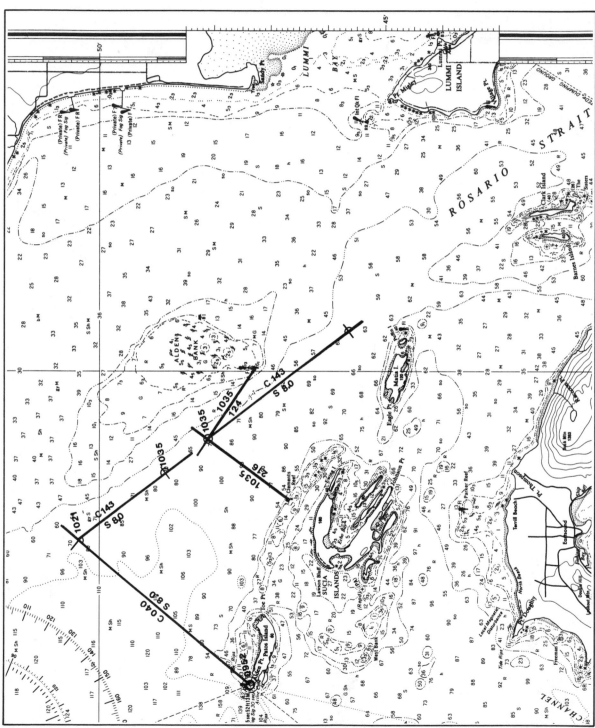

Chartlet IX

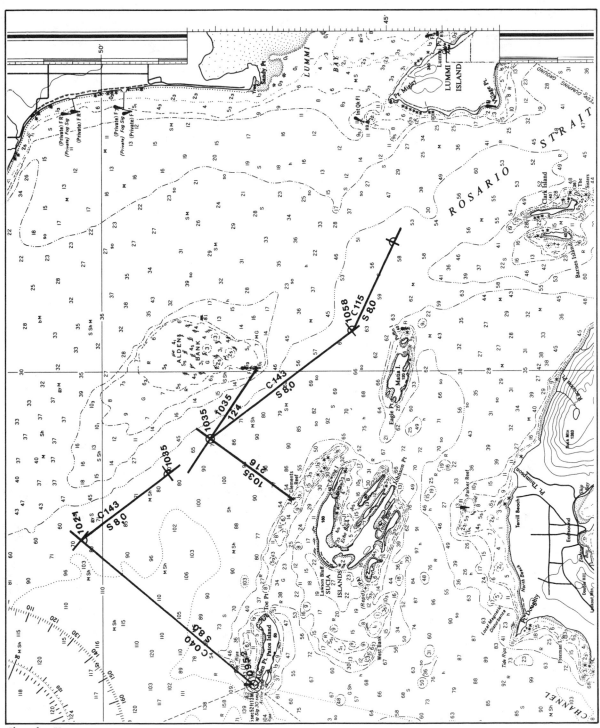

Chartlet X

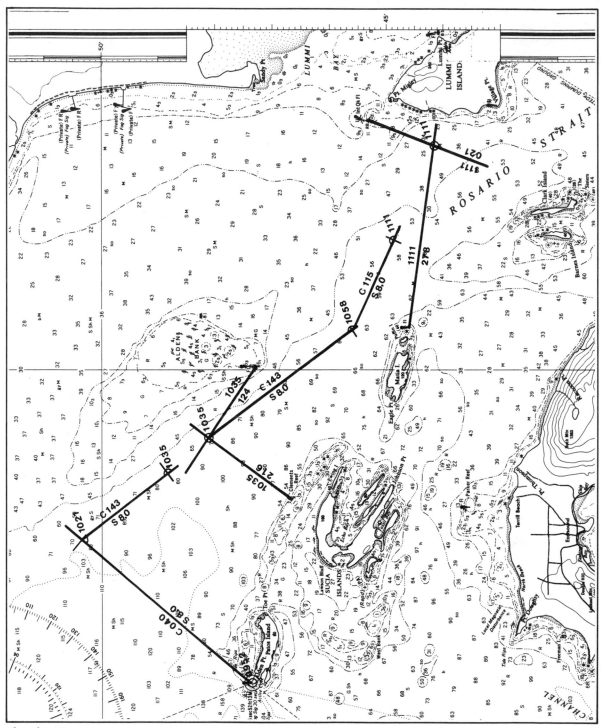

Chartlet XI

12. Running Fixes

"A really good navigator can always prove that he was going to where he got to." SAUNDERS' LAW OF NAVIGATION #9

ADVANCING A LINE OF POSITION

A fix, as you know, is usually the intersection of two or more lines of position established by taking bearings on two or more different charted objects at approximately the same point in time. As we saw in Chapter 10, there are occasions when we must almost immediately obtain a fix (or at least a distance off) when we can see only one charted object. We can do this by means of bow and beam or beam and quarter bearings. For the bow and beam method of obtaining distance off as one (circular) line of position, we must maintain course and speed between the two bearings.

Let us now consider a condition where we can see only one charted object but decide we have no need to establish a fix or that we cannot obtain a distance off circular LOP for any of a number of reasons. Nevertheless, we would be wise to take a bearing on the object while we can, just in case we need it later.

For the examples in this chapter and those in the remainder of the book, including the practice cruise, use the interpolated entries in the Deviation Table given in Appendix C.

Take the bearing (either relative or compass) and note it, together with the time, in your log. Maintain a log of your various courses and speeds or maintain a DR plot (or both) from that moment on.

At some later time (many minutes or several hours) you see a different charted object (and only one object), and you deem it wise or necessary to obtain a fix. To do so you:

1. Take a bearing on the second object.
2. Convert it to a true bearing and plot the LOP.
3. Convert the first bearing to a true bearing.
4. Advance the first LOP to the time of second LOP and plot this advanced LOP.
5. The intersection of these two LOPs is the position of your running fix at the time of the second bearing.
6. You must have noted in your Log:

a) Time and direction of each of the two bearings and your course at the time of each bearing.

b) Course and speed and the time and details of any changes in course or speed between the two bearings.

Example

Visualize the advancement of an LOP as follows, based on Figures 116 to 121.

1. Plot your DR position at the time of the first bearing (1040).

2. The visible, charted object is, of course, already plotted (LH1A on Fig. 119). The object may not be a lighthouse, but we will refer to any type of charted object as a lighthouse (LH) for simplicity.

3. Plot your DR position at the time of the second bearing (1250). You will also have plotted all intermediate DR positions in order to arrive at your 1250 DR location, but we have no further interest in these intermediate DRs.

4. With your parallel rules, determine the direction from the 1040 DR to the 1250 DR. It is usually not necessary to draw this line on your chart, because it may cause later confusion. But if you do, for the purpose of measuring the distance, draw it as a broken line or construction line. (See Fig. 118.) Use interpolated entries, Appendix C.

5. Draw a line (or portion of it) from LH-1A in the direction 1040 DR to 1250DR as in step 4 above. (See Fig. 119.)

6. Determine the distance from the 1040 DR to the 1250 DR with your dividers.

7. Mark this distance (step 6) on the line from LH-1A (step 5) and mark the position of LH-1B. (See Fig. 119.) It does not matter that LH-1B may be in the water or on the side of a cliff. It is a reference point only. You have now "moved" the object of the first bearing in the direction of and for the distance of your *net* travel between bearings. You have "built" and charted a new object (LH-1B) which, at the time of the second bearing, is in the same position relative to you as it was at the time of the first bearing. *You have now advanced the object.*

8. Continuing on in this series of figures, convert your first bearing (on LH-1A) from compass or relative to true.

9. Plot this true bearing through LH-1B. This line is the advanced LOP. (See Fig. 120.)

10. Label this LOP with the time of the first bearing *and* the time of the second bearing and with the true direction.

11. Plot and label the true bearing on the second object; we have called this LH-2. (See Fig. 120.)

12. The intersection of these two lines of position is your running fix

position at the time of the bearing on the second object. Continue your DR plot from this RFix. (See Fig. 121). *You have advanced a line of position and established a running fix.* In this case you have used two different objects, probably because both objects were not simultaneously visible at a time when the angle of cut of the two LOPs would be satisfactory.

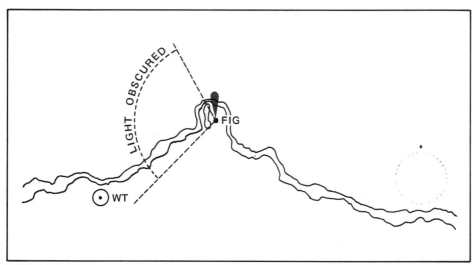

FIG. 116

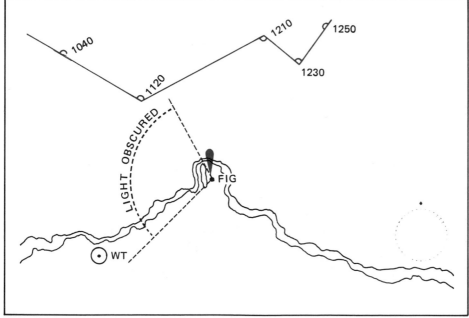

FIG. 117

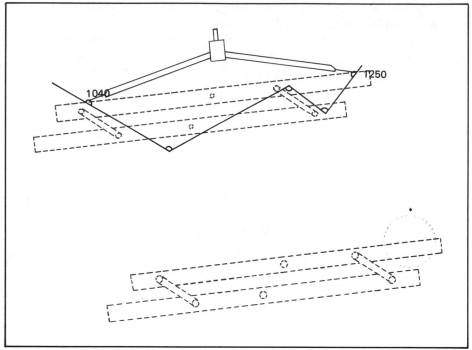

FIG. 118

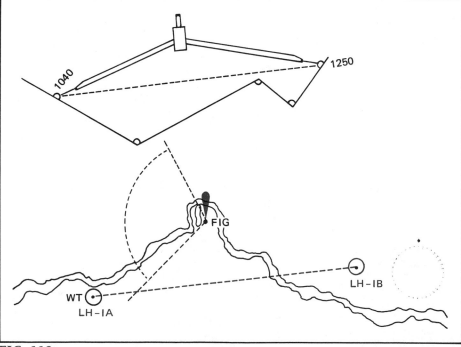

FIG. 119

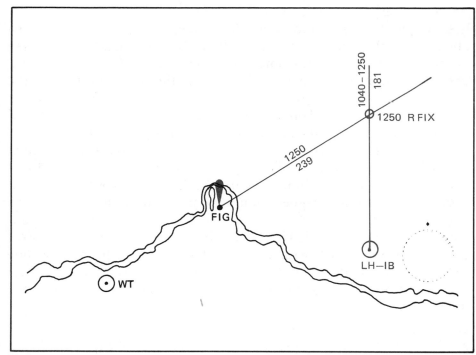

FIG. 120

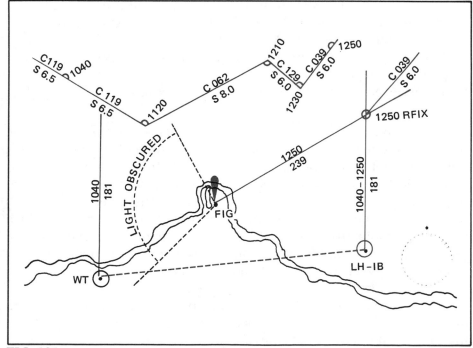

FIG. 121

RUNNING FIX — ONE CHARTED OBJECT

It may well be that some time after taking the bearing on the first object, the only visible object may still be the same one. You may then advance the first LOP to the time of the second LOP on the same object. The intersection of the two LOPs would be the fix at the time of the second LOP.

In the example based on Figures 122 to 124, it happens that the two bearings are on opposite sides of the vessel because of the change of course that occurred between the bearings. It is important to remember that, once you obtain a running fix, you abandon the previous DR plot and start a new DR plot from the running fix. Do not confuse your DR course lines with LOPs in determining your fix location.

RETARDING A LINE OF POSITION

In some rare circumstances, you may have taken a bearing on one object, then at a later time taken a bearing on the same (or another) object, and you may wish to know what your position was at the earlier time. Proceed as follows:

1. Plot the first line of position.
2. Plot the DR track from the DR position of the first bearing (DR-1) to the DR of the second bearing (DR-2).
3. Determine the direction from DR-2 to DR-1 and the distance.
4. Plot the second object (LH-2B) in the same direction and for the same distance from LH-2A (step 3).
5. Draw the true bearing (second bearing) through the "new" LH-2 plotted in step 4.
6. The intersection of the two LOPs is your fix at the time of the first bearing.

If you have not maintained a log or DR plot prior to the first bearing, but you have maintained a log starting at the time of the first bearing, you would not know your DR position (DR-1) from which to run your plot to DR-2. To solve this problem, merely select any convenient point on the *same* chart and call it "DR-1." The "convenient" point will probably be in open water (or land) well away from any area in which you expect to do any later plotting. It will probably also be one where you will be able to plot from the convenient point in a general direction of your net travel between DR-1 and DR-2. From DR-1 plot course lines and distances from your log to obtain a DR-2.

Use the convenient DR-1 and DR-2 to establish the direction and distance for advancing your first bearing or retarding your second bearing in the same manner as shown earlier.

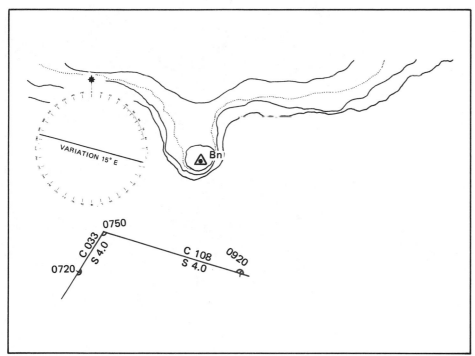

FIG. 122

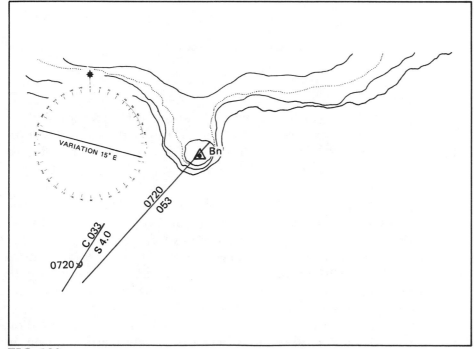

FIG. 123

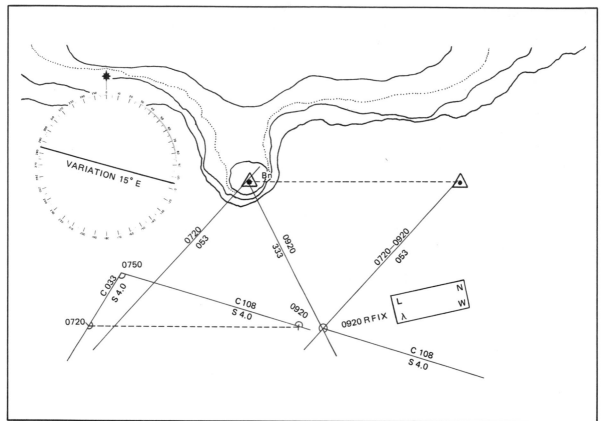

FIG. 124

ACCURACY

The line of position which has been advanced (or retarded) will be subject to any errors in your determination of distance and direction between the two DR locations. However, there are three benefits to be derived from such a running fix, even though it may be subject to some degree of error.

First, the amount of error will be limited to that occurring over the period of time between bearings, whereas the DR plot will contain the inaccuracies accumulating since the previous fix.

Second, if you have not maintained a DR plot or list of log entries since the last fix, or if you drifted for some considerable period (as in fishing), the running fix may be your only means to fix your position before approaching some hazardous area.

Third, the running fix can also serve as a check on your DR plot. Significant differences in the result of your DR position and running fix may reveal an inaccuracy in your DR position.

TIME	LOCATION L λ	DIST n.m.	SPEED Knots	SHIP'S HEADING OR BEARING					RPM	CALCULATIONS/COMMENTS
				True	V	Mag.	D	Comp		
1040		47.2	6.5	119°	13°W	132°	12°E	120°		
1040		47.2		181°	13°W	194°	12°E	182°		Bearing on water tower.
1120		51.5	8.0	062°	13°W	075°	4°E	071°		Changed course and speed.
1210		58.2	6.0	129°	13°W	142°	11°E	131°		Changed course and speed.
1230		60.2	6.0	039°	13°W	052°	1°E	051°		Changed course.
1250		62.2		239°	13°W	252°	1°E	251°		Bearing on Flashing Green Light.
1250	__°__.__'N __°__.__'W	62.2	6.0	—						Running fix. End of cruise.

LOG OF THE **Example 'A'**   DATE _____

VARIATION EAST MAGNETIC LEAST
VARIATION WEST MAGNETIC BEST
DEVIATION EAST COMPASS LEAST
DEVIATION WEST COMPASS BEST

60D = St
$S = \frac{60D}{t}$
$t = \frac{60D}{S}$

Log for Figures 117 to 121

Problems and Examples

The following problem situation is based on Figure 116. You are travelling on a compass course of 120° and have travelled 47.2 miles since leaving harbour. The variation (from chartlet) is 13°W. As you approach the shoreline, you see a water tower on a knoll. You take a compass bearing on the water tower at 1040 and note this and your speed and course in the log. You cannot see the flashing green light further along the shore, because the light is obscured by high ground.

At 1120 you change course and speed to stay well offshore. At 1210 you change speed. At 1210 and again at 1230 you change course.

As you leave the coast on compass course 051°, you decide to get a fix, but you can see only one charted object: the mast with the flashing green light. You take a compass bearing on the light tower at 1250.

By referring to the diagrams in Figures 117 to 121 and the log, you will see the solution to this problem unfold.

The following example of advancing a line of position is based on

LOG OF THE _Example 'B'_   DATE _____

TIME	LOCATION L λ	DIST n.m.	SPEED Knots	SHIP'S HEADING OR BEARING					RPM	CALCULATIONS/COMMENTS
				True	V	Mag.	D	Comp		
0720		6.4	4.0	033°	15°E	018°	4°W	022°		Relative bearing on beacon 020°.
0720		6.4		053°						Changed course.
0750		8.4	4.0	108°	15°E	093°	6°W	087°		Relative bearing on beacon 225°.
0920		14.4		333°						Running fix.
0920	_°__.'N _°__.'W	14.4	4.0	—						End of cruise.

VARIATION EAST MAGNETIC LEAST   60D = St
VARIATION WEST MAGNETIC BEST   S = $\frac{60D}{t}$
DEVIATION EAST COMPASS LEAST
DEVIATION WEST COMPASS BEST   t = $\frac{60D}{S}$

Log for Figures 122 to 124

Figure 117. It represents the chart of the area in Figure 116 with your DR course plotted from the log entries (page 167) after all courses and bearings have been converted to true bearings. Deviation is according to ship's heading.

Note that if you had not been maintaining a log or a DR plot earlier than 1040, you could establish a location anywhere that you wish on the same chart and label it as 1040 DR. From that arbitrary location, you could then plot a DR plot using the entries in your log.

Referring to your plot and ignoring everything except the DR locations at the time of each bearing, determine the direction and distance between these two DR locations (1040 and 1250). There is no need to draw any lines on the chart. Enter the information in the log. (See Fig. 118.)

On your chart, draw a broken line through the real water tower, which we call lighthouse-1A (LH-1A), in the direction determined from Figure 118. Measure along this line the distance from Figure 118 and relocate the water tower, which we call lighthouse-1B (LH-1B) as in Figure 119.

Plot the true bearings (directions in the log) for each bearing. Through LH-1B draw the line of position of the bearing to LH-1A (181° true). Through LH-2 (the flashing green light tower) draw the line of position of the bearing to LH-2 (239° true). The intersection of these two lines of position is the location of your running fix. (See Fig. 120.)

Label the RFix and continue your DR plot from there. Enter the RFix latitude and longitude in your log, or label it on your chart. (See Fig. 121.)

In this example, based on Figures 122 to 124, we will advance an object to get an advanced line of position. The second line of position will be a later bearing taken on the same object. Relative bearings have been taken using a pelorus.

While travelling on a compass course of 022°, you take a relative bearing of 020° on the day beacon at 0720. At 0750 you change course to 087° compass, and at 0920 you take another relative bearing on the same beacon as 225°. The log on page 170 contains the entries for this example. Figure 123 shows the plotting of the course and bearing at 0720. Figure 122 illustrates the line of position on the beacon advanced from 0720 to 0920 for the *net* course and distance and the line of position on the same beacon at 0920. The running fix at 0920 is the intersection of these two LOPs. Continue your plot from that point. (See Fig. 124.)

SUMMARY

A wise vessel operator will periodically obtain a fix or record bearings, even though they may not all be plotted. If the demand should arise, he or she will be able to quickly plot the latest data and obtain either a fix or a running fix.

A single bearing on only one object, while insufficient to plot a fix, may be used at a later time in conjunction with a later bearing on either the same object or a different object to obtain a running fix.

There must be a sufficient angle of cut between the two bearings to ensure accuracy just as was discussed in Chapter 9.

A running fix may be obtained by advancing (or retarding) a line of position, even though a DR plot or log was not maintained before the first of the two bearings, or you have made a number of changes in course and/or speed between the two bearings.

You *must* maintain a log or DR plot for the period of time between the two bearings. Otherwise, you will be unable to determine the direction or distance to advance (or retard) the bearing.

13. Leeway and Drift

"Many a man gets to the top of the ladder only to find that it has been leaning against the wrong wall."   TRUISM BY SAUNDERS

ACCURACY

From previous sections you have learned that, after obtaining a fix, you may not be located where you thought you were according to your DR position. This difference in position may be due to helmsmanship, compass error, plotting and calculation error or speed error. You should re-check your plotting and calculations. For compass bearings, remember that deviation is according to ship's heading. Periodically re-check your compass and deviation table for accuracy; for example, every time you "run a range." Also check your RPM/speed curve and Sum-log (cumulative distance measuring device) at each opportunity.

You will be unable, in a small craft, to run a course for an extended period of time closer than 5° to your intended course. You may allow the vessel to fall off course for various periods of time by 10° to 15°. Remember to steer "higher" than your intended course by 10° to 15° for equal periods of time in order to average out to your intended course.

Assuming that you are reasonably confident of the accuracy of these factors, then the difference in position between DR and fix must be due to leeway or drift (wind or current). Leeway is the difference between the course steered and the "course made good" (CMG) caused by wind, or the sideways movement or distance that a vessel is blown off course by wind. Drift is the difference between the course steered and the course made good (CMG) caused by current (water movement), or the sideways movement or distance that the vessel is floated off course by current. For simplicity, both factors are combined into one term — drift. When we speak of drift we are referring to the net combined effect of current and/or wind.

The term set is used to describe the true direction of drift, the direction *toward* which the vessel will be set by wind or current. Drift is the rate in knots (unless otherwise specified) at which the current/wind is moving the vessel. Refer now to Figure 125.

Assume that you wish to travel from town Alpha to town Bravo across the Echo River at a time of year when there is no current flow in

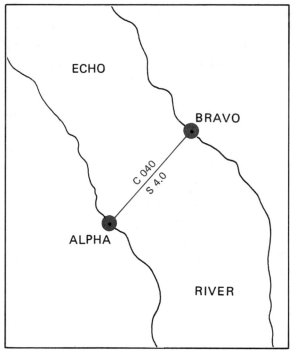

FIG. 125

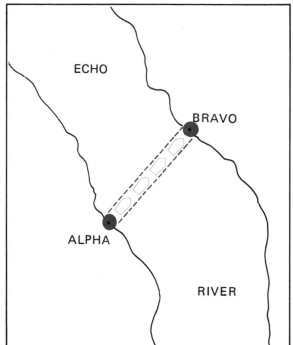

FIG. 126

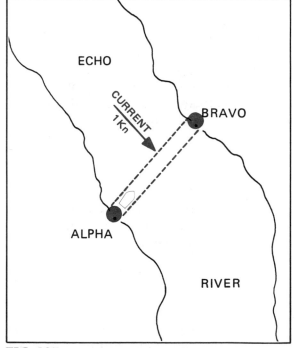

FIG. 127

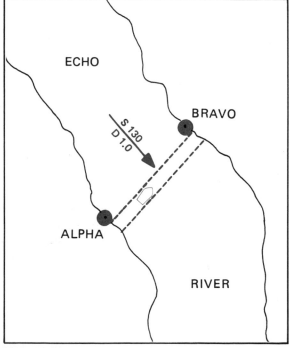

FIG. 128

the river and on a day when there is no wind. You check your chart and determine that the distance from Alpha to Bravo is 1.0 mile on a true course of 040°. Your vessel is capable of cruising at 4.0 knots. You will set your boat on true course 040° and 15 minutes later arrive at Bravo. You will have travelled straight across the river through a stationary "slice" of the river. (Fig. 126.)

If, at a later time of year, there were a current of 1.0 knot throughout the river, what would happen if you repeated the same journey? Again you set yourself on course 040° true at 4.0 knots and travel through your "slice" of water for 15 minutes. However, as you travel the "slice" is travelling (setting) downstream at the rate of 1.0 knot. Refer to the diagrams in Figures 127 and 128.

At the end of 15 minutes, the river will have moved downstream ¼ of a mile. You will be ¼ mile from your destination. That is, you will be ¼ mile off course. In this case, you would have travelled from Alpha to Charlie in 15 minutes.

The course that you actually travelled (CMG) was in a true direction of 054°, and the distance made good (DMG) in 15 minutes (Alpha to Charlie) was 1.03 miles which results in a speed made good (SMG) of 4.1 knots. You were set in a direction of 130° (Alpha to Charlie) for a distance of ¼ mile in 15 minutes at a rate of drift of 1.0 knot.

Set — 130°
Drift — 1 knot

In a similar manner, you can picture the effect of a wind *from* a direction of 310° (towards 130°) at a rate sufficient to blow you sideways at a rate of 1.0 knot. If there were no current, you would be travelling through a "slice" of air moving at 1.0 knot, and you would be blown through the water and across the ground in a direction of 130° at a rate of speed of 1.0 knot. We would call this leeway.

Set — 130°
Drift — 1.0 knot

Accumulative Effect of Wind and Current

If the wind and current were both going in the same direction, the wind would transfer you from "slice" to "slice" of water each of which would be travelling downstream. The result would be:

Set — 130°
Drift — 2.0 knots

A Simple Solution to the Problem of Drift

In order to arrive at town Bravo from Alpha when there is a current of 1.0 knot setting in a direction of 130°, you could start out on course

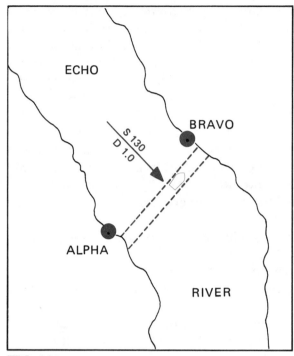

FIG. 129

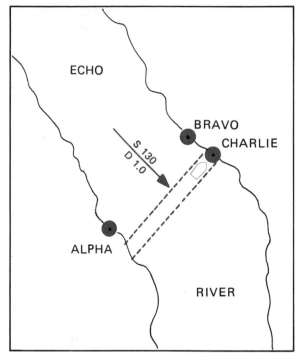

FIG. 130

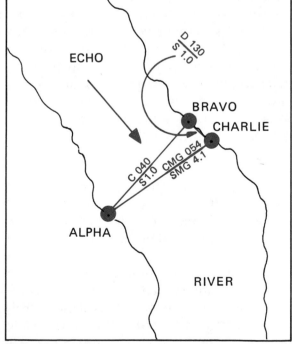

FIG. 131

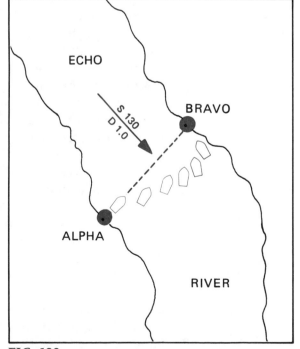

FIG. 132

040° true and, as you drift off course, keep changing your heading to keep your bow pointed at Bravo. The result would be that you would have described a course made good (CMG) something like Figure 132.

In addition to not being the most efficient method, there are times when it would be dangerous or impossible; if, for example, there were a hazard downstream from course 040°, or if there were fog so that you could not see Bravo from a distance greater than 0.2 miles. Therefore, we must know how to pre-compute our course to steer in order to obtain the desired CMG. We must determine this heading in advance of our trip. To do so we must be able to establish, or at least estimate, the probable set and drift due to wind and current. This is done by:

- Computation of current from government publications (see Chapter 17).
- Estimates based on current data supplied on some coastal charts or pilot charts. (See Chapter 17.)
- Knowledge from experience or from local boaters.
- Previous personal experience with the boat under various conditions.
- From your plotting, a determination of recent historical results (over the past few hours or days). We will discuss this further as Case III, page 181.

There are two possibilities for pre-computing a course (heading) to steer to obtain a desired course made good (CMG), sometimes called a course over the ground (COG). The first is to maintain a predetermined speed through the water which may be determined by your most economical or most comfortable cruising speed. The second is to establish a pre-determined time of arrival which may be required to meet a specific schedule. In order to solve each problem we will draw a current vector diagram which is simply a pictorial solution to the problem rather than a complicated mathematical solution.

VECTOR DIAGRAMS

A vector is a line representing both the direction and magnitude of some force, such as the direction and speed of wind, the direction and speed of current flow, the course steered and speed through the water, the effect of the combination of wind and current on a vessel (set and drift).

A vector diagram to solve leeway and drift problems consists of a triangle. One side (vector) portrays one force, such as course and speed, and another side (vector) portrays a second force, such as set and drift. In this example, the third side (resultant) will portray the course made good and speed made good as a result of the other two forces.

If the data is known (direction and speed) for any two sides, the two vectors can be drawn anywhere on a chart or piece of paper to any convenient scale and the resultant will represent the solution, because the direction and length of the resultant can be measured.

In drawing these diagrams, measure and draw all distances so that they represent one hour of time. In this manner, a measurement of the length of a vector will also represent the rate of speed. The vector diagram is a representation of what occurs during a one hour period of time, and also represents what is occurring during the whole period of time that a set of conditions prevails. The following examples will explain how these diagrams are used.

Case I

1. Note in your log the estimated set and drift that you expect to experience on the average over the length of time of your trip. (See Fig. 133.) In travelling from the Port of Delta to the Port of Foxtrot, you estimate a set of 315° and drift of 0.6 knots. You wish to travel at a speed through the water of 7.0 knots.

2. With your parallel rulers, determine the direction from Delta to Foxtrot (060° true).

3. Mark a point at some convenient location on the chart to represent Delta and from it draw a line in the direction of set (315°) 0.6 miles long. Label the line.

4. Draw a line approximately 2 miles long from point Delta in a direction the same as the intended course line (060° true).

5. Using a drafting compass or dividers, set one point on the location 0.6 miles from Delta and with the dividers set for a space of 7.0 miles sweep an arc. Determine the intersection of the arc with the course line drawn in 4 above.

6. Draw a line connecting the points at each end of the dividers in step 5. Determine the direction of this line; it is the true course to be steered to make good a course of 060°.

7. Convert the true course to compass course through TVMDC.

8. See Figure 134.

9. If you wish to know your SMG (speed made good), measure the distance from the convenient delta along the intended course line to the intersection with the course to steer line. This is the distance which will be travelled in 1 hour (SMG), because all measurements have been based on 1 hour of time. You can now compute your ETA.

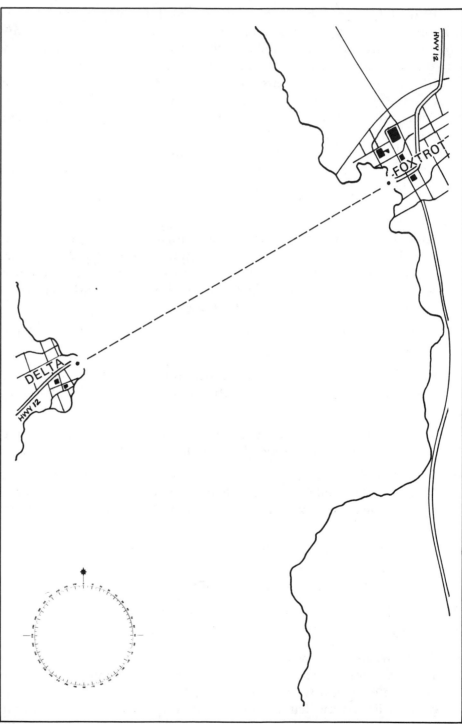

FIG. 133

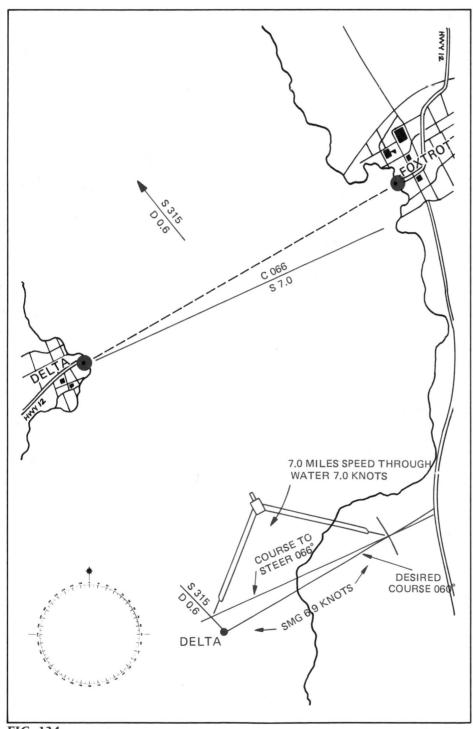

S 315
D 0.6

C 066
S 7.0

FOXTROT

HWY 12

DELTA

HWY 12

7.0 MILES SPEED THROUGH WATER 7.0 KNOTS

COURSE TO STEER 066°

S 315
D 0.6

DESIRED COURSE 060°

SMG 6.9 KNOTS

DELTA

FIG. 134

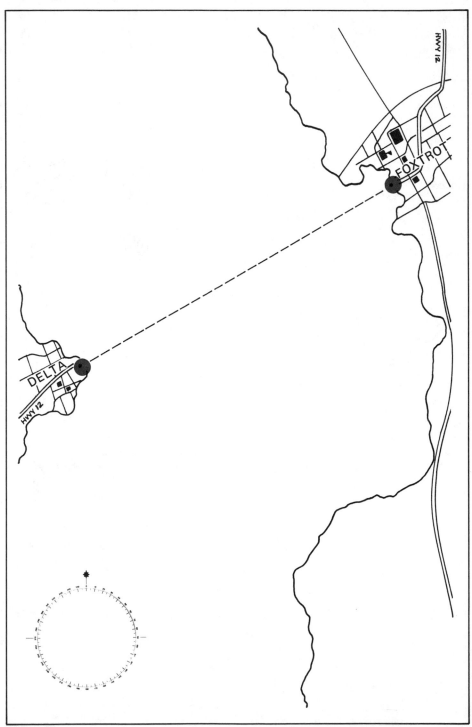

FIG. 135

Case II

1. Note in your log the estimated set and drift that you expect to experience on the average over the length of your trip. (See Fig. 135.) In travelling from the Port of Delta to the Port of Foxtrot, you estimate a set of 315° and drift of 0.6 knots. You desire an SMG of 7.0 knots.

2. Follow steps 2 through 4 in Case I as they apply to the vector diagram in Figure 136.

3. Set the dividers on 7.0 miles and measure from convenient Delta along the intended course line that distance.

4. From that point draw a line to the end of the set drift line. (0.6 miles from Delta).

5. Determine the direction and length of this line.

6. The direction will be the course to steer. The distance will be the required speed — distance to travel in one hour because all measurements have been based on 1 hour of time.

If your drawings are too small for accurate measurement, you may draw them double size merely by considering each minute of latitude to be ½ mile *strictly* for the purpose of the vector diagram solutions.

In both Case I and Case II we wanted to obtain an answer at the *beginning of the trip*. We therefore drew the set/drift line from the point where we would begin the trip.

There are two more possibilities when computing CMG, SMG, set or drift at the conclusion of a voyage or at some given time during the voyage. First, having obtained a fix and determined that you are not at the DR position, you may calculate the set and drift that caused this difference. Second, realizing during a voyage that you are experiencing some set and drift, and after estimating the amount, you may calculate the estimated position (EP) at the end of the voyage or some given time.

Again, we will solve these problems with simple vector diagrams. Just as in Case I, you can either draw the vector diagram right on top of our DR plot, or to avoid confusion you can draw them elsewhere on the chart at any convenient location remote from your plotting. You may also draw them to any scale that you please.

Because we are determining some information at the *conclusion* or *intermediate destination* of the voyage, we will draw our set/drift vector from that point.

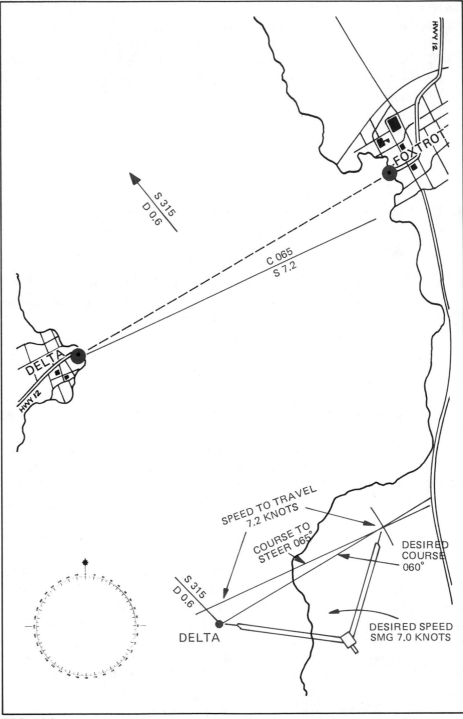

FIG. 136

Case III

1. Point of departure, Town of Golf at 0915. (See Fig. 137.) Determine set and drift as a result of the 1100 fix.
2. DR Course at 0915 is 260°. Speed 7.0. Change course at 0955 to 325°. Speed 5.0. At 1100 plot DR. At 1100 obtain 2-bearing fix and plot. (Solution: Fig. 138.)
3. Plot Golf at any convenient location on the chart.
4. Determine the distance and direction of a line between Golf and 1100 DR. Transfer this to the conveniently located Golf (step 1).
5. Determine the distance and direction of a line between Golf and 1100 fix. Transfer this line to convenient golf.
6. Draw a line connecting 1100 DR and 1100 fix on the vector diagram and determine direction and distance.
7. Refer to the line in step 5. This is course made good. Label it.
8. Refer to the line in step 6. Direction *from DR to fix* is the set. Label it.
9. Refer to the line in step 8. Distance is the total drift since the last fix at Golf 0915.

   Drift = Speed in 60D St formula

   $$(\text{Drift}) \; S = \frac{60D}{t} = \frac{60D \times \text{Total Drift}}{\text{Time (Fix to Fix)}}$$

   Label it.

Case IV

1. Point of departure, Charlie Marina at 1420. (See Fig. 139.) Determine your estimated position (EP) considering estimated current set and drift.
2. DR Course at 1420 is 255°. Speed 5.0 At 1620 plot DR. At 1620 determine your EP if you estimate current set at 025° and drift 1.1 knots. (Solution: Fig. 140.)
3. Calculate total drift between 1420 and 1620 (2.2 miles).
4. From DR 1620 (on DR plot) draw a broken line in the direction of the set (025°) for a distance of 2.2 miles (total drift) and mark that point as your EP.

ESTIMATING DRIFT

An estimate of leeway can be only just that — an estimate. It will vary between boats, and according to wind, water conditions, relative directions, etc. Leeway may be in the same direction as the current or at any relative angle. It may have greater or lesser impact on drift than current, depending on conditions. Current estimates may be very accurate predictions or may be personal estimates. The effect on the craft will depend on the attributes of a specific hull; planing or displacement, for example. Having arrived at our best estimates for each, we must esti-

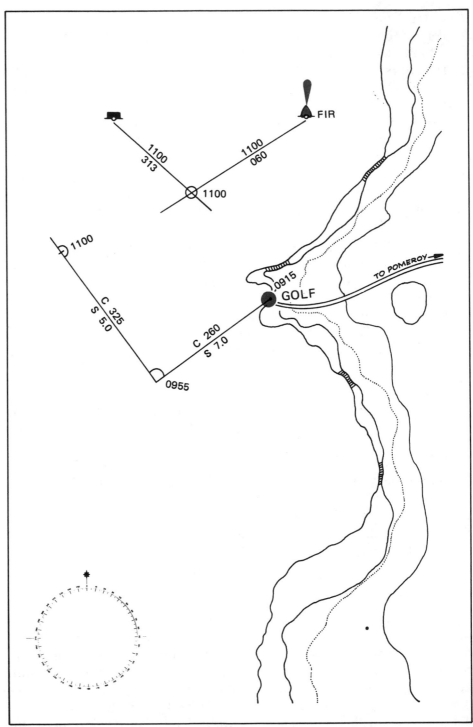

FIG. 137

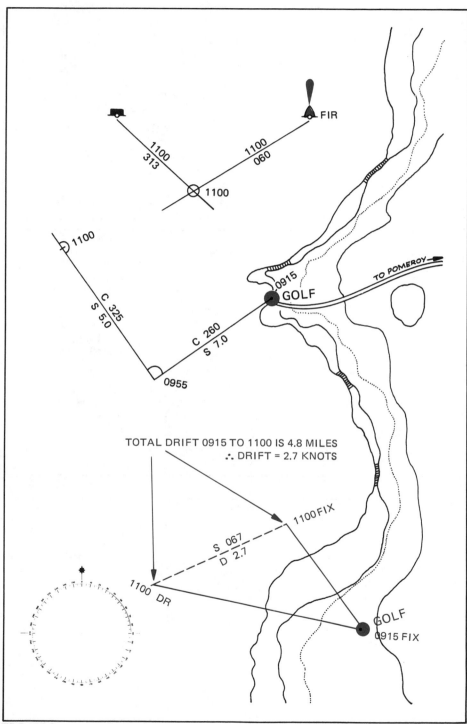

TOTAL DRIFT 0915 TO 1100 IS 4.8 MILES
∴ DRIFT = 2.7 KNOTS

FIG. 138

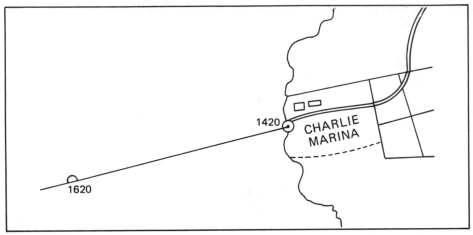

FIG. 139

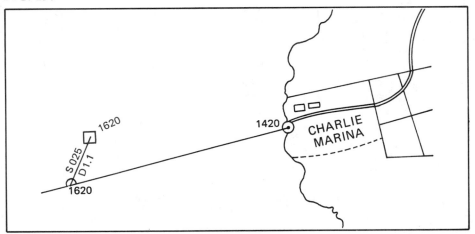

FIG. 140

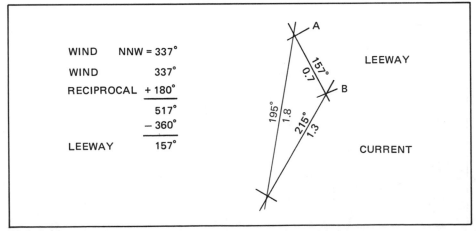

FIG. 141

mate their combined effect. This is probably best done with a vector diagram.

In figure 141 assume you have estimated drift for leeway under existing conditions at 0.7 knots and the wind is from the NNW (337° and therefore blowing in a direction of 157°, the reciprocal of 337°). You have estimated drift for current under existing conditions at 1.3 knots and the current direction is given as 215° true.

What set and drift should be used for the combined result? To solve the problem:

1. Select any convenient point on the chart as "A."
2. Draw line AB in the direction of leeway. Caution: *wind directions* are known as the direction *from which they blow*. Leeway must be drawn in the reciprocal direction of the name of the wind. Draw this line AB of a length equal to the estimated drift rate (0.7 miles).
3. From B draw line BC in the direction of the current and for a length equal to the drift rate (1.3 miles).
4. The combined result will be AC.
   The direction of AC will be the set 195°.
   The length of AC will be the drift 1.8 knots.

This diagram may be drawn to any convenient scale so long as the distance for 1 mile is the same for all lines (AB, BC, CA).

SET/DRIFT CALCULATIONS USING A RUNNING FIX

When you have obtained a running fix and determined that it gives you a different position than your DR, you *may* use these two positions to estimate drift since your previous fix as shown in Figure 138. However, you must recall that the accuracy of an RFix is more questionable than of a fix. Any such inaccuracy will be transferred to your drift estimates. Similarly, you should avoid calculating drift between an RFix and a fix. Where possible, determine drift between 2 or 3 bearing fixes.

In actual practice it may be that the speed of the vessel is great compared to the drift, the interval between bearings of an RFix is comparatively short, or the time interval to the last fix is much greater than the interval to the RFix. In such situations it is quite reasonable to calculate drift from an RFix to a fix as a temporary measure until you can properly calculate set and drift between two fixes.

SUMMARY

- By calculating in advance a course that you should steer to offset drift from leeway or current, you will travel the shortest possible distance to your destination.

- A difference in position between a DR and a fix may be due to drift.
- Although wind and current speeds may be accurately predicted or measured, their effect on each boat under varying conditions may be considerably different. Calculate the drift experienced frequently so that you may become a better judge of its effect on your boat under varying conditions.
- Vector diagrams are used to solve problems caused by the effect of wind and current on your vessel's course and speed.
- To determine course and/or speed to offset current before the voyage, draw the drift vector at the point of departure.
- To determine set and drift or EP after an interval of time or end of voyage, draw the drift vector at the point of destination.
- Wind directions are *from*. Use reciprocal for direction of set. Current directions are given as direction of set.
- Heading, course steered (C) and course to steer (C) are equivalent terms. They represent the direction in which the vessel should be pointed, is pointed or was pointed.
- Course made good (CMG) and course over the ground (COG) are equivalent. They represent the direction in which the vessel actually travelled or actually will travel with respect to the surface of the earth.
- The difference in direction between these two groups of terms is due to set caused by leeway from the wind and drift from the current.
- Speed through the water, speed travelled as indicated by knotmeter, tachometer, etc. (S); speed to travel as indicated by knotmeter, tachometer, etc. (S) are equivalent. They represent the speed at which the vessel is travelling (or will travel) through the water as indicated by conventional instruments aboard a pleasure vessel.
- Speed made good (SMG) and speed over the ground (SOG) are equivalent. They represent the speed at which the vessel actually travelled (or will travel) with respect to the surface of the earth.
- The difference in speed between this second two groups of terms is due to drift caused by leeway from the wind and drift from the current.

14. Positioning Review

"If you put a hole in one end of a boat, both ends will fill up."
SAUNDERS' LAW OF BUOYANCY.

A fix is a positive, accurate determination of a ship's position. As we have learned, this position may be determined by the methods reviewed below. This chapter will also discuss further methods of determining estimated position (EP), most probable position (MPP), and outline others yet to be covered.

To be moored is to be secured to a jetty or wharf which is shown on a chart.

To be close aboard is to be alongside of or passing (within a few yards) a buoy or some other charted object.

A fix is at the intersection of two or more lines of position, such as: the intersection of two ranges. (Fig. 142), the intersection of two bearing LOPs (Fig. 143), the intersection of a range and a bearing (Fig. 144).

A running fix (RFix) is a positive, somewhat accurate determination of a ship's position. Although less accurate than a fix, it is still a highly reliable means of determining a position. The degree of accuracy is, to a large extent, dependent upon external influences, such as wind and current, and also upon the time lapse between bearings. A time lapse of half an hour or less will usually provide a position nearly as accurate as a fix. A running fix may be determined by:

- Advancing an LOP — The intersection of an LOP (range, bearing, distance off, etc.) and an LOP which has been advanced, or retarded, from some other time. (See Fig. 145.)

- Bow and beam — The intersection of a beam bearing LOP on an object and a circular LOP on the same object determined by means of a bow and beam bearing (or two other bearings with a distance having been run between the two events, beam and quarter bearing for example. (See Fig. 146.)

A dead-reckon position (DR) is an indication of a ship's position based on calculations of course, speed, and distance plotted on a chart. The accuracy of such a position is highly dependent upon outside influences, such as wind and current, as well as other factors, such as steering errors, equipment (e.g., compass) errors, etc. Unless the outside influences and/or errors are significant relative to the elapsed time and vessel's rate of speed, the DR position is usually a reasonable indication of the ship's position at any time. (See Fig. 147.)

ESTIMATED POSITION

An estimated position (EP) is arrived at by applying an estimate of the result of outside influences to a DR position. This estimate may be obtained by some other accurate information, such as a bearing (single LOP) on an object or by estimates of the effect on the vessel of set and drift (current). We will now learn how to determine and plot an EP.

EP with No Current   Assume that, after having obtained a fix at 1100, you have travelled on a course 075° true at a speed of 6.0 knots. At 1350 you take a bearing on a structural buoy with a green light. Plot your EP. (See Fig. 148.)

From your 1100 fix draw a course line in the direction of 075° true and measure along this line a distance of 17 miles. Plot and label your 1350 DR. At 1350 you took a bearing on the buoy and converted it to a true bearing of 325°. You note that you must be somewhere on that LOP, and yet you calculate that you are at your 1350 DR. You therefore conclude that a good estimate of your position (EP) would be a point on the line closest to your DR. To locate that point draw a broken line from your DR so that it will intersect your LOP at 90°. That intersection is your 1350 EP (no current) and should be labelled as in Figure 148 with a square surrounding the location and with the time, 1350.

EP with Current   Assume that, after having obtained a fix at 1500, you have travelled on a course of 300° true at a speed of 8.0 knots. At 1900, after plotting your DR, you decide to plot your EP taking into account your estimate of the effect of the wind and current over the past 4 hours. You estimate the set at 225° and drift at 1.0 knot. From your 1900 DR draw a broken line in the direction of 225° for a distance of 4 miles. That point would be your 1900 EP. Plot and label accordingly. (See Fig. 149.)

In the preceding example, if you had obtained a bearing on the black-can-buoy of 190° true, instead of labelling the above point as your EP, you would draw a broken line from that point at 90° to your 1900 LOP and label that point as your EP. (See Fig. 150.)

Any EP, particularly one taking into account the effect of wind and current or other estimated factors, should be used with discretion. It is only one input of data to assist the navigator, and does not replace the obligation to use judgment. After plotting an EP, continue to run your DR plot from your last DR. (See Fig. 151.) An EP is *not* a fix. Do *not* continue your plotting from the EP.

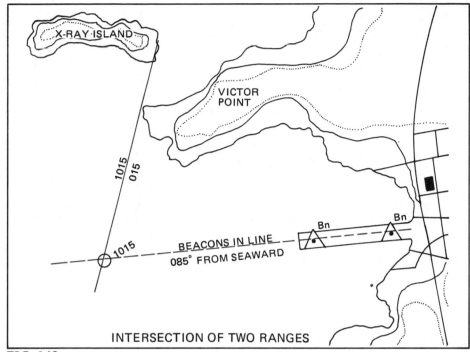

FIG. 142

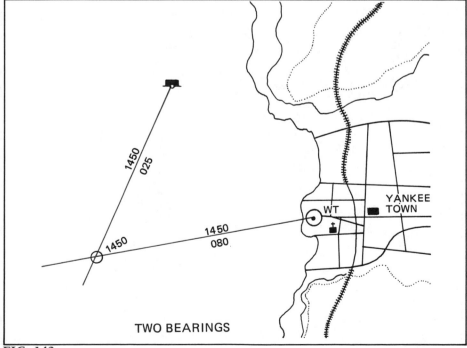

FIG. 143

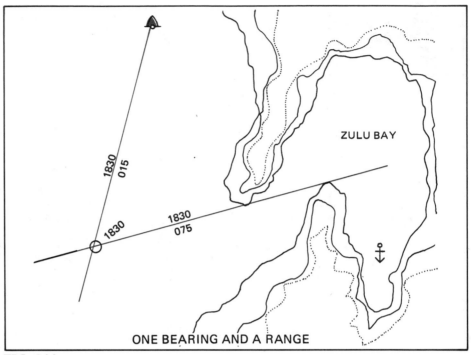

ZULU BAY

1830
015

1830

1830
075

ONE BEARING AND A RANGE

FIG. 144

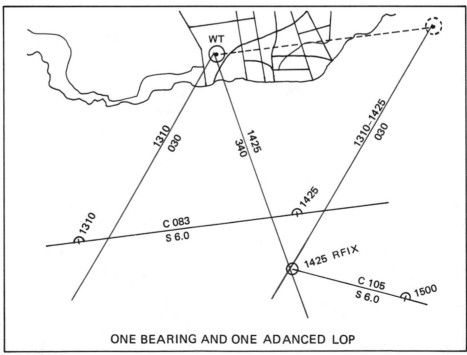

WT

1310
030

1425
340

1310-1425
030

1310

C 083
S 6.0

1425

1310

1425 RFIX

C 105
S 6.0

1500

ONE BEARING AND ONE ADANCED LOP

FIG. 145

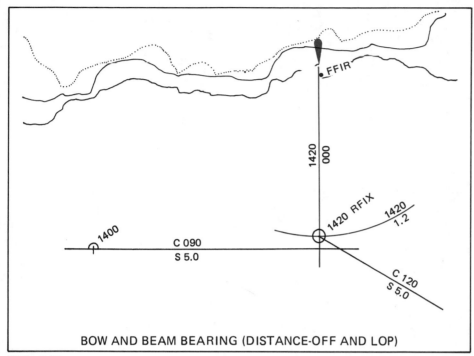

BOW AND BEAM BEARING (DISTANCE-OFF AND LOP)

FIG. 146

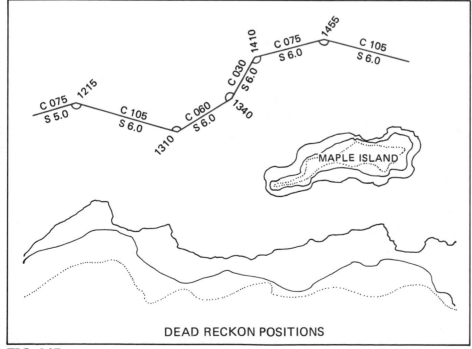

DEAD RECKON POSITIONS

FIG. 147

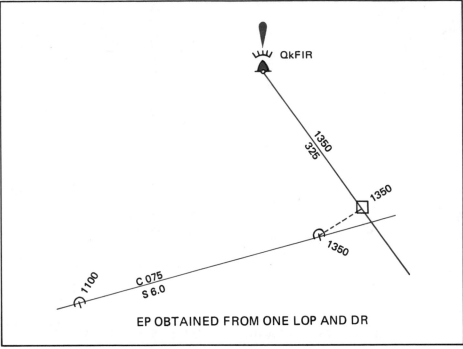

FIG. 148

EP OBTAINED FROM ONE LOP AND DR

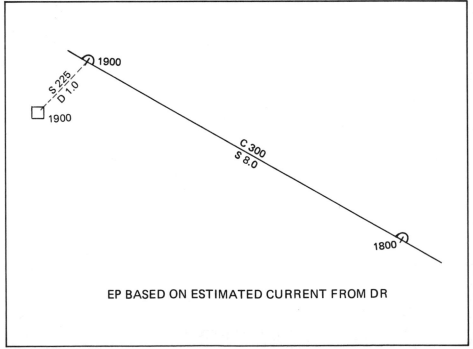

FIG. 149

EP BASED ON ESTIMATED CURRENT FROM DR

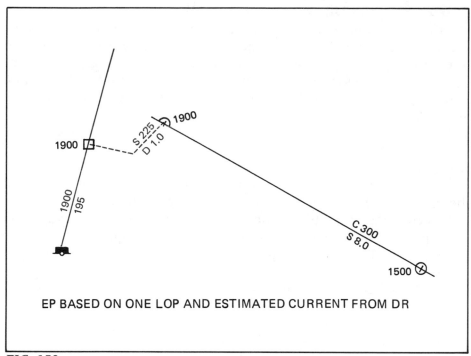

EP BASED ON ONE LOP AND ESTIMATED CURRENT FROM DR

FIG. 150

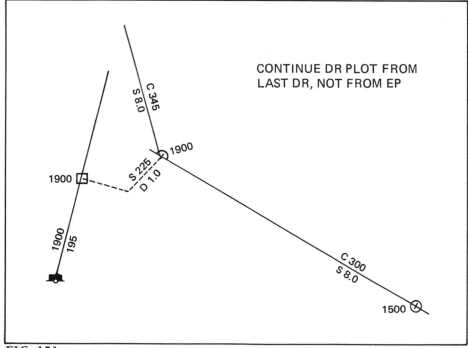

CONTINUE DR PLOT FROM
LAST DR, NOT FROM EP

FIG. 151

MOST PROBABLE POSITION (MPP)

This term is interchangeable with and means the same as estimated position. The letters EP are used here, because they are a reminder that the position is, after all, only an estimate.

An EP involving an LOP is naturally to be considered far more reliable than an EP based on estimates or judgments, only because by definition you must be somewhere on the LOP.

POSITIONING

Early in this chapter we defined methods of obtaining a fix. We will now add to this list. Some of these methods are yet to be covered here, including the appendices, and some (as noted) are beyond the intended scope of the book. The following methods of positioning will be explained in the remaining chapters and in the appendices:

- LOP by line of soundings.
- LOP by radio direction finding (RDF).
- LOP (circular) from distance off by sextant.
- LOP by station-finding.

Considered beyond the scope of this book are:

- LOPs by radar, bearings and distance off.
- LOPs by distance-finding station.
- LOPs (circular) from distance off by range finder.
- LOPs by loran or other electronic equipment.
- LOPs by nautical astronomy.

The Bibliography will suggest books that cover these very advanced techniques.

Considered to be of limited use and doubtful accuracy are:

- LOP (circular) from distance off by sound echo.
- LOP (circular) from distance off from an object on the horizon.

15. Danger Bearings and Angles

"Navigation is what tells you where you are, even when you aren't."
C. COLUMBUS.

SAFE PASSAGE

There may be times during the course of a voyage that you must maintain a minimum (or maximum) distance offshore, or that you must negotiate a narrow passage in order to avoid a shoal area or underwater hazard that is not marked by an aid to navigation. The solution to a safe passage may lie in the use of danger bearings or danger angles.

To ensure safe passage while underway, any one of the following methods may be used: danger bearings, with a compass or pelorus; danger angles (Horizontal), with a pelorus or sextant; danger angles (Vertical), with a sextant.

DANGER BEARINGS

Figure 152 describes a potentially hazardous situation. You leave Port Departure bound for Port Destination some 12 miles North-northeast and somewhere up the coast. Along the way you know from your chart that up the coast of Wreck Inlet lies an unmarked area of foul ground and rocks awash that is not marked by any aid to navigation. You plot a course to go well out to sea before turning onto a true course of 045°. However, you know that wind or current could cause you to make good a course that would take you into foul ground. How do you avoid this situation? Establish a danger bearing.

Select some object along the shoreline well beyond the hazard and which is shown on the chart. In Figure 152 we have selected the "conspicuous tree." Draw a line from that object tangent to (touching) the hazard so that the hazard will lie inshore of the line. Allow a little extra room for safety's sake. Determine the true direction of this line *toward* the object. (See Fig. 153.)

I suggest that you plot and label the line as shown; it is a danger bearing. In this example if, at any time when you are in the vicinity, you take a bearing on this object and your true bearing is less than the danger bearing you will be to seaward of the foul ground and therefore in a safe area. If your true bearing is greater, you are in danger. Keep in mind that as you travel you must convert your compass bearing on the object to a true bearing to compare it with your true danger bearing. You can prove this to your own satisfaction by referring to Figure 154.

You are somewhere in the vicinity of area A, and we have established a danger bearing of 010° true. If you take a bearing on the object as 000° true, then you must be on that LOP which does not pass through the foul ground. On the other hand, if your bearing at any time is 020° true, you must be on *that* line; it does pass through the foul ground. If you persist on that bearing, you may end up in the foul ground.

Whether to maintain a bearing greater or lesser than the danger bearing depends on your direction of travel and on which side of you the hazard lies. Determine this by inspection after plotting your danger bearing.

Let us leave Port Departure and apply this knowledge to ensure a safe passage. Refer to Figure 155. We propose to follow course 100° true until we have reached a distance offshore that will allow us to safely clear the foul ground after turning onto our intended course of 045° true. We have plotted our danger bearing 010° true. The safest way would be to continue course 100° until we have crossed the danger bearing before turning onto course 045° true. However, the proposed method is satisfactory. After turning onto course 045°, we frequently take a bearing on the "conspicuous tree." If this true bearing does not become 010° or less by the time that we reach the vicinity of the foul ground, then we had best change course to starboard and sail offshore until we are on the proper side of the danger bearing. We continue to take bearings on the object until we are well beyond the hazardous area.

DANGER ANGLES — COMPASS BEARINGS

We have consistently referred to true courses and true bearings. You would have converted these in your log to compass bearings. The compass danger bearing will be calculated using the deviation of the intended compass course. *Deviation is according to ship's heading.*

RELATIVE BEARING DANGER ANGLES — PELORUS

The relative bearing of the danger bearing while on course 045° may be quickly determined by subtracting the course (true) from the danger bearing (true): Relative Bearing = Danger Bearing (True) − True Course. Or in the example:

$$010° − 045° =$$
$$(010° + 360°) − 045° =$$
$$370° − 045° = 325° \text{ Relative Danger Bearing}$$

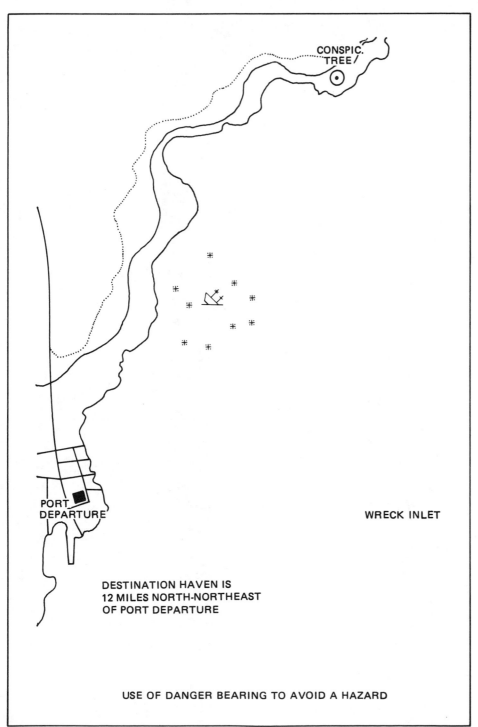

CONSPIC.
TREE

WRECK INLET

PORT
DEPARTURE

DESTINATION HAVEN IS
12 MILES NORTH-NORTHEAST
OF PORT DEPARTURE

USE OF DANGER BEARING TO AVOID A HAZARD

FIG. 152

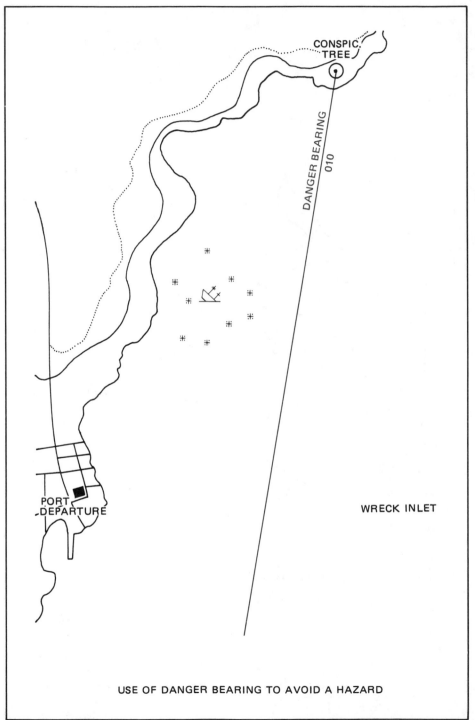

USE OF DANGER BEARING TO AVOID A HAZARD

FIG. 153

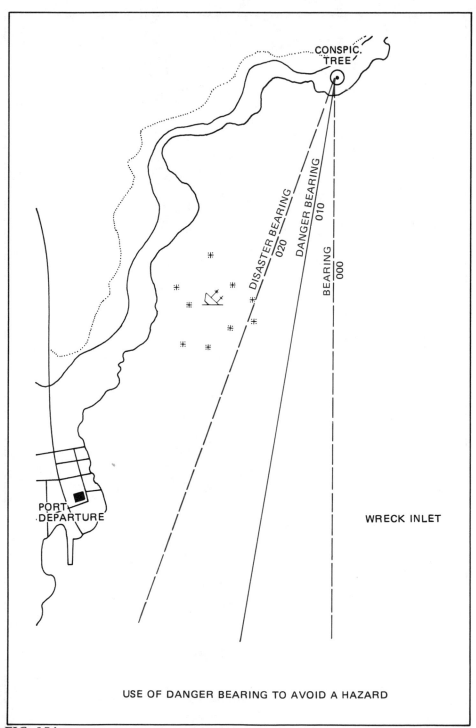

USE OF DANGER BEARING TO AVOID A HAZARD

FIG. 154

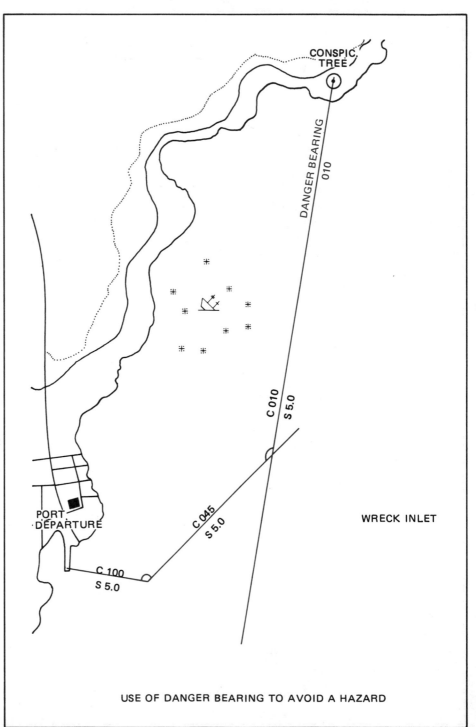

CONSPIC
TREE

DANGER BEARING 010

C 010
S 5.0

WRECK INLET

PORT
DEPARTURE

C 045
S 5.0

C 100
S 5.0

USE OF DANGER BEARING TO AVOID A HAZARD

FIG. 155

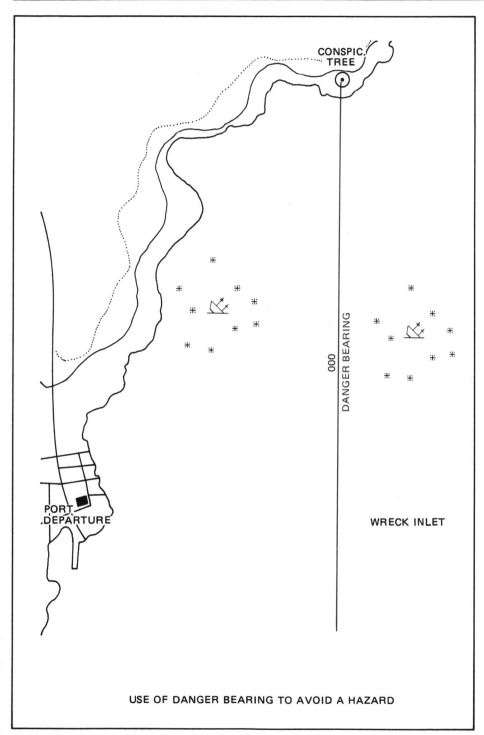

CONSPIC.
TREE

DANGER BEARING

000

PORT
DEPARTURE

WRECK INLET

USE OF DANGER BEARING TO AVOID A HAZARD

FIG. 156

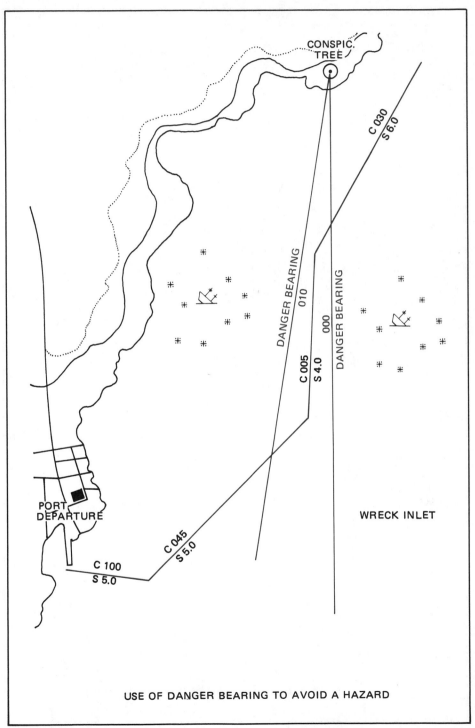

USE OF DANGER BEARING TO AVOID A HAZARD

FIG. 157

While on your intended compass course equivalent to true course 045° and with your pelorus set at 325° relative, periodically ensure that your pelorus sighting is on the proper (in this case seaward) side of the object. Otherwise, move further offshore until the proper conditions exist.

Similarly, a danger bearing may be used to stay inshore of an outlying hazard (Fig. 156) or to thread a passage between two hazards (Fig. 157.) There is no need that the object be on the landward side or that it be ahead of you. You can, of course, take the bearing over starboard, quarter or stern.

DANGER ANGLES — HORIZONTAL

You may not be fortunate enough to have an object in sight in the desired location. In that case you may be able to obtain a circular danger bearing or "danger circle." The principle is the same as in geometry. The angle at any point on the circumference of a circle between the lines from that point to two other points on the circumference will remain unchanged if that point is moved to any other location on the circumference of the same circle. (See Fig. 158.)

If we apply this fact to the situation in Figure 159, we can establish a method of safely avoiding a hazard. In this example, we must be certain to maintain a minimum distance offshore as we pass the area of foul

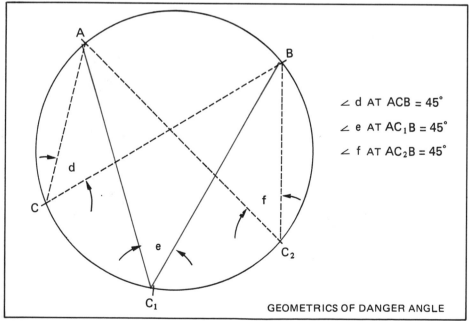

∠ d AT ACB = 45°

∠ e AT AC$_1$B = 45°

∠ f AT AC$_2$B = 45°

GEOMETRICS OF DANGER ANGLE

FIG. 158

ground. The solution is shown in Figure 160 and involves these steps:

- Draw a line between the two objects.
- Draw a perpendicular bisector of this line.
- With a drafting compass, and by trial and error, construct a circle whose circumference passes through the two objects and passes comfortably clear of the limit of the area of the hazard. The centre of the circle will lie on the bisector.
- Select any convenient point on the circumference of the circle and label it "C."
- Measure angle S subtended at C by lines from WT to C and from Cupola to C.
- Refer now to Figure 161.

Any point where the angle is greater than S in Figure 161 will lie inside the circle. Any point where the angle is less than S will lie outside the circle. It follows, then, that if you measure the angle between the two objects as you travel your intended course and the *angle remains less* than S, you *will be outside the circle* and safe of the foul ground. Angle S is termed the "danger angle."

In a similar manner, you can construct a circle and determine an angle so that you will stay inside of an offshore or outlying hazard. You may also construct circles and determine angles so as to stay within a

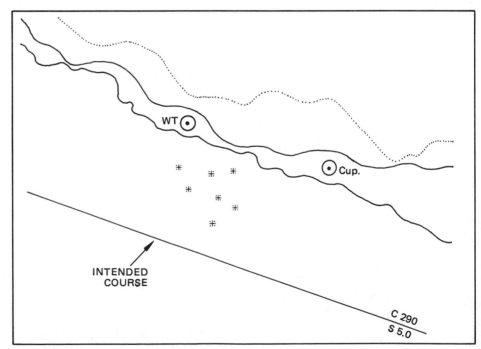

FIG. 159

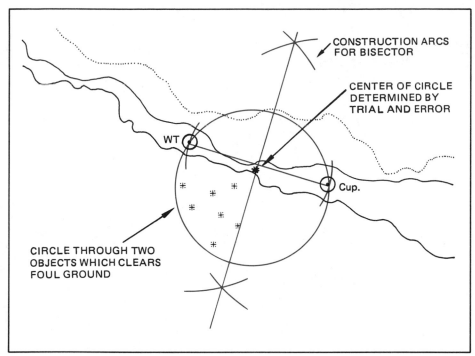

FIG. 160

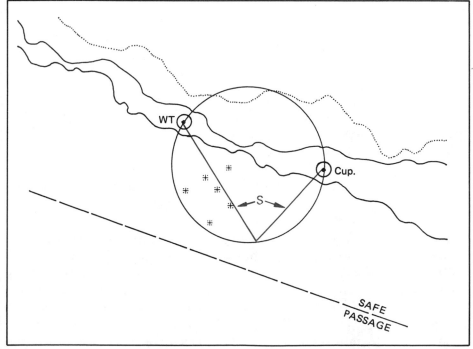

FIG. 161

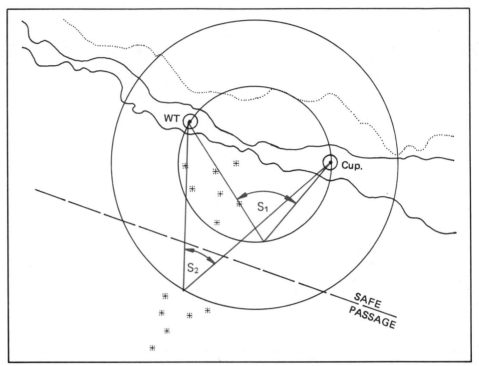

FIG. 162

safe passage between two hazards. (See Fig. 162.) Safe passage will result if you maintain a position such that the angle between bearings taken simultaneously (or nearly so) on the two objects is between angle S1 and angle S2.

Measuring the Danger Angle   Danger angles can be measured in the following ways:

- The difference between two compass bearings taken nearly simultaneously on each of two objects while on a constant course.
- The difference between two relative bearings taken with a pelorus nearly simultaneously on each of two objects while on a constant course.
- The direct measurement of the angle with a marine sextant held in a horizontal position, called a ''horizontal sextant angle'' (HSA).

Of these methods, the sextant angle is the quickest, most nearly constant in read-out and the most accurate. The compass and relative bearing methods are the same as discussed in the earlier section on danger bearings.

With the sextant, you may prefer to calculate the angle which you should read to go midway between the hazards and leave the sextant set at that angle. A member of the crew can then keep an almost constant reading on the object and advise the helmsman to steer port or starboard as the view in the sextant dictates.

A Word about Sextants A treatise on sextants is beyond the scope of this book. Usually, you either own one or you will be using the sextant of a friend, an association or school. If using your own sextant, you probably have a book or booklet describing its use and care. If using a sextant belonging to someone else, you presumably have access to that person's elementary instructions on its use and care. In any case, there are a number of books on the market treating the subject of sextants in excellent fashion. Suffice it to say that when using the sextant on "nearby" objects for coastal navigation as opposed to "distant" objects for celestial navigation, the index error must be determined by viewing one of the "nearby" objects to be used.

DANGER ANGLES — VERTICAL

There may well be occasions when only one object is available and it is not in a position for use to obtain a danger bearing. Under these conditions a circle of position may be used as a danger circle by taking a vertical sextant angle (VSA) reading. This procedure is detailed in Figure 163.

The distance away from the base of the object to the observer is calculated by the formula:

$$D \text{ (distance)} = \frac{h \text{ (height)} \times .565}{A \text{ (angle)}}$$

$$D = \frac{h \times .565}{A}$$

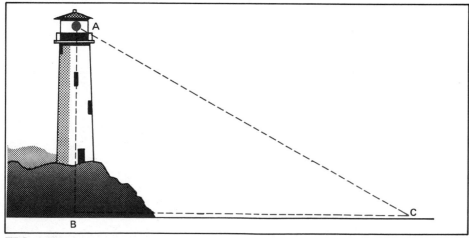

FIG. 163

D is the distance from the observer to the base of the object in nautical miles. Height (h) is the vertical height of the object from the surface of the water at the time and location of observation measured in feet. A is the sextant angle in minutes of arc after correction for index error and/or instrument error. When height is in feet, .565 in a constant. When height is in meters, the same formula is used, but the constant is 1.854:

$$D = \frac{h \times 1.854.}{A}$$

Again, if we apply this information to a real situation, such as Figure 164, we can safely avoid the hazard. From the charted location of the object we sweep an arc so as to comfortably miss the hazard and then measure the radius of the arc using the latitude scale. In this case it is 0.8 nautical miles. We obtain the height of the object from the chart or lights list and determine what our sextant must read to be 0.8 miles away from the base of the object. Because height is measured in feet on this chart, the solution is:

$$D = \frac{h \times .565}{A}$$

$$A = \frac{h \times .565}{D} = \frac{105 \times .565}{0.8} = 74.2 \text{ minutes of arc}$$

$$A = 1° \, 14'$$

If the angle of the sextant reading is greater than 1° 14', we will be closer than 0.8 miles from the light and could be in danger. The object, then, is to pilot the vessel so as to maintain a vertical sextant angle of 1° 14' or less (assuming no sextant errors).

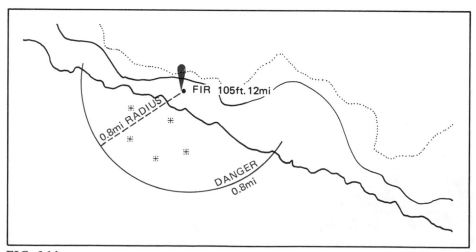

FIG. 164

In a manner similar to horizontal sextant angles, we can determine the angle to stay inside of a danger or we can determine a combination of angles to ensure a safe passage between hazards. As is also true for horizontal angles, distance measurements are *from* the object, *not* the shoreline

DISTANCE OFF BY SEXTANT

The vertical sextant angle method is quite acceptable as an accurate method of determining distances. However, the pilot should be aware of some inherent inaccuracies and limitations.

The formula is not precise. It is an arithmetic approximate solution of a trigonometric problem. It is nonetheless totally acceptable in accuracy for coastal navigation and piloting.

The height of object must be accurately known. Therefore, the variance from chart datum at the time of the measurement must be determined. This can only be accomplished by close approximation through tide tables or inland water level tables.

The exact location for height measurement must be known. For official aid to navigation lights, this is the centre of the filament or source of light.

If the base of the object is "over the horizon" some inaccuracy will result. However, for all practical purposes if you are within approximately 3-4 miles of the object; if the object's height above water is approximately 100' or more per mile of distance; and if the observer's height above water is 6 to 14 feet; then no appreciable error will result. (See Fig. 165.)

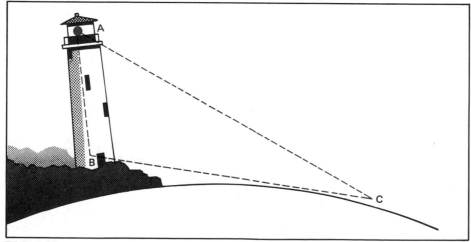

FIG. 165

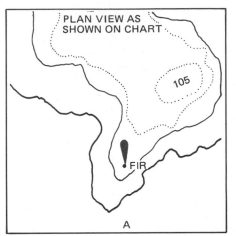

PLAN VIEW AS
SHOWN ON CHART

105

FIR

A

FIG. 166

PROFILE VIEW

FIG. 167

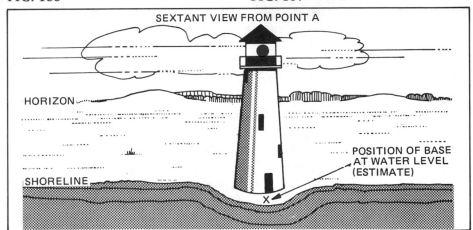

SEXTANT VIEW FROM POINT A

HORIZON

POSITION OF BASE
AT WATER LEVEL
(ESTIMATE)

SHORELINE

X

FIG. 168

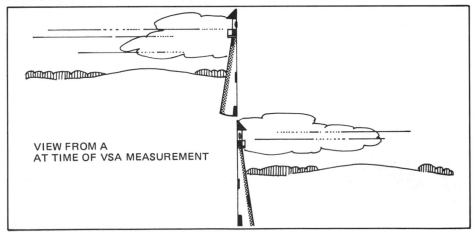

VIEW FROM A
AT TIME OF VSA MEASUREMENT

FIG. 169

The calculations are based on height being vertically above the base at water level. Seldom can the base be seen as it is usually inland somewhat. The actual base position must be estimated when taking the sextant reading.(See Figs. 166-169.) The alternative to this estimating is a complex series of steps using special tables, given as 9 and 22 in *The American Practical Navigator*. Their use is seldom justified in practical applications aboard small vessels. A good method, in some instances, is to use the structure only. If the height of land on which the structure is located is shown on the chart, deduct the land height from the charted height of the structure to obtain the structure height only. Bring the centre of the lantern down to the base of the structure to measure the angle. Since both measurements are from the same chart datum, the height of tide is not required in order to calculate the distance.

If the object is beyond the horizon, more than approximately 4 miles distant, you may determine the distance accurately by use of Table 9 in Bowditch (*The American Practical Navigator*) or equivalent publications.

SUMMARY:

Unmarked hazards may be avoided without an accurate determination of your position by means of:

- Danger Bearing — Maintaining a minimum (or maximum) bearing on a charted object. In effect, "staying on the proper side of the line." This may be a compass bearing or a relative bearing.
- Danger Angle (Horizontal) — Maintaining a minimum (or maximum) horizontal angle between two charted objects. The horizontal angle may be measured as the difference between the bearings on the object or measured directly as an angle with a sextant held in a horizontal position.
- Danger Angle (Vertical) — Maintaining a minimum (or maximum) vertical sextant angle on one charted object. The greater the angle the less distant the object is from you.

16. The Sextant and Coastal Piloting

"There's a solution to every problem; the only difficulty is finding it."
SAUNDERS' SAGE SAYING

CIRCULAR LINES OF POSITION
You have seen in the previous chapter how the sextant can be used to obtain circles of distance off by either horizontal or vertical sextant angles. These circles, which we used as danger circles without determining our position, are circular lines of position.

As you know, the intersection of two such circular lines of position or the intersection of one circular line and some other line of position, such as a bearing on any charted object taken nearly simultaneously, would constitute a fix. Even though one LOP is circular and may be a distance off, it is still a fix, rather than a running fix, because the distance off was obtained at almost the same instant as the other LOP.

HORIZONTAL SEXTANT ANGLE ON TWO OBJECTS
To plot a line of position based on a horizontal sextant angle (HSA), refer to Figures 170 to 172. The angle between the lighthouse and water tower in this example is 54° 37′, and the steps are as follows:
1. Draw a line between the two objects (base line).
2. Deduct the sextant angle (rounded to the closest whole degree) from 90°: 90° − 55° = 35°.
3. Draw a line at the resultant angle (35°) to the base line from each of the two objects. Both lines are drawn on the same side of the base line as you are located. (You know certainly if you are to the NW or SE.)
4. Draw the lines lightly, as they are construction lines only and must not be confused with lines of position.
5. From the intersection of the lines from each object draw a circular line of position whose radius is the distance between the intersection and either object. This LOP will pass through both objects.
6. Label this LOP with the time and sextant angle as shown.
7. You are located somewhere on that line at the time of the measurement.

If the sextant angle exceeds 90°, the result of step 2 will be a minus

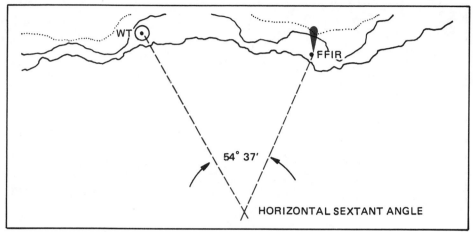

FIG. 170

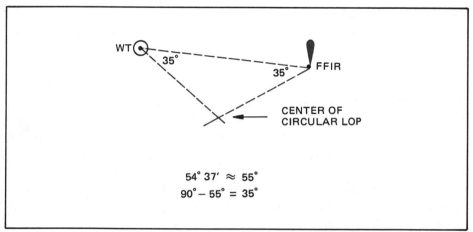

54° 37′ ≈ 55°
90° − 55° = 35°

FIG. 171

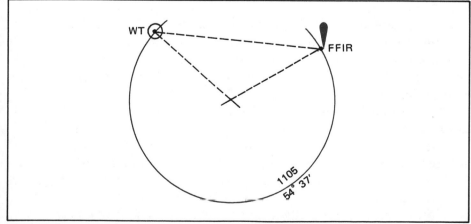

FIG. 172

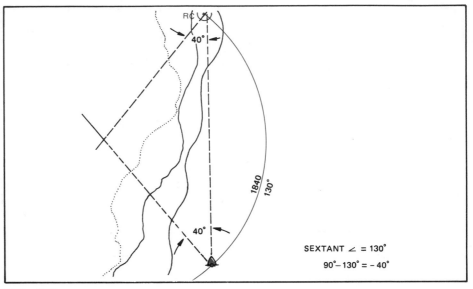

SEXTANT ∠ = 130°

90°– 130° = – 40°

FIG. 173

number. Most sextants will measure up to a maximum of approximately 140°. In the example shown in Figure 173, the HSA is 130°, and therefore the result would be: $90° - 130° = -40°$. Now draw lines from the objects at an angle of 40° to the base line on the side of the base line opposite to the one on which you are located. From that intersection draw the circular LOP in the same manner as previously described. Maximum accuracy will be obtained if objects can be selected which will result in a horizontal sextant angle between 15° and 75°, or between 105° and 140°.

HORIZONTAL SEXTANT ANGLE — OBTAINING A FIX

Having obtained one line of position in the preceding fashion, the second LOP may be a range; in some instances a bearing on one of the two objects discussed above: a bearing on some other object; a circular line of position on two other objects (in a similar manner); or an advanced line of position. (See Figs. 174 to 178.)

The second LOP, whether a bearing or another circular LOP, may result in two intersections. Obviously, only one of these intersections can be your fix. These intersections will be sufficiently far apart and so located relative to the objects that you will have no difficulty in selecting and labelling the proper one. Through experience you will be able to select combinations of objects so that the LOPs intersect as close as possible to 90° to a line tangent to the circle at the point of intersection. Refer to Figures 179 and 180 for examples.

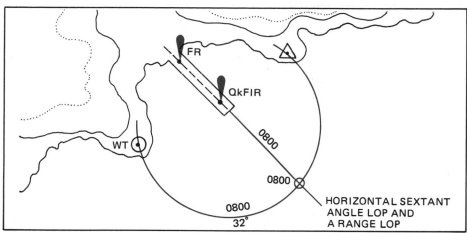

FIG. 174

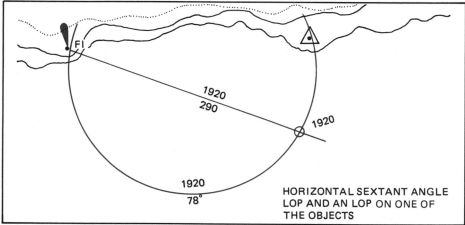

FIG. 175

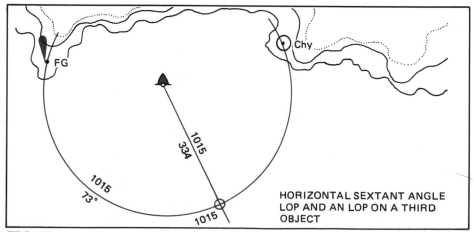

FIG. 176

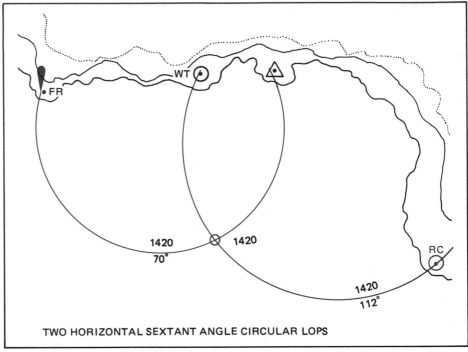

TWO HORIZONTAL SEXTANT ANGLE CIRCULAR LOPS

FIG. 177

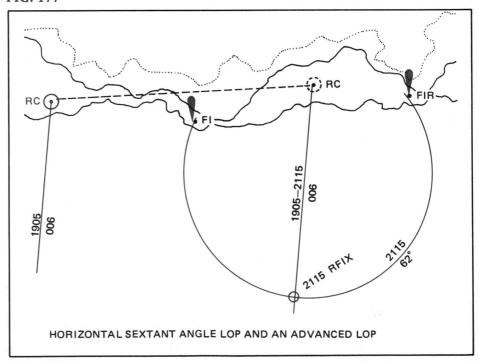

HORIZONTAL SEXTANT ANGLE LOP AND AN ADVANCED LOP

FIG. 178

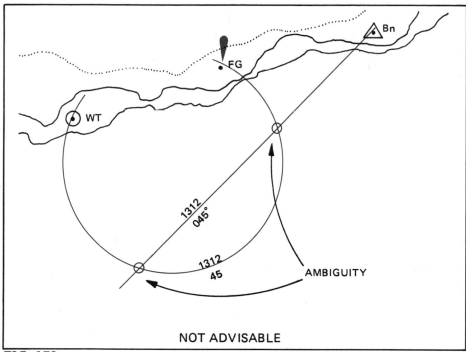

NOT ADVISABLE

FIG. 179

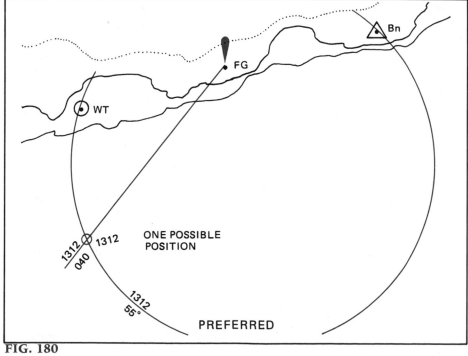

ONE POSSIBLE
POSITION

PREFERRED

FIG. 180

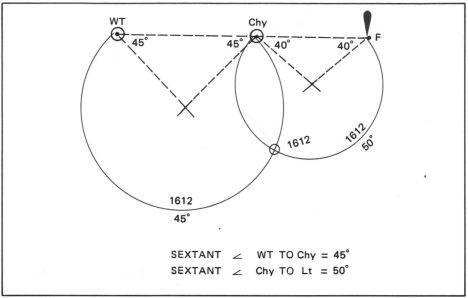

SEXTANT ∠ WT TO Chy = 45°
SEXTANT ∠ Chy TO Lt = 50°

FIG. 181

TWO HORIZONTAL SEXTANT ANGLES ON THREE OBJECTS

If only three aids to navigation are available from which to obtain a fix by horizontal angles, it may be determined in one of three ways:

1. Treat the three aids as two pairs of two objects and obtain two intersecting circular LOPs as previously outlined. (See Fig. 181.)

2. Using the two angles obtained as in Figure 181, set a three-arm protractor at the appropriate sextant angles and move it around until each arm goes through one object. Your fix is then at the centre of the instrument; the protractor has a hole so you may mark the chart at that point. (See Fig. 182.) Alternatively, you may mark the three intersecting lines on tracing paper, and slide the tracing around until each line goes through an object. Your fix is the point of intersection of the lines. (See Fig. 183.) In either of these methods there are two possible locations. The correct one should be obvious.

3. Use a station-pointer to measure the angles. This instrument can then be used as the three-arm protractor. (See Fig. 182.) It essentially is a three-arm protractor equipped with mirrors to allow the setting of the arms by sighting the objects. It is less expensive than many high-class sextants but equivalent to an acceptable quality plastic sextant. However, the sextant is probably more accurate and far more versatile in that it can be used to obtain vertical angles and also for celestial navigation.

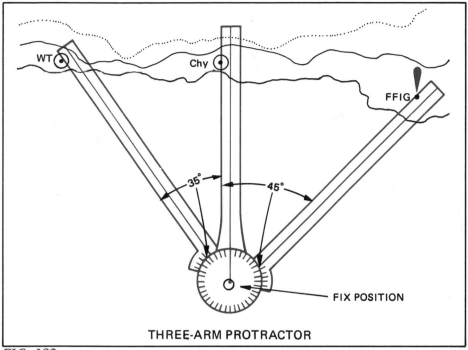

THREE-ARM PROTRACTOR

FIG. 182

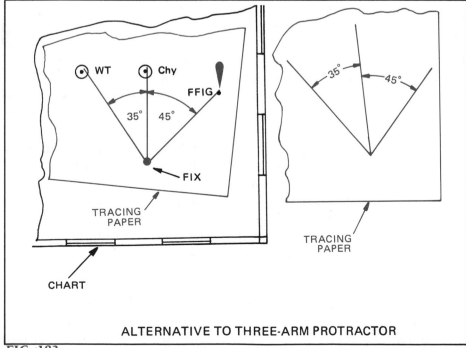

ALTERNATIVE TO THREE-ARM PROTRACTOR

FIG. 183

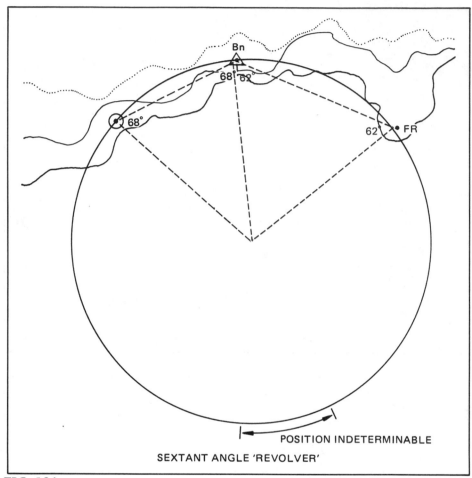

SEXTANT ANGLE 'REVOLVER'

FIG. 184

Revolvers   A word of caution when obtaining two angles from three objects. The objects could lie on the circumference of the same circle, or nearly so. (See Fig. 184.) In such a case your position may be indeterminable or of extremely doubtful accuracy. This situation is termed a "revolver." Selection of the three objects so that they are nearly in a line, or so that the centre object is closest to you, will eliminate the problem.

VERTICAL SEXTANT ANGLE

In Chapter 15 we learned how to obtain distance off by calculation. With this distance as a radius you can draw a circular LOP. You may then obtain a second line of position, and the intersection of the two LOPs is your fix.

Horizontal sextant angles probably result in the most accurate method to obtain a fix that is available to small craft vessel operators. Under some conditions, radar might be a possible exception. These horizontal (or vertical) angle circles of position can be advanced (or retarded) in the same way as any other line of position.

SUMMARY

- Fixes established by lines intersecting at nearly 90° are most accurate.
- When using two angles on three objects, avoid a "revolver" (indeterminate position) by ensuring that the centre object is closest to the observer.
- Horizontal sextant angles to establish circular lines of position tend to result in the most accurate fix that can be obtained by a small boat skipper.

17. Tides and Currents

"When the draft of the vessel exceeds the depth of the water, you are most assuredly aground."   SAUNDERS' LAW OF NAVIGATION *#10*

Tides are the vertical rise and fall in the height of water caused by the gravitational effects of various bodies in the solar system, principally the moon and sun. The single greatest cause of tides is the moon. When the moon is new (in conjunction with the sun) or when the moon is full (in opposition with the sun), the maximum change in tidal height occurs. These are known as spring tides, although there is no connection with the season. The minimum change in heights occurs when the moon is in quadrature (first and last quarter). These minimum tides are known as neap tides. (See Figs. 185 to 188.)

Because the lunar month (new moon to new moon) is approximately 29 days, spring tides occur approximately every two weeks and neap tides occur one week after spring tides. Because the moon rises approximately 50 minutes later each day, the maximum effect of lunar gravity, and thus the tides, occurs at any given point on earth approximately 50 minutes later each day. Because of man's knowledge of the solar system, the times of these occurrences are accurately predictable. However, other factors affect the timing and height of tides: size of the body of water, latitude of the area, direction of rotation of the earth, shape of the coastline, contour of the bottom, and so on. Because of these and still other factors, we have situations where there is one high water and one low water daily (diurnal); two high waters and two low waters daily (semi-diurnal) which may be equal or unequal; and differences in height between high and low water of a few inches or forty feet. (See Figs. 189 to 191.)

FIG. 185

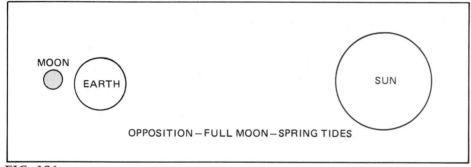

FIG. 186

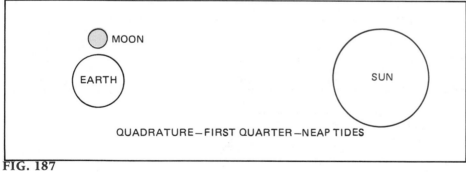

FIG. 187

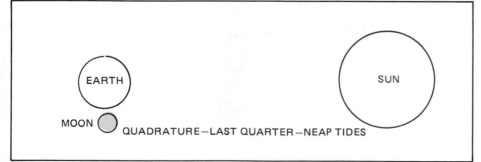

FIG. 188

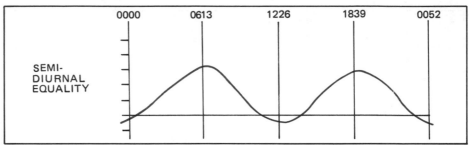

FIG. 189

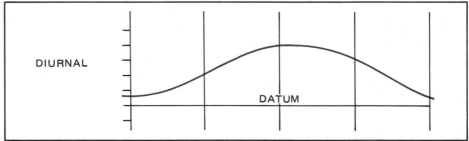

FIG. 190

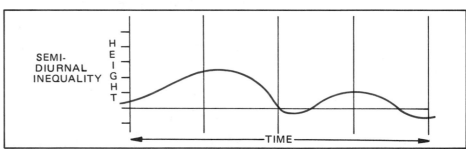

FIG. 191

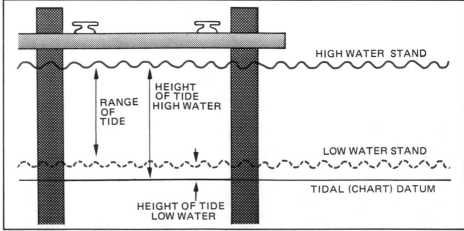

FIG. 192

TERMINOLOGY

High-water Stand: that point at which the water is neither rising nor falling (no vertical movement) and at which it has reached its maximum height for any given tidal occurrence.

Low-water Stand: that point at which the water is neither rising nor falling (no vertical movement) and at which it has reached its minimum height for any given tidal occurrence.

Range: the difference in height between any succeeding high-water and low-water stand or any succeeding low-water and high-water stand. (See Fig. 192.)

Tidal Datum: that level from which high- and low-water stands (and intermediate points) are measured. Low-water stands can be below tidal datum and are then listed as negative figures.

Chart Datum for Tidal Heights: this datum varies from country to country, as does the terminology, but can generally be described as the maximum height of high-water stand experienced on the average. Note that this height may be exceeded from time to time.

Chart Datum for Depths: similar to datum for heights, except that it is the minimum height of low-water stand experienced on the average.

Charted Heights and Depths: These are the minimum heights (as clearance) and depths experienced on the average.

TIDAL HEIGHT PREDICTIONS

The prime factors contributing to tides are precisely predictable. However, the many contributing influences are less accurately predictable. In addition to those previously listed are barometric pressure, wind direction (strength and constancy), storm surges, geographic "storms" (earthquakes, volcanoes), spring or rain "run-off" due to severe rains or melting snow.

Thus, although we have published tidal height predictions available for a vast number of locations around the world, *tide tables are predictions only* and are subject to many other influences. Tide predictions must be viewed as approximations only and the navigator must apply a great deal of judgment to their use.

TIDE TABLES

Tidal prediction tables are published by many countries and are generally available for any part of the world through leading chart dealers.

Canadian tables covering all the tidal areas of Canada are published by the Fisheries and Oceans Department of the Government of Canada. U.S. tables covering the world are published in various volumes by the U.S. Department of Commerce, National Oceanic and Atmospheric Administration. *Reed's Nautical Almanac*, published in various volumes, covers the world and includes much other useful data. It is available from Thomas Reed Publications Limited, London, England.

Tide tables are generally divided into two sections. The first gives tidal height predictions for a few specific ports or locations within the area of coverage. These are reference ports. On a daily basis, these tables predict the time of each high-water stand and height of water above tide datum. The tables also predict the time of each low-water stand and the height of water above or below tide datum. Detailed instructions are included for the purpose of predicting the height of tide at any intermediate time or predicting the time at which any given height of tide will occur.

The second section lists tidal height and time differences for many other locations within the area of coverage. These are secondary ports. These tables predict the difference in time by which a tidal event (high or low water) at a given location (secondary port) will precede or follow that same event at the reference port. It also gives the difference in height, if any, from the height at the reference port.

These tables are predictions only and must not be taken as absolutely accurate. Tidal events at some other unlisted location may vary significantly from either the reference port or secondary port, even though geographically close.

Tidal prediction summaries are frequently listed in the major daily newspapers in tidal water areas.

NON-TIDAL AREA WATER LEVELS

Major navigational areas, such as the Great Lakes area of the St. Lawrence Seaway in the U.S. and Canada, and lesser navigable areas, such as the Trent-Severn Waterway, are subject to significant differences in water surface height through the course of a year and also year to year. In such non-tidal waters, chart datum is usually an arbitrarily selected height above mean-sea-level which represents the mean-water-level over a period of years. The charted depths and heights are in reference to this datum.

If depths or clearances are critical, the navigator should know the actual level, not merely that listed on the chart. This information can be obtained from: VHF marine weather broadcasts for inland areas; a local port authority office; the weather or operations office of an airport located on or near the waterway; or from a monthly water level bulletin published for the area by a governmental agency and usually available by subscription or from your local chart dealer.

TIDAL CURRENTS

The flow of water from one location or area toward some other location which is caused by variances in height generated by tidal height differences is called a tidal current. This current is indirectly influenced by the solar system gravity that causes tides. The direction of flow, strength of flow and timing is therefore a factor of tidal conditions, shape of coast or constrictions, contour of the bottom, the out-flow of current from a feeder river or stream and so on.

Flood current flow is defined as that moving toward land from sea, up a river from open water, into a bay or inlet or flow in any direction caused by one of these conditions.

Ebb current flow is defined as that moving outward from land, downstream toward open water, outward from a bay or inlet or generally, but not always, in the reciprocal direction of a flood current.

Slack water is defined as the time and condition of still water occurring between an ebb flow and flood flow (or vice versa) where there is no horizontal movement of water. This period rarely occurs coincidental with high-water stand or low-water stand. There is, however, a slack-water occurrence for each high-water stand and each low-water stand. Slack water occurs four times daily in the case of semi-diurnal tide.

TIDAL CURRENT TABLES

Predictions of tidal currents are published by the same agencies as tide tables and are also available from your chart dealer. The predictions are developed from historical data and their relationship to tides. Their layout and use is similar to tide tables.

Data on slack-water time, maximum-flow time and current strength for both ebb and flood currents are also listed. In addition, the average directions of both flood and ebb during maximum flow are given in true directions. This data is included for reference ports, with a separate listing of differences for secondary ports. These differences are in the rate of maximum flow, the time difference for slack and maximum, and the true directions of flood and ebb currents.

The time of tidal current events can be determined for any reference or secondary station. The rate of flow at a specific time or the time at which the flow is at a specific rate may also be predicted. This information may be vital to ensure a safe passage through an area where the current flow could be dangerously fast, except at times near to slack water.

Again, you are cautioned that, although precise calculations are used, the data that result are not precise; they are estimated predictions only. Caution is also advised in areas of strong tidal current flow, particularly when the wind is opposite to the current, where the flow is around a headland or where the flow is near or over rapidly shoaling areas.

ROTARY CURRENTS

Rotary tidal currents are not to be confused with whirlpools or swirling water. A rotary tidal current is one that, at some specific location, is constantly changing direction through a period of time so that it will flow briefly in each direction as the tide changes from ebb to flood to ebb. The direction of the flow will be listed in the current tables as a separate item giving the direction of flow for periods of time after maximum flood flow at a reference port.

TIDAL CURRENT CHARTS

Tidal current in larger bays, inlets, sounds, etc. may flow at different rates or in different directions within the various areas of the body of water. As these cannot be readily included in the current tables, they are usually listed in auxiliary current charts and/or on specific areas of the navigation chart. Arrows denoting current direction on such charts use the symbol ⇒ for flood current direction (feathered = flood) and ⟶ for ebb current direction.

NON-TIDAL CURRENTS — GEOGRAPHIC AND HYDRAULIC

An example of a geographic non-tidal current is the Gulf Stream which is basically a continuous clockwise rotary flow of water in the North Atlantic. Data giving the direction and rate of such streams or currents (and there are many world-wide) are shown on pilot charts, such as the North Atlantic Pilot Chart. These charts are also available from your chart dealer.

The flow of water caused by a difference in altitude of the surface of two bodies of water is a hydraulic current. Currents of this kind are generally found in a series of rivers or lakes. Generally they are fairly constant, except during periods of heavy seasonal run-off from rains or melting snow. Information about the strengths and directions of such currents is usually obtainable from charts, sailing directions or local sailors.

USING THE TABLES

Instructions for using tide and tidal current tables are included in the United States, Canadian and English publications. Examples are given in these guides, and hence they have not been repeated here.

APPROXIMATING TIDAL HEIGHTS

For those small vessel operators using the daily newspaper summary to obtain the times of high water and low water, this rule of thumb for approximating the time or height of intermediate occurrences may be helpful.

1. Determine the difference in height between low tide and high tide. The result is the range of the tide.

2. The tide will rise or fall according to the following list:

	SEMI-DIURNAL	DIURNAL
At the end of 1 hour	$1/12$ of range	
At the end of 2 hours	$3/12$ of range	$1/12$ of range
At the end of 3 hours	$6/12$ of range	
At the end of 4 hours	$9/12$ of range	$3/12$ of range
At the end of 5 hours	$11/12$ of range	
At the end of 6 hours	Total range	$6/12$ of range
At the end of 8 hours	Not applicable	$9/12$ of range
At the end of 10 hours	Not applicable	$11/12$ of range
At the end of 12 hours	Not applicable	Total range

If, for example, you wanted to know the height of the tide 4 hours after high water in a semi-diurnal location, and you had the figures 10.3 feet for high tide, −1.6 feet for low tide and a range in feet of 11.9, then you would consult the list above: 4 hours = $9/12$ of range = of 11.9 = 8.9 feet approximately. That is, the tide has dropped 8.9 feet from a high of 10.3 feet, and the height of the tide is 10.3 − 8.9 = 1.4 feet.

SUMMARY

- Tides are the vertical rise and fall of water caused primarily by the relative motion of the moon.
- The greatest range, the difference between high and low water, occurs at the new moon and the full moon.
- Water heights due to tide can be predicted by the use of tide tables.
- Tidal predictions are approximate forecasts only and should be treated accordingly.

- Tidal currents are the horizontal movement of water due to the difference in height of water caused by tides.
- Flood current is generally the inflow or shoreward direction of a tidal current.
- Ebb current is generally the outflow or seaward direction of a tidal current.
- Tidal current flow can be predicted with the use of tidal current tables.
- Non-tidal ocean currents (e.g., Gulf Stream) are usually depicted on pilot charts.
- Significant inland river currents are called hydraulic currents and are caused by the difference in height between waterways. They are described in sailing directions.

18. Final Cruise

"That quantity which, when multiplied by, divided by, added to or subtracted from the answer you get, gives you the answer you should have got."   FLANAGAN'S FINAGLING FACTOR

This final practice cruise is an opportunity for you to employ each of the principles learned in this book. It is performed on Chart 3450-T (Canadian), and the answers are given in the diagrams and step-by-step solutions.

We are in a 32 foot (10 m) fin-keel sloop, having a draft of 4'9" (1.4 m) and equipped with a 30 h.p. Perkins diesel inboard auxiliary engine. The variation is 23°E, and deviation is according to the table in Appendix C, *with interpolation.*

PART I
At 1000 on August 20th, we leave close aboard the black-can-buoy at the entrance to Drayton Harbour, near L 48° 59.7'N, λ 122° 46.7' on our way to Point Roberts. The wind is from the SSE at 20-25 knots. We are on a close reach steering a compass course of 241° and travelling at an average speed of 6.0 knots according to the knotmeter. See the logs on pages 232 & 233 for all entries and the chart illustrations for plotting.

At 1059 you take a compass bearing of 194° on the buoy with a Fl light which is on the horizon off your port bow. You have already plotted your DR course line of 262° true and measured 5.9 miles along this line from the Drayton Harbour black-can-buoy. This established your 1059 DR position as plotted:

$$60D = St \qquad D = \frac{6 \times 59}{60} = 5.9 \text{ miles}$$

You also plot and label the LOP from your compass bearing, which is 215° true. Noting that the LOP does not pass through your DR position, you drop a construction line from your DR perpendicular to the LOP in order to determine your estimated position. Continuing your compass course of 241° until 1104, you come to port on a new course of 172° compass (201° true) reducing speed to 4.0 knots.

At 1151 you take another compass bearing on the same light, which is now on your starboard quarter. The compass bearing is 293°. Plot the

LOG OF THE _Alzarc_   DATE August 20, 198–

TIME	LOCATION L λ	DIST n.m.	SPEED Knots	SHIP'S HEADING OR BEARING					RPM	CALCULATIONS/COMMENTS
				True	V	Mag.	D	Comp		
1000	Drayton Hbr.	0.0	6.0	262°	23°E	239°	2°W	241°		Black can buoy close aboard.
1059		5.9		215°	23°E	192°	2°W	194°		Compass bearing on Flashing White Light off port bow.
1104		6.4	4.0	201°	23°E	178°	6°E	172°		Changed course and speed.
1151		9.5		322°	23°E	299°	6°E	293°		Compass bearing on Fl W.
1151	48°56.8'N 122°58.7'W	9.5	5.5	290°	23°E	267°	6°W	273°		R fix. Changed course and speed. ETA Point Roberts 1238.
1152		9.6	5.5	287°	23°E	264°	6°W	270°		Steer 3° to port to allow for leeway. Revised ETA 1235 (SOG 5.9). End cruise II Part I

VARIATION EAST MAGNETIC LEAST   60D = St
VARIATION WEST MAGNETIC BEST
DEVIATION EAST COMPASS LEAST $S = \frac{60D}{t}$
DEVIATION WEST COMPASS BEST $t = \frac{60D}{S}$

LOP in a true direction of 322°. Plot the 1151 DR 3.1 miles from the 1104 DR in the true direction 201°.

You decide to advance the 1059 LOP to a time of 1151 to obtain a running fix. Measure the direction (208° true) and distance (3.4 miles) between the 1059 DR and 1151 DR. Plot the flashing white light 3.4 miles in a true direction of 208° and from that point draw the 1059 LOP, which is now the 1059-1151 advanced LOP. The intersection of this advanced LOP and 1151 LOP is your running fix location at 1151: L 48° 56.8'N, λ 122° 58.7'W. Note that your RFix is approximately 1.0 mile North-westerly of your DR at 1151. Probably this is due primarily to the wind.

Estimating your speed at 5.5 knots on a compass course of 273° (290° true) you further estimate your ETA at Point Roberts as 1238. However, you also know that if the conditions remain constant over the next hour, you will be set to the north approximately 1/2 mile. You should, therefore, steer about 3° less (270° compass) to make Point Roberts light. Refer to the vector diagrams on the chart. Part I ends at

LOG OF THE **Alzarc**   DATE **August 21, 198–**

TIME	LOCATION L λ	DIST n.m.	SPEED Knots	SHIP'S HEADING OR BEARING					RPM	CALCULATIONS/COMMENTS
				True	V	Mag.	D	Comp		
1115	Gossip Shoals	0.0	7.0	060°	23°E	037°	1°W	038°		Depart Gossip Shoals Light.
1242		10.2		012°	23°E	349°	1°W	350°		Compass bearing on Pt. Roberts.
1242		10.2		083°	23°E	060°	1°W	061°		Compass bearing on Flashing White.
1242	48°56.6'N 123°05.5'W	10.2	7.0	012°	23°E	349°	7°W	356°		Fix. Changed course to Pt. Roberts.
										End of Cruise II Part II

VARIATION EAST MAGNETIC LEAST
VARIATION WEST MAGNETIC BEST
DEVIATION EAST COMPASS LEAST
DEVIATION WEST COMPASS BEST

$60D = St$

$S = \dfrac{60D}{t}$

$t = \dfrac{60D}{S}$

Gossip Shoals; Part II will continue the cruise to Point Roberts on the following day.

PART II

You leave Gossip Shoals (L 48°53.1'N, λ 123°18.3'W) at 1115 bound for Point Roberts and determine that you should sail a course 060° true. This requires you to steer a compass course of 038°. You estimate a speed of 7.0 knots, which would result in an ETA of:

$$60D = St \quad T = \frac{60D}{S} = \frac{60 \times 10.2}{7.0} = 87 \text{ minutes} = 1 \text{ hour } 27 \text{ minutes}$$

$$
\begin{array}{rl}
11 \quad 15 & \text{Departure} \\
+ \quad 1 \quad 27 & \text{Travel time} \\
\hline
12 \quad 42 & \text{ETA}
\end{array}
$$

Not having arrived at 1242 and seeing Point Roberts light coming almost abeam to port, you take a compass bearing of 350° on the light and a compass bearing of 061° on the flashing white light fine on your starboard bow. You plot the two lines of position and plot your 1242 fix.

To determine your set and drift, you draw a line from your 1242DR (your destination) to your 1242 fix. The direction of this line is 192° true; it is the set. The total length of the line (1.7 miles) is the total drift over 1 hour and 27 minutes:

$$S = \frac{60D}{T} = \frac{60 \times 1.7}{87} = 1.17. \text{ The drift is 1.2 knots.}$$

To determine course made good and speed made good you draw a line from your departure point to your 1242 fix. The direction of this line (067°) is your CMG. The total length of the line is 9.2 miles, a distance you travelled in 87 minutes.

$$60D = St \quad S = \frac{60D}{T} = \frac{60 \times 9.2}{87} = 6.3 \text{ knots SMG}$$

PART III

You leave the junction buoy (interrupted quick flashing white light) at Lummi Bay and wish to pass close aboard the flashing white light on Alden Bank at 1415 after leaving the Lummi light at 1300.

You decide to motor for this trip. What compass course should you steer and at what speed must you travel to reach Alden Bank at 1415? From previous experience and considering the state of tide and tidal current, you estimate that you will likely experience a set in the direction of 035° true and drift at the rate of 0.6 knots. The solution requires a vector diagram. It is an example of Case II, Chapter 13, because we know that the drift is 0.6 knots, the set is 035° and the desired SMG is 3.8 knots. The SMG is calculated from: time of departure (1300) desired ETA (1415), or a time of 75 minutes (1 hour, 15 minutes). The distance from Lummi light to Alden Bank light is 4.7 miles by measurement.

$$\text{Therefore, SMG} = \frac{60 \times 4.7}{75} = 3.76 = 3.8 \text{ knots}$$

We want to know what course to steer and what speed to travel through the water at the beginning of the voyage. Select L 48° 40.0'N, λ 122° 50.0'W as your convenient location. Draw a line from this convenient location in the direction of your intended CMG (295° true); that is, Lummi light to Alden Bank light is 295° true. Mark a point on this line 3.8 miles from the convenient location that represents your desired SMG of 3.8 knots. Label it as point B. Draw a line from the convenient location in the direction of estimated set (035° true). Mark a point on this line 0.6 miles from the convenient location that represents your estimated drift of 0.6 knots. Label it as Point A.

Now measure the direction of a line from A to B. This direction (286°) is your required course.

T	V	M	D	C
286°	23°	263°	6°W	269°

The compass course to steer is 269°.

Measure the distance from A to B. This distance (4.0 miles) is your required distance to travel each hour through the water. Therefore, your speed through the water should be 4.0 knots.

PART IV

After drifting and trolling for a few hours in the vicinity of L 48° 50.0′N, λ 123° 00.0′W, you wish to fix your position before returning to Point Roberts at 1620. You can see Rosenfeld Rock light, Alden Point light and the IntQkFl white light inside Boundary Pass. You wish to obtain an accurate position but do not have a pelorus or azimuth ring. You decide to establish a circle of position using your sextant and the Rosenfeld Rock and Alden Point lights. Following this procedure, you "aim" your boat at the Boundary Pass light to obtain an accurate compass bearing. Your horizontal sextant angle, after superimposing the two lights, is 47°. Your compass course reads 167° when the boat is aimed at Boundary Pass light.

The solution has two parts:

1. 90° − 47° = 43°.
   Draw a base line between the two lights.
   Draw a line from each light at an angle of 43° to the base line.
   Both lines must be drawn on the same side of the base line as you are located.
   With the intersection of the two lines as a centre, draw a circle whose radius is the distance between this intersection and either light. You now have a circular LOP.
2. Convert your compass course (bearing) to true and plot it through Boundary Pass light (197° true).

T	V	M	D	C
197°	23°E	174°	7°E	167°

The bearing intersects the circular LOP in two locations. Your position is easily determined by inspection.
You are located at L 48° 50.4′N, λ 122° 58.7′W.
The compass course to Point Roberts is 320°:

T	V	M	D	C
333°	23°E	310°	10°W	320°

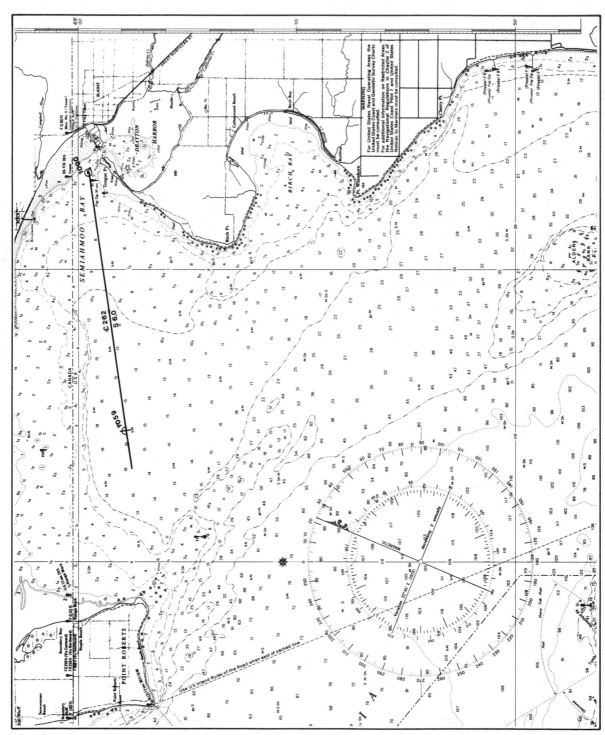

Chartlet I

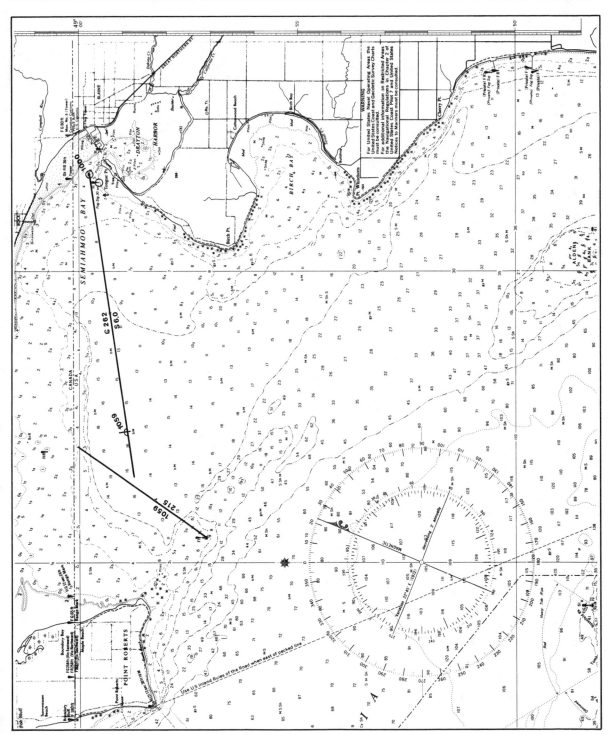

Chartlet II

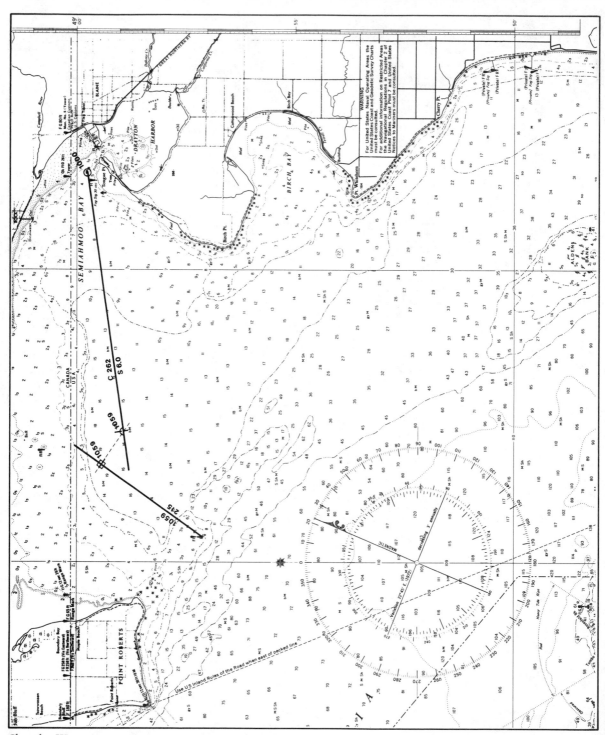

Chartlet III

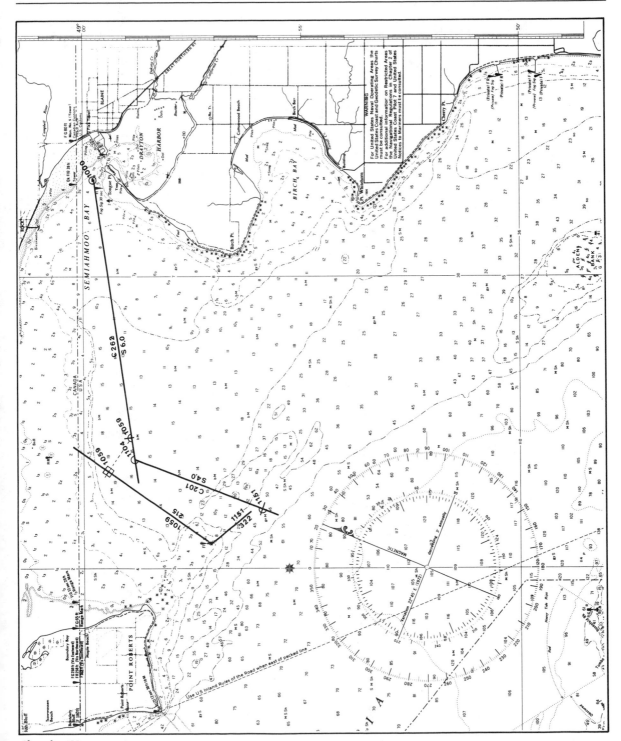

Chartlet IV

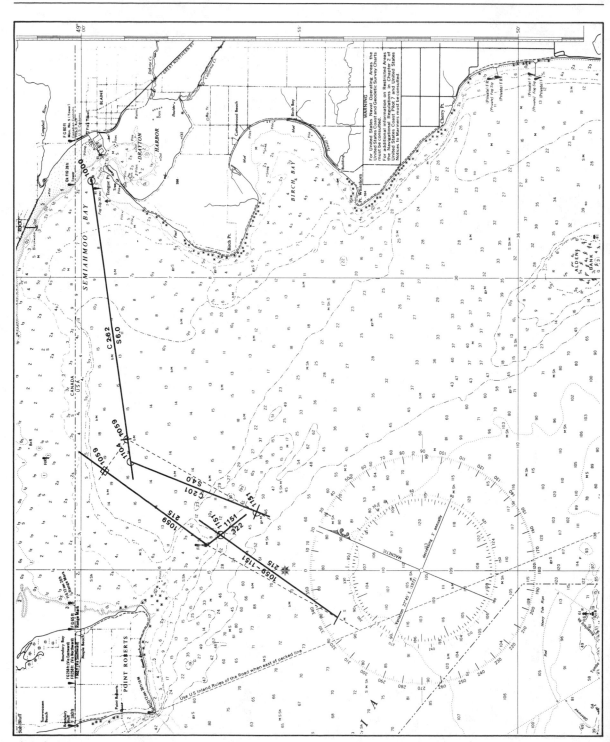

Chartlet V

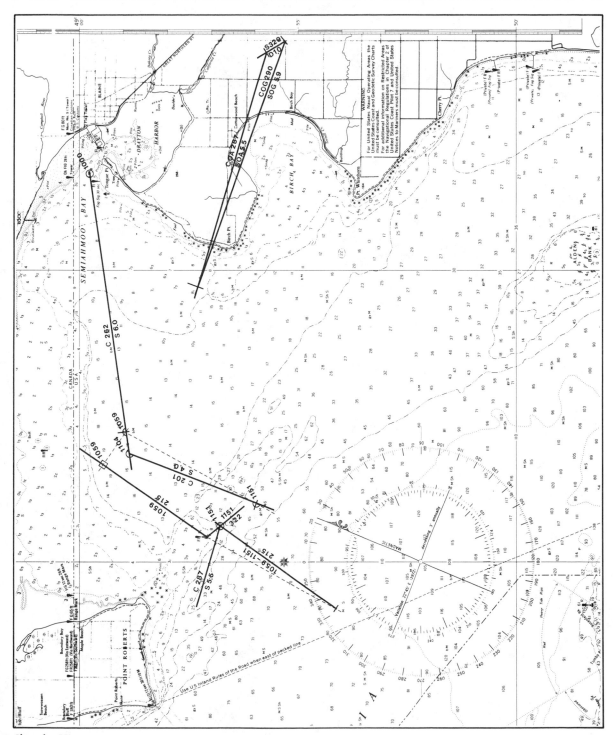

Chartlet VI

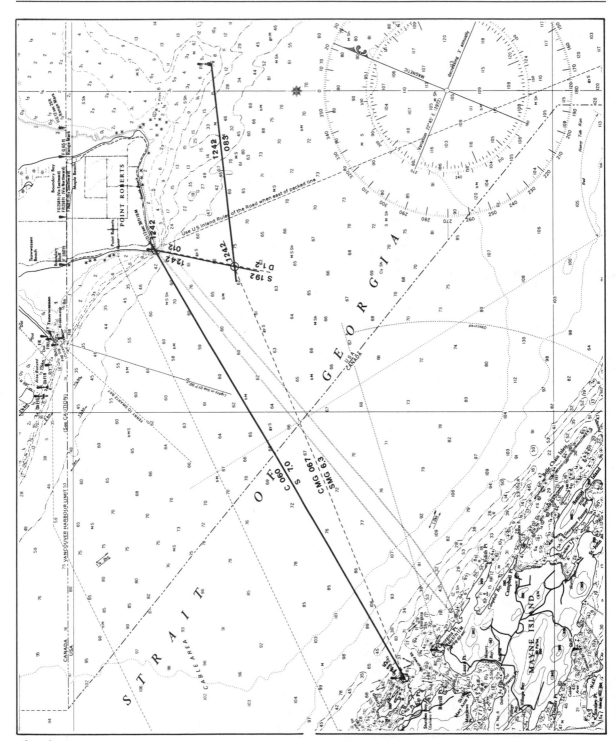

Chartlet VII

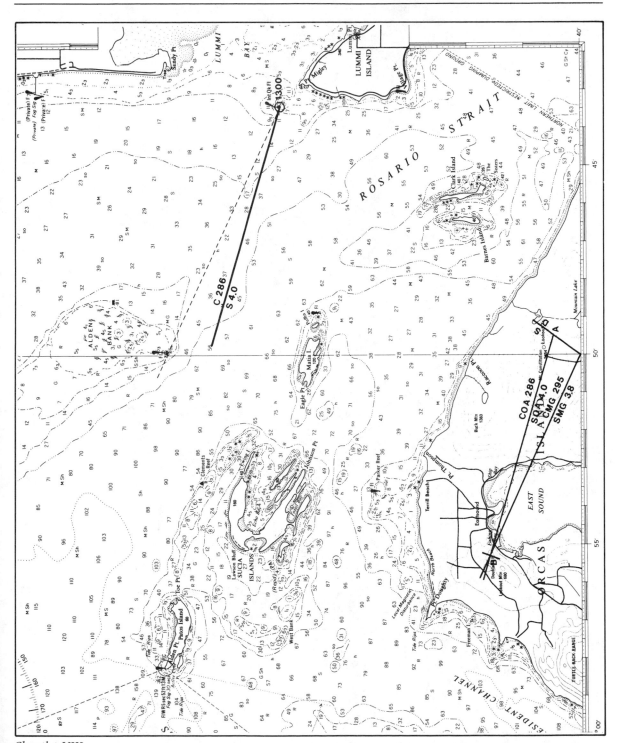

Chartlet VIII

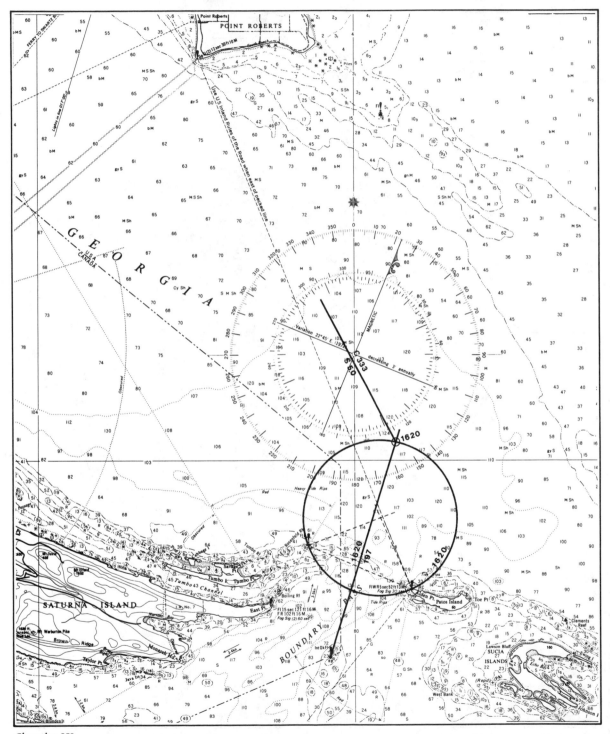

Chartlet IX

APPENDIX A
Compensating a Compass

"No amount of planning can ever replace dumb luck."
SAUNDERS' LAW OF NAVIGATION *#11*

Having installed your compass with due regard to the considerations outlined in Chapter 4, you will want to check it for accuracy and, if necessary, adjust or compensate it for the magnetic properties of your boat. In addition to performing this operation annually, you are advised to then re-establish your deviation table. The magnetic properties of your boat may change over the period in storage. You should also check the compass and deviation table for accuracy after the replacement of any major engine parts, or the installation of equipment that may have magnetic properties.

COMPENSATING

Follow the compass manufacturer's instructions. If none are available, store all gear aboard as for normal cruising and set all switches as would most frequently prevail. Select a sunny day in an area relatively free of traffic and with fairly calm water. Perform the following exercise under sail or power as you most frequently operate the boat.

1. Set the Devi-Sun on some spot where it is fairly level and in the sunlight. For instructions on how to make a Devi-Sun, the author's name for this handy gadget, see page 247.
2. Steer a course 000° according to your compass, and at the same time have a crew member rotate the shadow plate of the Devi-Sun so that the cursor makes a shadow on any line.
3. Reverse your course so that the cursor makes a shadow on the reciprocal line (180° opposite to the original line). *Do not steer by compass.*
4. While on this reciprocal course, use a non-magnetic screwdriver (see page 248) to turn the N-S screw in the compass case so as to remove ½ of any error by which the compass does not read

180°. You have approximately 4 minutes from the time that you set the Devi-Sun while travelling North until you must complete the adjustment in step 4.

5. Turn onto course 090° according to your compass and adjust the Devi-Sun shadow plate so that the cursor shadow falls on any line.

6. Reverse your course so that the cursor shadow falls on the reciprocal line to that in step 5. *Do not steer by compass*.

7. Rotate the E-W adjusting screw so as to remove $1/2$ of any error by which your compass does not read 270°. Again, you have 4 minutes from the time that you set the Devi-Sun while travelling East until you must complete the adjustment in step 7.

8. Turn onto compass course 000°.

9. Reset your Devi-Sun.

10. Turn onto reciprocal course according to the Devi-Sun.

11. Remove $1/2$ of error from 180° using N-S screw.

12. Turn onto compass course 090°.

13. Reset your Devi-Sun.

14. Turn onto reciprocal course according to the Devi-Sun.

15. Remove $1/2$ of error from 270° using E-W screw.

16. Repeat steps 8 to 15 until you are satisfied that you have the minimal or acceptable error.

17. Establish a deviation table as in Appendix B.

Compensation Summary
- Steer course 000° compass.
- Set Devi-Sun shadow.
- Steer reciprocal course per Devi-Sun shadow.
- Adjust N-S screw to $1/2$ error from 180°.
- Steer course 090° compass.
- Set Devi-Sun shadow.
- Steer reciprocal course per Devi-Sun shadow.
- Adjust E-W screw to $1/2$ error from 270°.
- Repeat all the steps as often as necessary.

DEVI-SUN CONSTRUCTION
Materials:

Two pieces of 6" square × $1/8$" thick tempered masonite, or plexiglass (opaque), or laminated plastic

One brass toilet tank valve lifter rod, approximately $1/16$" dia. × 8" long with ring ($1/4$" inside diameter) formed at 90° on one end.

One $1/4$" ×1" long brass bolt and brass nut. The nut should have a "capture insert" so that it will not turn freely when only snug.

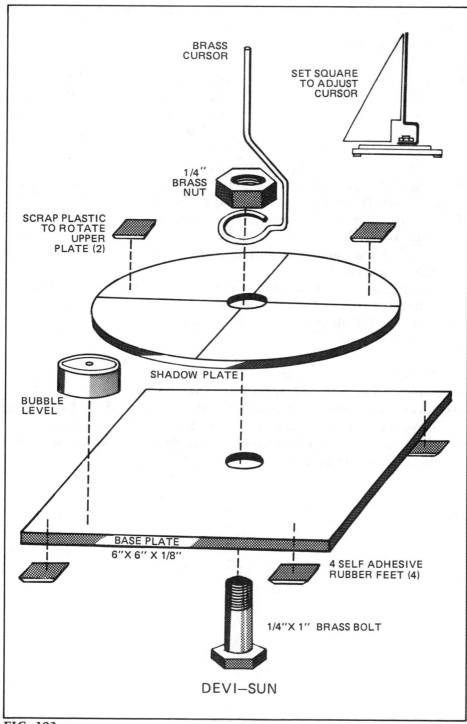

BRASS
CURSOR

SET SQUARE
TO ADJUST
CURSOR

1/4''
BRASS
NUT

SCRAP PLASTIC
TO ROTATE
UPPER
PLATE (2)

SHADOW PLATE

BUBBLE
LEVEL

BASE PLATE
6''X 6'' X 1/8''

4 SELF ADHESIVE
RUBBER FEET (4)

1/4''X 1'' BRASS BOLT

DEVI—SUN

FIG. 193

One circular bubble level with adhesive back, as used on music record turntables.

Four self-adhesive, non-skid feet.

Method:

1. Scribe a line through the centre of one of the plastic plates. Scribe another line through the centre at 90° to the first line. Fill the scribed lines with paint if necessary so they are readily visible against the white (or light) background of the plate.

2. Drill a $1/4''$ hole through the centre of both plates.

3. Cut the scribed plate to $5^3/4''$ diameter.

4. Cement two $1/4'' \times 1/2''$ pieces of scrap plate on top of the circular plate as shown. The exact position is not important.

5. Form the brass rod approximately as shown so that the rod will be concentric with the hole. The rod must be perpendicular to the base plate. Use a set square as shown to adjust by bending and re-check each time used.

6. Assemble as shown. Tighten the nut so that the top plate may be rotated but so that the rod does not wobble.

7. Install the bubble level on the base plate.

8. Install feet.

NON-MAGNETIC SCREWDRIVERS

Purchase a set of alignment tools from a radio parts supply store. These are plastic or aluminum "screwdriver-like" tools used for fine tuning of coils or transformers in radios or television sets. They are inexpensive and the end can be easily filed if necessary to fit the compensating screws on your compass.

APPENDIX B
Developing a Deviation Table

"Only that which is thought to be difficult is, in fact, difficult." ANON.

You will need:
- 1 boat.
- 1 compass, properly mounted so that a line between the centre of the compass card and the lubber line on the compass case is parallel to the vessel's keel.
- 1 pelorus.
- 1 pencil.
- 1 pad of paper.
- 1 parallel ruler.
- 1 chart of the area.
- 3 people (preferred), 2 people minimum.
- 2 to 3 hours of time.

SELECTING THE LOCATION
- You must be on a charted waterway.
- On smooth water; i.e., calm day and little traffic.
- In an area of water sufficient to allow running the vessel on a straight course at normal cruising speed for a minimum of 2 minutes ($1/2$ mile).
- Able to see a charted object at least 2 and preferably 6 miles distant from the selected location.

KNOWLEDGE AND ABILITY REQUIRED
- How to steer a compass course for a distance of at least $1/8$ of a mile.
- How to take a relative bearing with a pelorus.
- How to plot a line of position on a chart.
- How to convert true directions and magnetic directions to compass directions (TVMDC).
- How to add and subtract.

PREPARING THE VESSEL

Set the pelorus with the base lubber line parallel to keel; lubber line reads 000° on pelorus card; card as level as possible; and with a maximum radius of visibility of the entire horizon.

Establish your position; it should be the centre of a circle approximately ¼ mile or less in diameter and preferably close aboard a charted object, such as a floating aid to navigation.

Establish the position of some other visible, charted object, such as the CN Tower, steeple, water tower, conspicuous tree, centre of small island, etc.

Plot a line between your position and the other charted object. Determine the direction (true) of this line, consider variation and convert the true direction to magnetic direction (TVM).

Set all electrical switches to either on or off as would be their normal position when cruising.

OPERATING PROCEDURE

Pilot the vessel on a compass course 000° at normal cruising speed so you leave the floating, charted aid close aboard. The helmsman must concentrate on holding a steady course and continously saying "Mark" every time the vessel is on that course.

Because the helmsman is preoccupied with holding a constant course, it is strongly recommended that a lookout be standing by the helm to give warning of any potentially unsafe or discourteous situation. If the lookout detects such a situation, he immediately says "Danger" and takes over the helm. The lookout has responsibility and overall command of the vessel at all times.

At an instant that the helmsman has said "Mark," the bearing-taker notes the relative bearing of the distant object from the pelorus. The bearing-taker notes the compass course and the relative bearing on the work sheet.

The bearing-taker advises the helmsman of the next compass course to steer, say 015°. Fifteen degree increments are recommended. A new relative bearing on the distant object is taken for the new compass course and is noted on the work sheet opposite the new compass course. Continue this sequence until you have covered the complete circle by 15° increments.

Taking a Relative Bearing for Each Run Visually determine the approximate centre of your area of operation. (That point you used to determine the direction to the distant object.) If practical, drop a floating, anchored marker overboard at that point; a plastic bottle tied to a sash weight will suffice. This is not necessary if a floating aid is close by.

Assuming that your first compass course will be 000° compass, start at some point approximately South of the marker and steer course 000°.

The bearing-taker will continuously sight the distant object in the pelorus vanes. The helmsman will continuously say "mark" when exactly on the prescribed compass course. The lookout, in addition to being alert to potentially dangerous situations, will call "Marker Coming Up" when the vessel is approximately 100 yards from the point at which the marker will be abeam, and call "Marker Abeam" when the marker is abeam and "Marker Astern" when the marker is approximately 100 yards abaft the beam.

At some time between "Marker Coming Up" and "Marker Astern," and at a time that the helmsman is saying "Mark" and that the bearing-taker is satisfied the vessel is approximately level and on a stable course, the bearing-taker will note the relative bearing of the distant object. Enter the relative bearing on the work sheet opposite the appropriate compass course. Accuracy is improved the closer the vessel is to being "Marker Abeam" when the relative bearing is taken.

After noting the relative bearing, the bearing-taker states "Bearing Taken: Next Course XXX°." If no satisfactory bearing was taken, the bearing-taker will say, "No Bearing Taken: Repeat Run On Compass Course XXX°."

To make subsequent runs, repeat these procedures always starting the run so that the floating marker is approximately dead ahead when you are on the desired compass course. *Do not steer for the marker. Steer the specified compass course.* Having completed all runs at approximately 15° increments according to the compass and noted the appropriate relative bearings, adjourn to the clubhouse or quiet location to perform the necessary math (addition and subtraction only) which will result in an accurate deviation table for that particular vessel.

Figures 194 to 197 are sketches of a typical example of a location, how to follow these procedures, typical worksheets and the type of deviation table that will result. The hypothetical location is the entrance to Frenchman's Bay, Ontario. The sample latitudes, longitudes and directions are not necessarily correct! Establish your own locations and directions!

Accuracy

Distant object distance	6 miles	2 miles
Distance from marker when bearing taken	100 yards	25 yards
Error — less than	$1/2°$	$1/2°$

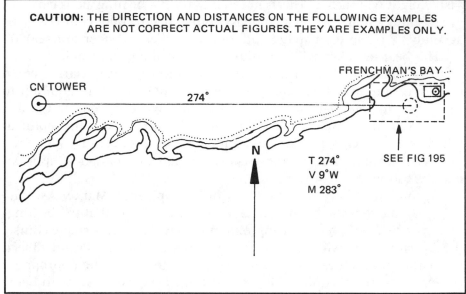

CAUTION: THE DIRECTION AND DISTANCES ON THE FOLLOWING EXAMPLES ARE NOT CORRECT ACTUAL FIGURES. THEY ARE EXAMPLES ONLY.

CN TOWER

274°

FRENCHMAN'S BAY

N

T 274°
V 9°W
M 283°

SEE FIG 195

FIG. 194

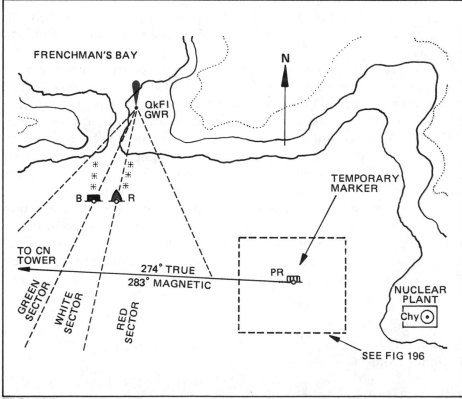

FRENCHMAN'S BAY

N

QkFl
GWR

B   R

TO CN
TOWER

274° TRUE
283° MAGNETIC

GREEN SECTOR

WHITE SECTOR

RED SECTOR

TEMPORARY
MARKER

PR

NUCLEAR
PLANT

Chy

SEE FIG 196

FIG. 195

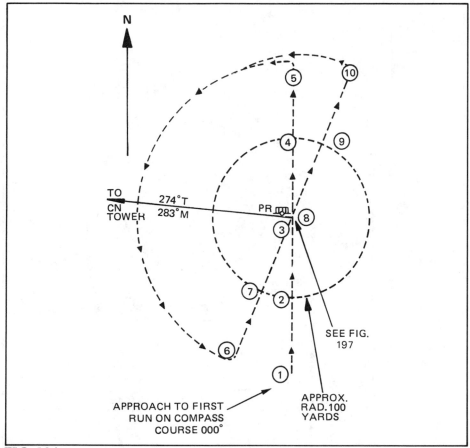

FIG. 196

Worksheet

VESSEL: MY VERY OWN

DATE: XX/XX/XX

1. Location of approximate centre
of deviation runs L   xx° xx.x′ N Or S
λ   xx° xx.x′ E or W
2. Location of distant object L   xx° xx.x′ N or S
λ   xx° xx.x′ E or W
3. Distance to distant object . . . . xx.x n.m.
4. True direction from point 1 to point 2 — xxx°
5. Magnetic direction from point 1 to point 2 — xxx°
T   xxx°
V   xx° E or W (from chart)
M   xxx° (enter in column D on worksheet)

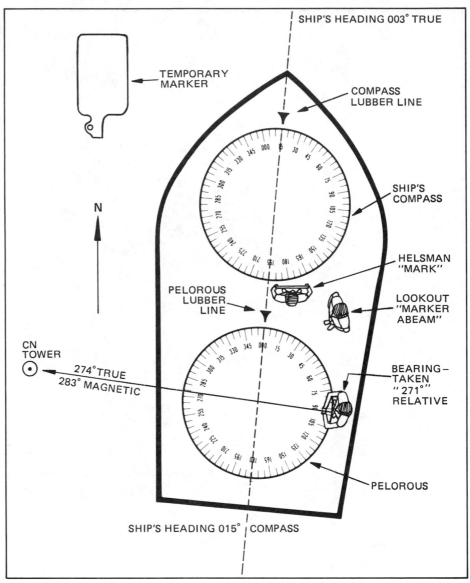

SHIP'S HEADING 003° TRUE

TEMPORARY MARKER

COMPASS LUBBER LINE

N

SHIP'S COMPASS

HELSMAN "MARK"

PELOROUS LUBBER LINE

LOOKOUT "MARKER ABEAM"

CN TOWER

274° TRUE
283° MAGNETIC

BEARING – TAKEN " 271°" RELATIVE

PELOROUS

SHIP'S HEADING 015° COMPASS

FIG. 197

6. __Pelorus card set at 000°.

__Pelorus lubber line parallel to keel.

__Speed of runs — _____knots, RPM _____.

__Switches/radios at normal position.

__Gear stowed as for normal cruising.

__Lookout authority and responsibility understood by all.

__No abnormal ferrous or electrical objects adjacent to compass.

DATA					
A Compass course + steered °	**B** Relative bearing = to dist. object °	**C** Compass bearing ~ to dist. object °	**D** Magnetic direction = to dist. object °	**E** Deviation amount °	**F** Deviation direction E or W
000	285	285	283	2	W
015	271	286	283	3	W
030	257	287	283	4	W
045	244	289	283	6	W
060	231	291	283	8	W
075	218	293	283	10	W
090	204	294	283	11	W
105	187	292	283	9	W
120	171	etc.	etc.	etc.	etc.
135	etc.	etc.	etc.	etc.	etc.
150	etc.				
165					
180					
etc.					
etc.					
360					

Deviation (Column E) is the difference between column C and column D while on the compass course in Column A. Deviation is West if column C is greater than column D.

PREPARING THE TABLE

With the compass course from column A and the deviation from column E calculate the magnetic course and rewrite columns A and E to your preferred format. The following format, for example, is that used in the deviation table for practice problems and examples in this book. It is similar to that employed by Canadian Power Squadrons in their "Basic Boating Course."

Do *not* use this table for your boat or any examples or problems in this book. For instructions on how to use a deviation table, see Appendix C, page 258.

SHIP'S HEADING MAGNETIC °	DEVIATION °	SHIP'S HEADING COMPASS °	SHIP'S HEADING MAGNETIC °	DEVIATION °	SHIP'S HEADING COMPASS °
358	2W	000	179	1W	180
012	3W	015	195	0	195
026	4W	030	212	2E	210
039	6W	045	228	3E	225
052	8W	060	245	5E	240
065	10W	075	265	10E	255
079	11W	090	283	13E	270
096	9W	105	etc.	etc.	285
etc.	8W	120	etc.	etc.	300
etc.	5W	135			315
	3W	150			330
	etc.	165			345
	etc.	180			360

Example

You select the area outside the entrance to Frenchman's Bay channel adjacent to the nuclear power station. Plot a circle approximately 0.1 to 0.2 miles in diameter and plot a line between the centre of this circle and the distant object (in this case the CN Tower). Determine the direction of this line toward the distant object by measurement on the outer compass rose. Label the direction (274°). Convert this true direction to magnetic (TVM):

$$\begin{array}{ccc} T & V & M \\ 274° & 9°W & 283° \end{array}$$

Refer to Figures 194 to 197, but be aware that the directions and distances are not correct, actual figures. They are examples only.

Run #1   Compass Course 000°

1. Turn onto compass course 000°
2. "Marker Coming Up"
3. "Marker Abeam"
4. "Marker Astern"
   — take relative bearing between 2 and 4
5. Turn to return for second run 015°

Run #2   Compass Course 015°

6. Turn onto compass course 015°: Caution: wait for your wake to subside.

7. "Marker Coming Up"

8. "Marker Abeam"

9. "Marker Astern"

10. Turn to return for third run 030° and continue the procedure.

CN Tower

True bearing	T	274°
Variation	V	9°W
Magnetic bearing	M	283°
Deviation	D	— Therefore deviation = 3°W
Compass bearing	C	286° — On compass course 015°

Compass Bearing = Compass Course 015° + Relative Bearing 271° = 286°

APPENDIX C

Practice Deviation Table

"The obvious may be devious."   AL'S COGENT COMMENT.

This is a theoretical table developed for examples in the text. You must construct a similar table for your own vessel based on your own figures. The amount of deviation shown here is more than one would expect in a well compensated, properly located compass. Your own deviation table must be checked annually or each time you relocate, change, add or delete any gear with magnetic properties. Installing a new cylinder head could, for example, affect deviation, because it may have significantly different magnetic properties than the old cylinder head.

HOW TO USE A DEVIATION TABLE
If you know the magnetic direction (course or bearing) and wish to know the compass direction (course or bearing):

> Enter the magnetic direction in the appropriate column in the table, say 168°.
> Use the closest magnetic direction (165°).
> Deviation is 8°E.
> Deviation East — Compass Least.
> Therefore, subtract 8° from 168° magnetic.
> Answer: 160° compass.

> If you know the compass direction (course or bearing) and wish to know the magnetic direction (course or bearing):

> Enter the compass direction in the appropriate column in the table, say 183°.
> Use the closest compass direction (191°)

MAGNETIC HEADING	DEVIATION	COMPASS HEADING	MAGNETIC HEADING	DEVIATION	COMPASS HEADING
000°	6°W	006°	180°	6°E	174°
015°	4°W	019°	195°	4°E	191°
030°	2°W	032°	210°	2°E	208°
045°	0°	045°	225°	0°	225°
060°	2°E	058°	240°	2°W	242°
075°	4°E	071°	255°	4°W	259°
090°	6°E	084°	270°	7°W	277°
105°	8°E	097°	285°	8°W	293°
120°	10°E	110°	300°	9°W	309°
135°	12°E	123°	315°	11°W	326°
150°	10°E	140°	330°	10°W	340°
165°	8°E	157°	345°	7°W	352°
180°	6°E	174°	360° (000°)	6°W	006°

Deviation is 4°E.
Deviation East — Compass Least,
Therefore, add 4° to 183° compass.
Answer: 187°.

If your known direction, either compass or magnetic falls exactly midway between two listed directions, use the deviation for the larger of the two entries. Say, for example, you require the deviation for 285° compass.

285° compass falls midway between 277° and 293° compass.
Using 293°, deviation would be 8°W deviation.

Answer: M   D   C
            277°   8°W   285°

For more accurate results, you should interpolate the deviation for all intermediate readings. This is especially true when the total deviation is extreme, as in the case of the theoretical boat used in examples in this book. Interpolation has *not* been used in the early problems. However, in Section III and in the final Practice Cruise, this more advanced technique has been employed.

INTERPOLATION

If you required an extremely accurate magnetic heading for the compass heading 250°, you would interpolate in the following manner:

Mag.	Dev.	Comp.	
240°	2°W	242°	Next lower tabulation
		250°	Required
255°	4°W	259°	Next higher tabulation

250° is closer to 242° than 259°.

250° is 8° from 242°.

The difference between the bracketed tabulations is

$$259° - 242° = 17°$$

The required deviation is $^8/_{17}$ of the difference in deviation between the tabulated entries plus the deviation of the closest heading:

$$\frac{8}{17} \times 2° \ (4°W - 2°W)$$

$$= \frac{8}{17} \times 2 = \frac{16}{17} = 1° \text{ (closest whole degree)}$$

Therefore, the required deviation is 1° from the deviation of 242° and is between the deviation for 242° and 259° (2°W + 1° = 3°W). The answer is:

M	D	C
247°	3°W	250°

If you required an interpolated compass heading for the magnetic heading of 265°, you would calculate in this manner:

M	D	C
255°	4°W	259°
265°		
270°	7°W	277°

$$\frac{5}{15} \times 3° = 1° \qquad 7°W - 1° = 6°W$$

The answer is:

M	D	C
265°	6°W	271°

APPENDIX D
Elementary Electronic Navigation

"Always be prepared for the worst. If it happens, you are ready for it. If it doesn't happen, you will be pleasantly surprised."   ANON.

DEPTH SOUNDERS AND RADIO DIRECTION FINDERS

It is assumed here that the reader has access to the installation and operating instructions for this elementary equipment. There are so many makes and models that it is not practical to offer detailed installation, operating, tuning and adjustment instructions. The intent is to offer a few suggestions on the use of depth sounders and radio direction finders in small boat navigation.

Both instruments have extremely similar characteristics, limitations and uses. They both require a source of power, either batteries or external power. They are both subject to electronic/electrical circuit failure caused by such things as vibration, moisture and contact corrosion. Both demand considerable experience for interpretation to their full potential. Their accuracy, range, etc. are highly dependent on location, adjustment and correction tables supplied by the manufacturer. Maximum value is obtained when they are used during periods of limited visibility or when making land fall in an unknown area, when it is dark or when there are few land marks or aids to navigation. You will require supplementary data: tide or water level tables and/or marine radio aids to navigation.

CAUTION should be exercised, because the data from a depth sounder or radio direction finder (RDF) will not generally be sufficiently accurate to negotiate in extremely confined waters, nor to result in as accurate an LOP as can be obtained by most other means. They do, however, provide valuable information for the navigator; in some cases they may be the only source of information.

Depth Sounder   The primary uses of a depth sounder are to obtain an LOP by establishing a line of soundings, determine distance off by depth or to run a contour course. In all of these cases, you must have a chart of the area, know the height of water relative to chart datum through the use of tide tables or inland water level charts, and you must know the vertical distance from the water surface to the transponder. You must also have a depth correction chart for the specific boat if the depth sounder has any significant non-adjustable errors.

Line of Soundings   To obtain an LOP by a line of soundings, steer a constant course at a constant speed and note a series of soundings well before reaching confining waters. Your chart should look like this example.

CHART — NON METRIC

Date — XXX/XX/XXXX
Approx. Location — YYYYYYYYYYYYYYYYYYY
Chart # — ZZZ
Depth of transponder of 3' included in listed depths.
Height of water above (below) datum —.
Speed — 5.0
Course (true) — 285°
Time of start — 1020
Time of finish — 1044

Elapsed Time (minutes)	Depth (in fathoms)	Distance
0.0	12	
2.4	12	0.2
4.8	11	0.4
7.2	11	0.6
9.6	10	0.8
12.0	8	1.0
14.4	9	1.2
16.8	11	1.4
19.2	12	1.6
21.6	13	1.8
24.0	12	2.0

Prepare a chart similar to the example and fill in date, approximate location, chart number of the area (largest scale available), the speed which you will maintain and the true course equivalent of the compass course which you will maintain.

Note the time at which you start to record the soundings and note the depth from the depth sounder read-out after adding the transponder depth.

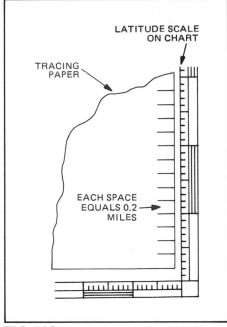

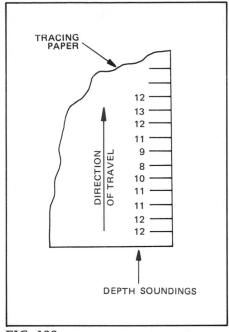

FIG. 198   **FIG. 199**

Take depth soundings at intervals of 0.2 of a nautical mile or 1216 feet and record the depth, including the transponder depth, and the distance from the first sounding and elapsed time between soundings. To take a reading each 0.2 miles you must establish the time required to travel 0.2 miles at your rate of speed. Use this formula: minutes of time = 12 ÷ speed (in knots). In this example,

$$\text{minutes} = \frac{12}{S} = \frac{12}{5} = 2.4 \text{ minutes} = 2 \text{ minutes, 24 seconds}$$

On one edge of a piece of tissue paper mark off intervals 0.2 miles by using the latitude scale of the chart. (See Fig. 198.) Note the corresponding depths on that (depth contour) piece of paper. (See Fig. 199.) Orient the edge of the paper on the chart so that it points in the true direction that you were travelling at the time of the soundings. Oriented in this fashion, slide the tissue around the chart in the general area of your DR position and match the depths on the paper as closely as possible to the soundings on the chart. At the point of closest match draw a line on the chart along the edge of the paper. (See Fig. 200.)

This line represents a line of position on which you can plot an EP, or that you can use with some other LOP to plot a fix. Although these positions may be of somewhat debatable accuracy, they may be the best available and are probably better than instinct.

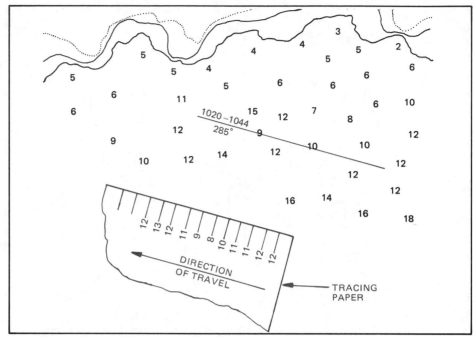

FIG. 200

Distance Off At the same time that a bearing is obtained on one shore-based object, record the depth (adding transponder depth) in your log. Under favourable conditions (a fairly constant and somewhat steep bottom contour), you will be able to determine your distance off from the object by noting the point along your LOP that the chart sounding approximately agrees with the depth noted in your log.

Running a Contour Course It is assumed that you are approaching a landfall and know on which side your destination lies. You may have "steered a Chichester" by keeping well to starboard of a course toward your destination, thus knowing that you must turn to port after making landfall. By examination of the chart you may be able to select a depth such that, if it is maintained, it will keep you on a safe course. Although it may be circuitous, a contour course of this kind will keep you well offshore yet within sight of landfall when visibility (or access to other LOP data) improves. Follow such a depth contour until you estimate that you are abeam of your destination and then anchor or stand-off until you are able to verify your position by some more accurate method.

RADIO DIRECTION FINDER

The primary uses of a radio direction finder (RDF) are to obtain one or more LOP to establish a fix, follow a (radio) danger bearing or to run a "homing" course.

You are urged to use marine radio stations intended primarily for the purpose of marine navigation. Their frequencies and signal characteristics are available in various government publications and, together with updated *Notices to Mariners*, are available from your chart dealer.

Avoid the use of aero-beacons or commercial broadcast stations. Aero station locations are shown on aerocharts and updated only by *Notices to Airmen*. Commercial station transmitters may not even be located in the same city as the call signal would indicate, and they could be using alternate or relocated facilities. In both cases, the transmitter may be situated well inland, increasing the error due to radiowave refraction. If your set lacks a sense antenna, be cautious of "reciprocal error," or an ambiguity of 180° error in reading.

You are advised to use the ship's compass only (not the RDF compass) for any aspect of navigation. You are also advised to set the RDF pelorus card so that 000°/180° is parallel to your keel and read all bearings as relative.

LOP by RDF   From the "Marine Aids to Navigation" obtain the location, latitude and longitude, frequency of transmission, call letters or signal characteristics, and times of broadcasts for one or more station. Select stations for the best "angle of cut" of LOPs for a fix, ideally 90° for a two-bearing fix.

Tune the station and identify it. Rotate the antenna for best null (minimum signal), keeping hand and body contact and interference to a minimum. Read the relative bearing and correct it for radio deviation only using the RDF deviation card and *radio signal relative bearing*. Add the corrected relative bearing to your true course. The result equals the true bearing to the radio transmitter location.

In a similar manner take a second RDF bearing or some other type of bearing, then plot and label your LOP and the resultant fix.

RDF Danger Bearing   In a way similar to determining a visual danger bearing angle as described in Chapter 15, it is possible to obtain a danger bearing using an RDF transmitting station. Maintain a course by RDF pelorus by using your RDF to tune for maximum null (minimum signal), rather than sighting with your standard pelorus.

Allow an extra 5° or 10° to clear the hazard due to the lesser accuracy of RDF. Always use visual aids when possible. Do not rely on RDF for "close quarters" navigation.

Homing Course by RDF   Select an RDF station at, or close to, your

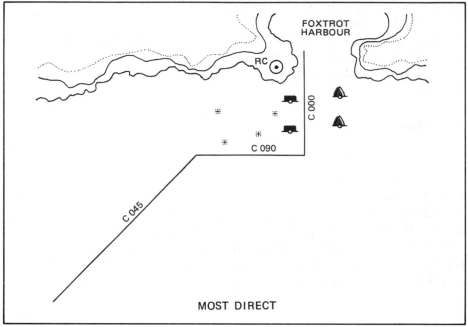

FIG. 201

destination or some convenient intermediate location. After tuning and identifying the receiver for the station and turning the antenna to locate null, determine the relative bearing from the RDF pelorus. Change course so that the relative RDF bearing will be 000°, and you will home in on the transmitter. In extremely limited visibility, it is obviously best that you do not approach too close. Be certain to establish from your chart that no hazard lies too close to your intended course.

If you find that you are continuously adjusting your course in one direction, it is probably due to current or leeway. Rotate the RDF antenna 5° (to starboard if you are continously adjusting course to port, or vice-versa) to allow for drift. If too much or too little, readjust until you can run a fairly constant course.

Homing Course to Finals   Due to excessive refraction close to a shoreline or other possible hazards, you may wish to stay somewhat offshore rather than taking the most direct route to the RDF station near a harbour entrance. (See Figs. 201-202.) In such a situation, follow this procedure:

1. Select station, tune RDF and identify signal, turn antenna for null and note relative bearing from RDF.
2. Add RDF relative bearing to true course to obtain true bearing.

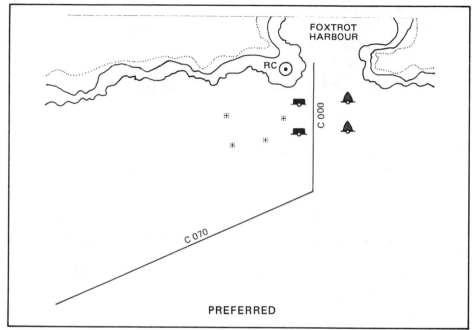

FIG. 202

3. If you wish to *leave the EDF Station on your port side* (as in Fig. 202), *add* 25° or 30° to the true bearing. The result is your true course to steer. Convert this to a compass course and steer that course. If you wish to *leave the RDF station on your starboard side*, *deduct* 25° or 30° from the true bearing. The result would be your true course to steer. The exact amount of addition (or deduction) between 25° and 30° is somewhat arbitrary. The amount of 25 – 30° is probably the optimum in the majority of cases.

4. While steering the course established in step 3, reset your RDF antenna to the true bearing of your final course (in this example 000° or 360°):
True Bearing = True Course + Relative Bearing
Relative Bearing = True Bearing – True Course
Relative Bearing = 360° – 070°
Relative Bearing = 290°

5. Leave RDF antenna on 290° relative. Steer true course 070° until RDF reaches maximum null then turn onto final course.

6. Reset RDF antenna to 000° relative and follow null until you see the outer channel markers or stand off until visibility improves.

APPENDIX E

RPM/Speed Curve

"It is more important to know where you are going than to get there fast."   SAUNDERS' LAW OF NAVIGATION #12

Some pleasure boats are equipped with knotmeters or speedometers that provide read-out in nautical miles per hour (knots) or statute miles per hour. These devices are operated by various means and vary widely in accuracy. Accurate results with such meters are not generally possible over a large range of operating speeds.

A good back-up for these instruments and/or an alternative method of obtaining a continuous read-out of speed through the water when operating under power is the engine tachometer (RPM indicator). A typical RPM/speed chart may look like this:

RPM (max. 4200) Speed (knots)	1000 2.0	1100	1200	1300 3.0	1400	1500 4.0	1600	1700 5.0	1800	1900 6.0
RPM Speed (knots)	2000 6.7	2100 7.4	2200 8.0	2300	2400 9.0	2500	2600	2700 10.0	2800 11.0	2900 13.0
RPM Speed (knots)	3000 14.0	3100 16.5	3200 19.0	3300 21.5	3400 24.0	3500 26.0	3600 *27.5	3700 28.5	3800 29.0	3900 29.5

*Maximum continuous RPM.

In addition, you may prefer to have a graph from which you can determine your speed for any engine RPM. (See Fig. 203.)

Distance measuring equipment may also be a part of the vessel's instrumentation, either as part of the speedometer or knotmeter, or as a separate instrument (Sumlog, for instance). These devices resemble a trip odometer in an automobile and can usually be reset to "0" in order to measure distance travelled through the water for each voyage or a part of each voyage. They are usually operated by an underwater impeller and are reasonably accurate.

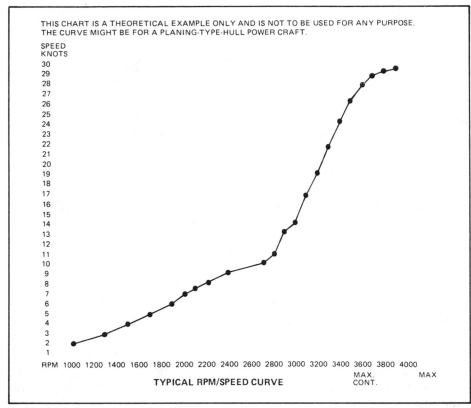

THIS CHART IS A THEORETICAL EXAMPLE ONLY AND IS NOT TO BE USED FOR ANY PURPOSE. THE CURVE MIGHT BE FOR A PLANING-TYPE-HULL POWER CRAFT.

TYPICAL RPM/SPEED CURVE

FIG. 203

DEVELOPING A SPEED CURVE

Select an area of light traffic with little or no current and little or no wind. There should be two aids or a combination of aids whose distance apart can be accurately determined. The aids should be at least one and preferably two miles apart; their situation should be such that a position abeam can be accurately determined. Two ranges two miles apart would be ideal.

Make two runs, one in each direction at increments of 100 RPM. With a stopwatch, time the run in each direction. Using the formula 60D = St, calculate the speed for the run in each direction. Do *not* add the times. Average the two speeds for each RPM setting. Plot and/or chart the results. Periodically and randomly check the chart for accuracy. The chart must be re-established if your propellers are changed, or if the trim or displacement of the boat is substantially altered.

The results will be incorrect if you average the time and then calculate the speed. You *must* calculate the speed for each direction and then average the two speeds.

APPENDIX F
Plotting Symbols and Abbreviations

"Navigation: The art of getting from here to there while still afloat."
A DEFINITION BY A. SAUNDERS

Symbols and practices for plotting and labelling vary from country to country and from one area to another. Those shown here should not be taken as absolute. They represent a combination of references to a number of leading texts on the subject, as well as the author's own experience. Significant deviations from common practice in your area of boating are discouraged. It is preferable that anyone involved in navigation or position finding on the vessel be familiar with the method used aboard that boat.

SYMBOL

USE

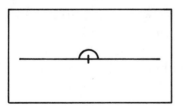

DR *(dead reckon position), position determined by calculations of course, speed and time.*

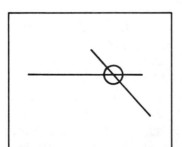

Fix, *lines of position established by compass, pelorus, sextant, echo sounding, line of sight (range), station pointer, or by being close aboard a charted object.*

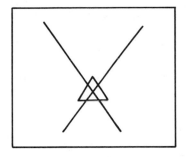

Fix, *at least one line of position was obtained by radar, radio direction finder or some other electronic signal receiver (e.g., Loran).*

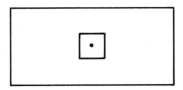

EP *(estimated position), position determined by course, speed and time. DR plus additional factors of estimates for leeway and drift or incomplete data such as one line of position. Sometimes referred to as most probable position (MPP).*

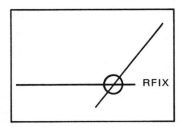

Running Fix *(R Fix), a position determined by lines of position where at least one line of position has been advanced or retarded in time and allowance made for DR movement between the times. Also where at least one line of position was determined over a period of time such as a distance-off by bow and beam bearings.*

Of these symbols, only the running fix need be labelled, as all others are self-explanatory. The time of determination of the position should be expressed in four digits of 24-hour time to the closest minute. A fix position (except close aboard a charted object) should also include a note of the vessel's position (latitude and longitude). Except for DR positions, labelling should be horizontal. The time of the DR should be at an acute angle to the horizontal.

SYMBOL   **USE**

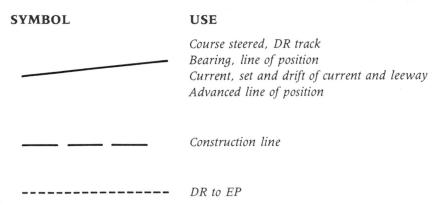

*Course steered, DR track
Bearing, line of position
Current, set and drift of current and leeway
Advanced line of position*

Construction line

DR to EP

PLOTTING AND LABELLING
Plot and label all directions as true.

EXAMPLE	REMARK

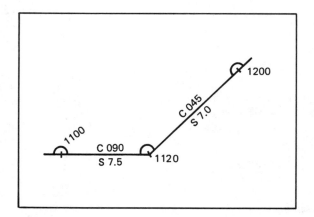

DR Track

Symbol at each hour.
Symbol at each change of course and/or speed.
Label time of each DR.
Label course line — DR track (course steered)

$$\frac{C090 \ (course)}{S6.0 \ (speed \ in \ knots)}$$

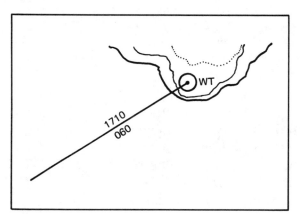

Bearing (LOP)

$$\frac{1710 \ (time \ of \ bearing)}{060 \ (direction \ \text{toward} \ object)}$$

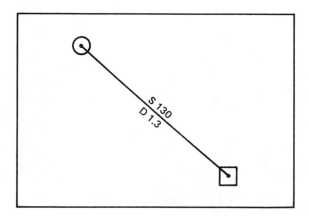

Current Set and Drift

$$\frac{S130 \ (direction \ \text{toward} \ which \ vessel}{is \ being \ set)}$$
$$\frac{}{D1.3 \ (rate, \ in \ knots, \ at \ which}{vessel \ is \ being \ set)}$$

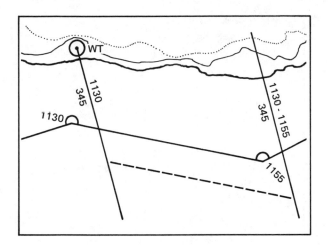

Advanced LOP

$$\frac{1130 \ (time \ of \ bearing)}{345 \ (direction \ \text{toward} \ object)}$$

1130–1155 (time of bearing) –
time to which bearing advanced)
345 *(direction* toward *object)*

Construction line from any point on LOP for net direction and distance of travel between DR establishes any point on advanced LOP.

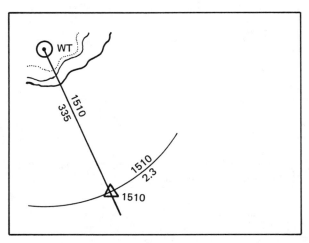

Radar Fix

$$\frac{1510 \ (time \ of \ bearing)}{335 \ (direction \ \text{toward} \ object)}$$
1510 (time of distance determination)
2.3 (distance-off in nautical miles)

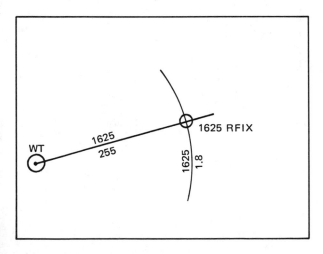

Running fix (distance-off by bow and beam bearings)

1625. Time of second bearing used to calculate distance off and beam bearing.
1.8 *(distance-off in nautical miles)*

Fix (close aboard a charted object)

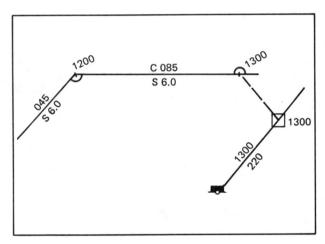

EP (determined without considering current)

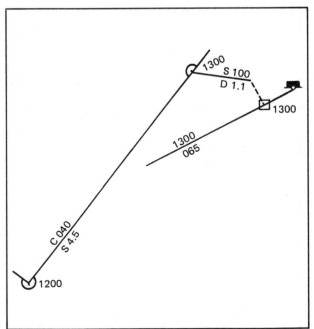

EP (determined taking into consideration estimated effect of wind and current)

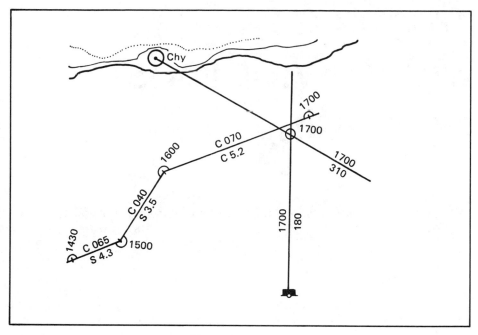

Two Bearing Fix

The fix position is the intersection of the LOP 1700 at 310° and the LOP 1700 at 180°.

The DR course line is no part of this fix. This is not *a three-bearing fix with a cocked hat.*

There are many other combinations of lines and plots to be labelled. They will be based on combinations of the above. The L and λ may be omitted from the chart for a fix or running fix if they are listed in your log.

APPENDIX G
Other Methods of Plotting

"If you know two things; you must forget two things in order to know nothing."
AN OBVIOUS TRUTH.

There are other methods of plotting than using the parallel rules discussed earlier in this book. The decision of which is best or fastest or most accurate is largely a matter of personal preference.

Visit your local chart dealer, and he will likely show you parallel rules, a Douglas protractor, a Paralline Plotter, plotting protractors and overlays, course protractors, circular protractors and semi-circular protractors. They will vary in price from $1.00 to $25.00 or $30.00. Some of the more expensive devices come with instruction sheets. The less expensive ones do not, but they are either self-explanatory or not worth the time of discussion.

The writer personally prefers a clear plastic straight edge and 30°/60° drafting set square; the total cost is approximately $4.00 for both a 15" straight edge and a 12" set square. The 12" square is ideal for large-size charts and a full-size plotting table. For smaller charts (folded or strip charts on smaller boats), buy an extra set consisting of a 9" straight edge and 6" set square for about $3.00.

PLOTTING WITH A STRAIGHT EDGE
AND SET SQUARE

With a permanent ink, felt-tipped, overhead foil marking pen, draw a straight red line on one surface of the set square along the hypotenuse, approximately ⅛" in from the edge. This serves as a reminder that that edge is always the measuring or drawing edge.

To draw a course line, bearing LOP, set and drift line in a specific direction, lay the set square on the closest compass rose with the

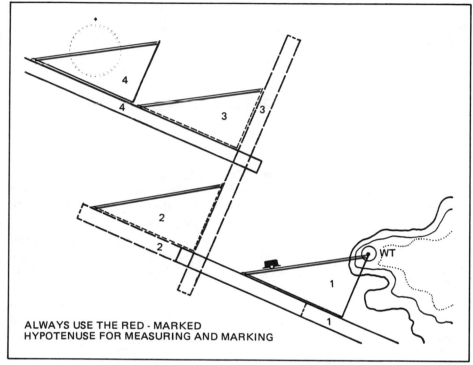

ALWAYS USE THE RED - MARKED
HYPOTENUSE FOR MEASURING AND MARKING

FIG. 204 *Example of moving set square to transfer line to rose for determining direction. Always use the red-marked hypotenuse for measuring and marking.*

hypotenuse lined up between the centre of the rose and the desired direction of the line. This is similar to using a parallel rule. While pressing heavily on the set square to prevent movement, bring the edge of the straight edge up to the longer or shorter side of the set square. Press heavily on the straight edge, while easing pressure on the set square and moving it in the desired direction. Alternate movement of each until the set square is in position to draw the desired line. The direction of travel of the set square is governed by the side of the set square against which the straight edge is held during movement of the set square.

To measure the direction of a line on the chart, set the reference edge of the set square on the line and move it to the compass rose by the same process, just as you would with parallel rules. (see Fig. 204.)

Glossary

"If you got there at all, you did something right." SAUNDERS' FINAL LAW OF NAVIGATION

Aid to Navigation An object, either man-made or natural, whose position is plotted on a chart and can be readily seen from the waterway.

Angle of Cut The angle of intersection of two plotted lines on a chart.

Azimuth Direction from one object to another, measured as an angle in degrees between a reference line between the vessel and the True North Pole and a line between the vessel and an object.

Azimuth Ring A circular device with sighting vanes that fits over the compass to enable accurate readings of compass bearings; also called an azimuth circle.

Beam Athwartships direction or structural member; also the maximum width of a vessel at the gunwale.

Beam Bearing See bearing.

Bear To be located, as in the buoy bears 065° relative: the buoy is located on a line which is at an angle of 65° to the ship's heading.

Bearing An angle, as in the angle between a line toward an object and some reference line, such as the ship's heading. A beam bearing is the bearing of an object from the vessel when it is abeam or has a relative bearing to the vessel of 090° (on the starboard side) or 270° (on the port side). A bow bearing is the bearing of an object from the vessel when a line toward the object is at an angle of 045° to the direction in which the ship is heading; 045° relative (starboard) or 315° (port). A quarter bearing is a relative bearing of 135° or 225°. See also danger bearing.

Bow Bearing See bearing.

CMG Course made good; the direction of actual progress between two points which was made by a vessel with respect to the surface of the earth.

COG Course over the ground; the direction of actual progress between two points being made by a vessel with respect to the surface of the earth.

Chart A graphic display of some portion of the earth's surface on a piece of paper intended for the planning or plotting of a vessel's movements; a map for nautical use.

Chartlet A portion of a chart.

Circular LOP See LOP.

Close Aboard Within a short distance of the vessel, so that for plotting purposes the vessel may be assumed to be in the same position as the object.

Close Reach When sailing, the vessel is headed so that the wind blows across the boat from a direction of approximately 60° to 80° either side of directly over the bow.

Cocked Hat A triangle enclosed by three lines of position which (due to some inaccuracies) do not intersect at one point.

Compass A device used aboard a vessel to determine directions of objects or the vessel's course with respect to compass North.

Compass Rose A circle graduated in degrees clockwise from 000° through 360° printed on charts; 000° indicates the direction of true North. On coastal and inland charts, a second much smaller circle may be superimposed so that 000° indicates the direction of magnetic North.

Compensation The process of adjusting magnets internally or externally on a compass so as to minimize the deviation error of other magnetic fields aboard the vessel.

Course The direction of the path or intended path of the vessel. A collision course is one that, if it remains unchanged, will result in a collision between the vessel and another object or vessel.

Course Made Good See CMG.

Course Over the Ground See COG.

Course Steered The direction in which the vessel is intended to head or to point so as to follow that direction through the water; the dead reckoning course.

Current The horizontal flow of water.

Cut The intersection of two lines plotted on a chart; see also angle of cut.

DR The process of establishing courses, speeds, positions based on calculations and ignoring variable factors, such as current, leeway, etc.

Danger Angle The horizontal angle between two charted objects or the vertical angle between two parts of one charted object as measured from the vessel. The vessel's position is maintained so that the angle will always be larger or smaller, and the vessel will pass closer to the larger or further from the smaller of the object(s).

Danger Bearing A bearing taken on a charted object from the vessel so that the vessel will traverse a safe passage if a course is steered to maintain a smaller or greater bearing dependant on the relative location of the hazard and the charted object. See bearing.

Danger Circle A circle described on a chart based on a vertical or horizontal danger angle, indicating the inner or outer approach to or from an object when maintaining the angle as measured from the vessel.

Datum A reference level from which other conditions or objects are measured: tidal water level, heights, depths.

Dead Reckoning See DR.

Depth Sounder A device aboard a vessel that indicates and/or records the depth of water directly under the boat from the position of a hull-mounted transponder.

Deviation The angular difference between the direction from the vessel to the Magnetic North Pole and the direction to the Magnetic North Pole as indicated by the compass.

Direction The horizontal relationship of one object or location to another without considering distance.

Diurnal A daily occurrence.

Draft The minimum depth of water required to float a vessel.

Drift The horizontal movement of a floating object caused by the movement of water or wind; also the distance of such movement, or the rate of speed of such movement.

EP Estimated position; the position of the vessel arrived at by adjusting the dead reckoning or calculated position by an amount to account for other (usually estimated) data, such as leeway, drift, a single line of position, etc. Also called MPP — most probable position.

ETA Estimated time of arrival; a precalculated determination of an arrival time at some destination based on the distance to be travelled and the predicted rate of travel.

Ebb The reduction in water height caused by tidal action or the outgoing flow of water (current) caused by a falling tide.

Echo Sounder See depth sounder.

Equator An imaginary line on the surface of the earth connecting all points which are equidistant from the North and South poles.

Estimated Position See EP.

Estimated Time of Arrival See ETA.

Fathom A unit of measure, usually depth, equal to 6 feet or 1.8 metres.

Fix A positive determination of the vessel's position at some specific point in time; frequently determined by the intersection of two or more lines of position. See Rfix.

Flood   A rise in the depth of water caused by tidal action. The shoreward movement of water (current) caused by tidal action.

Heading   The direction in which a vessel's bow is pointed at any instant in time; usually synonymous with course steered.

Horizontal Danger Angle   See danger angle.

Interpolation   A method of determining information from a table when the desired information falls between two table entries; usually a proportional determination of the desired intermediate value.

Knot   A nautical value for a measure of speed: 1 nautical mile per hour.

Knotmeter   A device aboard a vessel for measuring its rate of speed in knots (nautical miles per hour).

LOP   A line of position that can be plotted on a chart and on which the vessel is known to be located. An advanced LOP is one that has been relocated to reflect the movement (direction and distance) of the vessel since the line was determined; it is relocated to the later position of the vessel. A circular LOP is an arc of a circle whose radius represents the distance between the vessel and the object used to establish the LOP. A retarded LOP is a line of position that has been relocated to reflect the movement of the vessel since an earlier line was determined; it is relocated to the earlier position of the vessel.

Latitude   The distance North or South of the equator measured as an angle in degrees, minutes and tenths of minutes.

Leading Lights   A pair of lights located in line so that when the lights are observed to be in line the vessel is located in the desired position.

Leeway   The horizontal movement of a vessel caused by wind.

Line of Position   See LOP.

Log   A journal in which is recorded all pertinent data with respect to a vessel's movements. See Sumlog.

Longitude   The angular distance East or West of Greenwich measured in degrees, minutes and tenths of minutes.

Lubber Line   A line or mark on the compass case to indicate that point at which the compass course should be read from the compass card.

MPP   Most probable position. See E.P.

Magnetic Field   An area of magnetic influence where the molecules in iron or ferrous metals are lined up and thus attract or repel other pieces of iron.

Meridian   A reference line on a globe or chart that extends North from the South Pole directly to the North Pole. See longitude.

Most Probable Position   See MPP and EP.

Nautical Mile   The distance on the surface of the earth equivalent to 1 minute of arc of latitude; equal to 6080 feet or 1852 metres.

Neap Tide   See Tide.

Null   The lowest reading or strength of an incoming signal from the antenna to an RDF receiver.

Parallel   A reference line on a globe or chart parallel to the equator. See latitude.

Pelorus   An instrument similar to a compass with an azimuth ring, except that no magnets are fitted to the card which must be manually set at the desired reading; a "dumb" compass with sighting vanes.

Plot   The graphic representation of a ship's course, bearings and position drawn by the navigator as events occur.

Port   The left side of the vessel when facing toward the bow, and a land-based location for mooring or tying up vessels.

Position   A location of an object on the surface of the earth as depicted by a plot on a chart; usually the location of a vessel stated in terms of latitude and longitude.

Quarter Bearing   See Bearing.

RDF   A radio direction finder; a radio receiver specially equipped to receive long-wave marine radio signals; also equipped with a rotatable antenna of strong directional characteristics for the purpose of establishing radio signal lines of position. Some modern VHF receivers are equipped with RDF capability to establish lines of position from short wave signals.

RFix Running fix; a fix established by two or more lines of position, each of which were obtained at significantly different times, or if distance-off, the distance was established over a significantly long period of time. See fix.

Radio Direction Finder See RDF.

Range Two aids to navigation which, when in line, can be used to establish a line of position or a line of safe navigable waterway. A transit. See also Tide and Leading Lights.

Reciprocal A 180° difference in direction. The opposite or reverse course, or the opposite or reverse bearing.

Relative In bearings, a direction measured relative to or from a line representing the direction in which the vessel is heading at the time of the bearing.

Resultant A line in a vector diagram that displays the direction and magnitude of force or movement caused by the combination of the other two forces or movements displayed in the diagram.

Retarded LOP See LOP.

Revolver A situation resulting in a position being indeterminable by horizontal sextant angles and caused by circular lines of position being nearly identical.

Running Fix See RFix.

Running Free When sailing, the vessel is headed in a direction so that the wind blows across the boat from the stern or nearly over the stern.

SMG Speed made good; the speed of actual progress between two points which was made on the average by a vessel with respect to the surface of the earth.

SOG Speed over the ground; the speed of actual progress between two points being made

by a vessel with respect to the surface of the earth.

Sector An area within two radii and the arc of a circle.

Sector Light A light with an arc of visibility defining the limits of a sector which may be either a sector of safe passage or a sector of hazards.

Semi-diurnal Occurring twice daily.

Set The direction toward which a current flows.

Sextant An optical device for the measurement of angles.

Slack Water The time and condition of no horizontal movement of water due to tidal action.

Soundings The measurement of depth of water.

Speed Made Good See SMG.

Speed Over the Ground See SOG.

Stand The instant at high tide and low tide when there is no vertical movement of water.

Station-finder An optical device for simultaneous measurement of two angles between three objects; also used to plot those angles on a chart.

Station-pointer See station-finder.

Statute Mile A land mile of 5280 feet.

Sumlog A device aboard a vessel to indicate or record the distance travelled through the water.

Tack The heading of a sailing vessel relative to the wind when the wind is blowing across the boat from somewhat ahead of abeam to considerably aft of the beam but not directly astern as in running free. In a starboard tack, the wind is blowing across the vessel from the starboard side. In a port tack, the wind is blowing across the vessel from the port side. The term tack also describes the act of changing from a port tack to a starboard tack or vice versa.

Three-arm Protractor See Station-finder.

Tide   The vertical movement of water caused by gravitational effects of planetary system bodies, principally the moon. A neap tide has the lowest normal range in any particular location. The term tidal range is used to indicate the total vertical movement of water measured in feet or metres between successive high and low tides at a specific location. A spring tide is the tide of the highest normal range in a particular location; usually occurs at the new and full phases of the moon.

Transit   See Range

Transponder   The portion of a depth sounding device that transmits and receives a signal in order to determine the depth of water.

True   The determination of direction as measured with respect to the True (Geographic) North Pole.

Variation   The angular difference between the direction from the vessel to the True (Geographic) North Pole and the direction to the Magnetic North Pole.

Vector   A line plotted on a chart depicting the direction and speed or magnitude of some force acting on the vessel.

Vector Diagram   A graphic solution or diagram of various vectors in order to measure the direction and magnitude of the resultant.

Vertical Danger Angle   See Danger Angle.

Bibliography

"No man possesses all wisdom." KING SOLOMON

Bowditch, Nathaniel. *The American Practical Navigator*. 2 Vols. Washington, D.C.: Defense Mapping Agency, Hydrographic Center U.S.A., 1975–1977.

_____. *Bowditch for Yachtsmen: Piloting*. (Selected from *The American Practical Navigator*.) New York: David McKay Company, Inc., 1976.

Buchaned, J., and E. Bergin. *Piloting/Navigation with the Pocket Calculator*. Blue Ridge Summit, Pa.: Tab Books, 1976.

Budlong, John F. *Shoreline and Sextant: Practical Coastal Navigation*. Toronto: Van Nostrand Reinhold, 1977.

Campbell, Stafford. *The Yachtsman's Guide to Coastline Navigation*. New York: Ziff Davis Publishing, 1979.

Canadian Coast Guard, Department of Transport, Ottawa, Canada K1A 0N7. (Write the Director, Aids and Waterways, for a list of publications.)

Chapman, Charles F. *Piloting, Seamanship and Small Boat Handling*. New York: Motor Boating & Sailing, 1976.

Devereux, Frederick L., Jr. *Practical Navigation for the Yachtsman*. New York: W. W. Norton & Co., 1972.

Dunlap, G. D., and H. H. Shufeldt. *Dutton's Navigation and Piloting*. Annopolis, Md.: United States Naval Institute, 1969.

Gardner, A. C. *Navigation*. London: English Universities Press Ltd., 1958.

Griffiths, Garth. *Boating in Canada: Practical Piloting and Seamanship*. Toronto: University of Toronto Press, 1973.

Hydrographic Chart Distribution Office, Department of Fisheries and Oceans, P.O. Box 8080, 1675 Russell Road, Ottawa, Canada K1G 3H6. (Write for a list of charts and other publications.)

Kemp, Peter, ed. *The Oxford Companion to Ships and the Sea*. London: Oxford University Press, 1976.

Mixter, George W. *Primer of Navigation*. Princeton, N.J.: D. Van Nostrand, 1967.

Moody, Alton B. *Navigation Afloat: A Manual for the Seaman*. New York: Van Nostrand Reinhold, 1980.

Noel, John V. *Knight's Modern Seamanship*. London: Van Nostrand Reinhold, 1972.

Ogg, R. D. *Compasses and Compassing*. Portland, Me.: Danforth Division of the Eastern Company, 1977.

Pike, Dag. *Electronic Navigation for Small Craft*. London: Adlard Coles and Granada Publishing, 1977.

Shufeldt, H. H., and G. D. Dunlap. *Piloting and Dead Reckoning*. Annapolis, Md.: Naval Institute Press, 1975.

Simonsen, Svend T. *Simonsen's Navigation: Coastwise and Bluewater Navigation*. Englewood Cliffs, N.J.: Prentice-Hall, 1973.

Simpkin, Richard. *The Cruising Yachtman's Navigator*. London: Stanley Paul & Co., 1978.

Watts, Oswald M. *Reed's Nautical Almanac*. London: Thomas Reed Publications Ltd., 1980.

Wilkes, Kenneth. *Ocean Yacht Navigator*. New York: David McKay Company, Inc., 1976.

Index

"To know where to obtain knowledge . . . is to be knowledgeable." AL'S OLD ADAGE

AREA B: WESTERN HEMISPHERE

BUOY TYPE		BUOY SHAPE AND COLOUR			TOPMARK	LIGHT COLOUR	LIGHT CHARACTERS	CHART SYMBOLS
LATERAL								
PORT		PILLAR	CAN	SPAR	GREEN CAN	GREEN	Fl OR Q	G G / G G / BELL WHIS / G G
STARBOARD		PILLAR	CONICAL	SPAR	RED CONE	RED	Fl OR Q	R R / R R / BELL WHIS / R R
FAIRWAY		PILLAR	SPHERICAL	SPAR	RED SPHERE	WHITE	Mo(A) OR LFl	RW RW / RW RW / BELL WHIS / RW RW
BIFURCATION								
PORT		PILLAR	CAN	SPAR	GREEN CAN	GREEN	Fl(2+1)5S OR Fl(2+1)10S	GRG GRG / GRG GRG / BELL WHIS / GRG GRG
STARBOARD		PILLAR	CONICAL	SPAR	RED CONE	RED	Fl(2+1)5S OR Fl(2+1)10S	RGR RGR / RGR RGR / BELL WHI / RGR RGR
CARDINAL								
NORTH		PILLAR		SPAR	2 BLACK CONES POINTS UPWARD	WHITE	Q OR VQ	BY / BY BY / BELL WH / BY BY
EAST		PILLAR		SPAR	2 BLACK CONES BASE TO BASE	WHITE	Q(3)10S OR VQ(3)5S	BYB / BYB BYB / BELL WH / BYB BYB
SOUTH		PILLAR		SPAR	2 BLACK CONES POINTS DOWNWARD	WHITE	Q(6)+LFl15S OR VQ(6)+LFl 10S	YB / YB YB / BELL WH / YB YB
WEST		PILLAR		SPAR	2 BLACK CONES POINT TO POINT	WHITE	Q(9)15S OR VQ(9)10S	YBY / YBY YBY / BELL WH / YBY YBY